THRESHOLD

Cambridge Pre-GED Program in Writing Skills

Gloria Levine

 CAMBRIDGE Adult Education
Prentice Hall Regents
Englewood Cliffs, New Jersey 07632

Library of Congress Cataloging-in-Publication Data

Levine, Gloria
    Threshold: Cambridge pre-GED program in writing skills/Gloria
Levine.
    p.   cm.
    ISBN 0-13-110958-8
    1. English language—Composition and exercises—Examinations,
questions, etc. 2. General education and development tests.
I. Title.
LB1631.L415 1994
808.042'076—dc20   93—5349
                                        CIP
                                        AC

Publisher: **TINA B. CARVER**
Executive Editor: **JAMES W. BROWN**
Editorial Supervisor: **TIMOTHY A. FOOTE**
Managing Editor, Production: **SYLVIA MOORE**
Production Editor: **JANET S. JOHNSTON**
Desktop Production: **KEN LIAO**
Buyers and Schedulers: **RAY KEATING AND ED O'DOUGHERTY**
Interior designers: **JANET SCHMID, JANET S. JOHNSTON**
Cover coordinator: **MARIANNE FRASCO**
Cover designer: **BRUCE KENSELAAR**
Cover photo: Monument Valley, Arizona, at sunset
Courtesy of **FPG INTERNATIONAL**
Photo researcher: **ELLEN GRATKOWSKI**

©1994 by PRENTICE HALL REGENTS
Prentice-Hall, Inc.
A Paramount Communications Company
Englewood Cliffs, New Jersey 07632

Printed in the United Sates of America

10 9 8 7 6 5

ISBN 0-13-110958-8

PHOTO CREDITS

Page 1	Laimute E. Druskis
11	Marcia Key Keegan, from the collection of Martin W. Sandler
153	Laima Druskis
215	Bob David

Prentice-Hall International (UK) Limited, *London*
Prentice-Hall of Australia Pty. Limited, *Sydney*
Prentice-Hall Canada Inc., *Toronto*
Prentice-Hall Hispanoamericana, S.A., *Mexico*
Prentice-Hall of India Private Limited, *New Delhi*
Prentice-Hall of Japan, Inc., *Tokyo*
Simon & Schuster Asia Pte. Ltd., *Singapore*
Editora Prentice-Hall do Brasil, Ltda., *Rio de Janeiro*

CONTENTS

ACKNOWLEDGMENTS

CAMBRIDGE Adult Education thanks the men and women enrolled in ABE and Pre-GED courses who read parts of the Threshold manuscripts and offered valuable advice to the programs' authors and editors.

We also thank the following consultants for their many contributions throughout the preparation of the Threshold Pre-GED programs.

Cecily Kramer Bodnar
Consultant, Adult Learning
Adult Literacy Services
Central School District
Greece, New York

Pamela S. Buchanan
Instructor
Blue Ridge Job Corps Center
Marion, Virginia

Maureen Considine, M.A., M.S.

Learning Laboratory Supervisor
Great Neck Adult Learning Center
Great Neck, New York

ABE/HSE Projects Coordinator
National Center for Disability Services
Albertson, New York

Carole Deletiner
Instructor
Hunter College
New York, New York

Patricia Giglio
Remedial Reading Teacher
Johnstown ASACTC
Johnstown, New York

Diane Marinelli Hardison, M.S. Ed.
Mathematics Educator
San Diego, California

Margaret Banker Tinzmann, Ph. D.
Program Associate
The North Central Regional Educational Laboratory
Oak Brook, Illinois

INTRODUCTION

The *Threshold* Pre-GED Programs

Threshold provides a full-range entry-level course for adults whose goal is to earn a high school equivalency diploma. The men and women who use the six *Threshold* programs will learn—and profit from an abundance of sound practice in applying—the writing, problem-solving, and critical-reading and -thinking skills they'll need when they take the GED tests. They will gain a firm grounding in knowledge about social studies and science, and will read many excellent selections from the best of classical and contemporary literature. In short, *Threshold* offers adults the skills, knowledge, and practice that will enable them to approach GED-level test preparation with well-deserved confidence and solid ability.

The *Threshold* Writing Skills Program

Students should begin their study in this book by taking the Pretest. Like the Writing Skills Test of the GED, it has two parts. The parts can be administered at the same time or separately. The multiple-choice items in Part 1 cover usage, sentence structure, and mechanics. They are formatted like the items in Part 1 of the GED's Writing Skills Test. To facilitate placement, the test has at least one item related to each lesson in Unit 1 of this book, as the Skills Chart that follows it shows. In Part 2, students plan and write a paragraph on an assigned topic.

Students may work through all the lessons in this book in order or may work through Units 1 and 2 at the same time.

Unit 1 covers usage, sentence structure, and mechanics in four chapters. It addresses aspects of sentence structure and sentence clarity, subject-verb agreement, tense, pronoun reference, capitalization, punctuation, and spelling tested by Part 1 of the Writing Skills Test. Further, because of its content, Unit 1 offers students the tools they will need to revise and edit the original writing they do in Unit 2. The chapters in Unit 1 end with GED Practices to provide valuable test-taking experience. The Skills Chart that accompanies each Practice allows assessment of skill mastery. The 23 lessons in Unit 1 are typically divided into subskill segments, each with succinct instruction and examples that are carefully explained. Instruction uses as little technical vocabulary as possible. Most exercises in the lessons require both sentence correction and sentence composition using the skills addressed by the lesson.

Unit 2 covers paragraph writing by use of the writing process. Its 19 lessons are divided into three chapters. The first chapter provides activities designed to help students overcome blocks to writing. The second chapter covers the steps of the writing process and helps students develop a paragraph using that process. The third chapter explores five ways paragraphs are typically organized and assigns topics that require students to write original paragraphs using each of those organization patterns. The last lesson in the unit provides 60 topics students can use to practice paragraph writing.

The Posttest, formatted like the GED, provides a comprehensive review of all the material covered in this book.

The Answers and Explanations—on perforated pages at the back of this book—offer correct or sample answers for all the exercises in Unit 1 and for many of the exercises in Unit 2. Entries related to the Pretest, the GED Practices, and the Posttest explain *why* correct answer choices are correct and refer students to appropriate pages in the text for review.

This book's placement tool, its carefully presented instruction, its exercises, its Skills Charts, and its GED-like Pretest, GED Practices, and Posttest make it an excellent first course in preparation for the Writing Skills Test of the GED.

You will profit in several important ways by using this book as you begin to prepare for the writing skills test of the GED:

- You will improve your ability to write sentences and paragraphs.
- You will be able to write with greater ease than you now do.
- You will gain experience answering questions like those on the GED.
- You will become more confident of your abilities.

To Find Out About Your Current Writing Skills . . .

Take the **PRETEST**. When you have finished, refer to the **ANSWERS AND EXPLANATIONS** at the back of this book. The **SKILLS CHART** that follows the Pretest will give you an idea about which parts of Unit 1 you most need to concentrate on. It would be best to have a teacher evaluate the paragraph you write in Part 2 of the Pretest.

To Improve Your Writing Skills . . .

Study the **LESSONS**. They present instruction about the various writing skills. Each lesson includes one or more **EXAMPLES** and **EXERCISES** to help you apply and improve your writing skills.

This book is divided into two units. The first covers topics in usage, sentence structure, and mechanics—skills tested mainly by Part 1 of the GED Writing Skills Test. The second unit covers most of the skills you'll need when you write the essay for Part 2 of the test. Although you may work on Unit 1 first and then on Unit 2, it would probably be better if you worked through both units at the same time. They reinforce each other.

To Gain Experience with Items and Writing Assignments Like Those on the GED

Take the **GED PRACTICE** at the end of each chapter in Unit 1. These four GED Practices are made up largely of items similar to those on Part 1 of the Writing Skills test of the GED. The Practices offer test-taking experience that you will find useful when you take the GED. The **SKILLS CHART** following each practice allows you to assess your performance.

Before you finish with this book, take the **POSTTEST**. Like the GED Practices, it is similar to the GED's Writing Skills test. Look at the **SKILLS CHART** that follows the Posttest. If you compare your Pretest and Posttest performances, you will probably find that your writing skills improved as you worked through this book. The chart can give you an idea about which parts of this book you should review.

Pretest

The following Pretest is similar to the Writing Skills Test of the GED. Taking it will help you find out what you need to study most in this book.

Part 1 of the Pretest consists of 32 multiple-choice items based on paragraphs with numbered sentences. Most of the sentences contain errors or need improvement. After reading each set of paragraphs, answer the multiple-choice items that follow. Some items refer to sentences that are correct as written, but most refer to sentences that need to be corrected or made clearer. (Before you begin Part 1 of the Pretest, you may want to look ahead to pages 47–49 and 77–78 in this book. They give examples of test items and explain their parts.)

Part 2 of the Pretest asks you to write a short paragraph on an assigned topic.

Work through the Pretest at a pace that is comfortable for you. When you have finished, check your answers. After that, refer to the chart on page 9. It shows which lessons in this book contain instruction and practice related to each of the items in the Pretest.

WRITING SKILLS PRETEST

Part I

Directions: Choose the <u>one best answer</u> to each item.

<u>Items 1 through 11</u> refer to the following paragraphs.

(1) Until recently my wife and myself have had trouble sleeping. (2) Many nights neither her nor I slept a wink. (3) Anybody who often tosses all night know how miserable insomnia is.

(4) We did some research and discovered that there's many causes for sleeplessness. (5) Heart disease, lung disease, gall-bladder disease, and experiencing other physical problems can cause poor sleep. (6) Depression, as well as anxiety, frequently keep people from sleeping. (7) Certain prescription medicines and over-the-counter drugs contribute to sleeping problems. (8) Caffeine too close to bedtime keeps many people awake.

(9) Neither I nor my wife has trouble sleeping now. (10) No longer do my wife take the weight-loss medication her doctor prescribed. (11) Her club of dieters help her control her weight now. (12) I don't eat chocolate while I watches television in the evening anymore, so caffeine no longer keeps me awake.

1. Sentence 1: **Until recently <u>my wife and myself</u> have had trouble sleeping.**

   Which of the following is the best way to write the underlined portion of this sentence? If you think the original is the best way, choose option (1).

   (1) my wife and myself
   (2) my wife, as well as myself,
   (3) my wife and I
   (4) myself and my wife
   (5) I and my wife

2. Sentence 2: **Many nights neither <u>her nor I</u> slept a wink.**

   Which of the following is the best way to write the underlined portion of this sentence? If you think the original is the best way, choose option (1).

   (1) her nor I
   (2) her nor me
   (3) herself nor myself
   (4) she nor I
   (5) she nor me

3. Sentence 3: **Anybody who often tosses all night know how miserable insomnia is.**

   What correction should be made to this sentence?

   (1) insert a comma after <u>Anybody</u>
   (2) change <u>tosses</u> to <u>toss</u>
   (3) insert a comma after <u>night</u>
   (4) change <u>know</u> to <u>knows</u>
   (5) replace <u>is</u> with <u>was</u>

4. Sentence 4: **We did some research and discovered that there's many causes for sleeplessness.**

   What correction should be made to this sentence?

   (1) change <u>did</u> to <u>done</u>
   (2) insert a comma after <u>research</u>
   (3) change <u>discovered</u> to <u>discover</u>
   (4) replace <u>there's</u> with <u>there are</u>
   (5) no correction is necessary

5. Sentence 5: **Heart disease, lung disease, gall-bladder <u>disease, and experiencing other</u> physical problems can cause poor sleep.**

   Which of the following is the best way to write the underlined portion of this sentence? If you think the original is the best way, choose option (1).

   (1) disease, and experiencing other
   (2) disease and experiencing other
   (3) disease, and the experience of other
   (4) disease, and other
   (5) disease and other

6. Sentence 6: **Depression, as well as anxiety, frequently keep people from sleeping.**

   What correction should be made to this sentence?

   (1) remove the comma after <u>Depression</u>
   (2) remove the comma after <u>anxiety</u>
   (3) change <u>keep</u> to <u>keeps</u>
   (4) change <u>keep</u> to <u>kept</u>
   (5) no correction is necessary

7. Sentence 7: **Certain prescription medicines and over-the-counter drugs contribute to sleeping problems.**

   What correction should be made to this sentence?

   (1) insert a comma after <u>medicines</u>
   (2) insert a comma after <u>drugs</u>
   (3) change <u>contribute</u> to <u>contributes</u>
   (4) change <u>contribute</u> to <u>will contribute</u>
   (5) no correction is necessary

8. Sentence 9: **Neither <u>I nor my wife has</u> trouble sleeping now.**

   Which of the following is the best way to write the underlined portion of this sentence? If you think the original is the best way, choose option (1).

   (1) I nor my wife has
   (2) I nor my wife have
   (3) my wife nor I has
   (4) my wife nor I have
   (5) my wife nor I had

9. Sentence 10: **No longer do my wife take the weight-loss medication her doctor prescribed.**

   What correction should be made to this sentence?

   (1) change <u>do</u> to <u>does</u>
   (2) change <u>do</u> to <u>did</u>
   (3) insert a comma after <u>medication</u>
   (4) change <u>prescribed</u> to <u>will prescribe</u>
   (5) replace the period with a question mark

10. Sentence 11: **Her <u>club of dieters help</u> her control her weight now.**

    Which of the following is the best way to write the underlined portion of this sentence? If you think the original is the best way, choose option (1).

    (1) club of dieters help
    (2) club of dieters helps
    (3) club, of dieters, helps
    (4) club of dieters, help
    (5) club of dieters, helps

11. Sentence 12: **I don't eat chocolate while <u>I watches</u> television in the evening anymore, so caffeine no longer keeps me awake.**

    Which of the following is the best way to write the underlined portion of this sentence? If you think the original is the best way, choose option (1).

    (1) I watches
    (2) I'm watching
    (3) I watched
    (4) I have watched
    (5) I was watching

Items 12 through 23 refer to the following paragraphs.

(1) Computer electronics have changed the way telephone companies handle calls. (2) A telephone company, which serves millions of customers, use many computers. (3) Some of them has voices that sound human.

(4) Has you ever made a long-distance call from a pay telephone? (5) When anyone dials a long-distance number, you hear a voice that says to deposit money. (6) The voice came from a computer with about seventy words and numbers in its memory. (7) An actress once recorded those words and numbers, and it was then stored in the computer's memory.

(8) The computer senses each number dialed. (9) The computer controls calls made from pay phones. (10) Using the dialed information, the computer be able to figure the charge for your call. (11) Then sounds from the computer's "voice" tells you how much your call costs. (12) Until you put your money in the slot, the computer "hears" the coins clink and connects your call. (13) Throughout this process, a computer does everything that operators once done.

12. Sentence 1: **Computer electronics have changed the way telephone companies handle calls.**

What correction should be made to this sentence?

(1) change have to has
(2) change have to had
(3) insert a comma after changed
(4) change of companies to company's
(5) no correction is necessary

13. Sentence 2: **A telephone company, which serves millions of customers, use many computers.**

What correction should be made to this sentence?

(1) remove the comma after company
(2) change serves to served
(3) remove the comma after customers
(4) change use to uses
(5) no correction is necessary

14. Sentence 3: **Some of them has voices that sound human.**

Which of the following is the best way to write the underlined portion of this sentence? If you think the original is the best way, choose option (1).

(1) them has
(2) the companies has
(3) the customers have
(4) the computers has
(5) the computers have

15. Sentence 4: **Has you ever made a long-distance call from a pay telephone?**

What correction should be made to this sentence?

(1) change Has to Have
(2) change made to make
(3) change made to maked
(4) replace the question mark with a period
(5) no correction is necessary

16. Sentence 5: **When anyone dials a long-distance number, you hear a voice that says to deposit money.**

What correction should be made this sentence?

(1) replace anyone dials with you dial
(2) remove the comma after number
(3) replace you hear with he or she hears
(4) change says to said
(5) no correction is necessary

17. Sentence 6: **The voice came from a computer with about seventy words and numbers in its memory.**

What correction should be made to this sentence?

(1) change came to come
(2) change came to comes
(3) insert a comma after words
(4) change the spelling of its to it's
(5) no correction is necessary

18. Sentence 7: **An actress once recorded those words and numbers, and it was then stored in the computer's memory.**

Which of the following is the best way to write the underlined portion of this sentence? If you think the original is the best way, choose option (1).

(1) it was
(2) she was
(3) they was
(4) they were
(5) they are

19. Sentences 8 and 9: **The computer senses each number dialed. The computer controls calls made from pay phones.**

The most effective combination of sentences 8 and 9 would include which of the following groups of words?

(1) The computer's sense controls
(2) computer, which controls calls made from pay phones,
(3) computer that controls calls made from pay phones
(4) dialed even though it controls
(5) dialed, but it controls

20. Sentence 10: **Using the dialed information, the computer be able to figure the charge for your call.**

Which of the following is the best way to write the underlined portion of this sentence? If you think the original is the best way, choose option (1).

(1) be
(2) are
(3) is
(4) was
(5) were

21. Sentence 11: **Then sounds from the computer's "voice" tells you how much your call costs.**

What correction should be made to this sentence?

(1) change computer's to computers'
(2) change tells to tell
(3) change tells to told
(4) change costs to cost
(5) no correction is necessary

22. Sentence 12: **Until you put your money in the slot, the computer "hears" the coins clink and connects your call.**

What correction should be made to this sentence?

(1) replace Until with After
(2) remove the comma after slot
(3) change hears to heard
(4) change connects to connect
(5) no correction is necessary

23. Sentence 13: **Throughout this process, a computer does everything that operators once done.**

What correction should be made to this sentence?

(1) remove the comma after process
(2) change does to did
(3) change operators to operator's
(4) change done to did
(5) no correction is necessary

Items 24 through 32 refer to the following paragraphs.

(1) Last May 7 a letter appeared in the newspaper from Martin Peterson. (2) It was a nasty letter, the last line was especially spiteful. (3) It said the letter's author was sick of people living well on welfare. (4) I'm on welfare, and I had a hard time surviving. (5) I have grown sick of welfare lines, and food stamps. (6) I'm tired of employed people that look down on me. (7) I quit my job over a year ago most of my pay went for day care.

(8) A local community college has helped to launch excellent careers for many former welfare recipients. (9) I want to enroll.

(10) If Martin Peterson opened his eyes. (11) He would see people who do not live well eager to get off welfare.

24. Sentence 1: **Last May 7 a letter appeared in the newspaper from Martin Peterson.**

    Which of the following is the best way to write the underlined portion of this sentence? If you think the original is the best way, choose option (1).
    (1) a letter appeared in the newspaper from Martin Peterson
    (2) a letter appears in the newspaper from Martin Peterson
    (3) a letter will appear in the newspaper from Martin Peterson
    (4) a letter from Martin Peterson appeared in the newspaper
    (5) a letter appeared from Martin Peterson in the newspaper

25. Sentence 2: **It was a nasty letter, the last line was especially spiteful.**

    Which of the following is the best way to write the underlined portion of this sentence? If you think the original is the best way, choose option (1).
    (1) letter, the
    (2) letter the
    (3) letter. The
    (4) letter and the
    (5) letter, but the

26. Sentence 3: **It said the letter's author was sick of people living well on welfare.**

    What correction should be made to this sentence?
    (1) change said to says
    (2) change letter's to letter
    (3) change letter's to letters
    (4) change letter's to letters'
    (5) no correction is necessary

27. Sentence 4: **I'm on welfare, and I had a hard time surviving.**

    What correction should be made to this sentence?
    (1) change the spelling of I'm to I'am
    (2) remove the comma after welfare
    (3) replace and with or
    (4) replace I with you
    (5) change had to have

28. Sentence 5: **I have grown sick of welfare lines, and food stamps.**

    What correction should be made to this sentence?
    (1) change have to had
    (2) change grown to grow
    (3) change grown to growed
    (4) remove the comma after lines
    (5) no correction is necessary

29. Sentence 6: **I'm tired of employed people that look down on me.**

    Which of the following is the best way to write the underlined portion of this sentence? If you think the original is the best way, choose option (1).
    (1) people that look
    (2) people, that look
    (3) people who look
    (4) people which look
    (5) people, which look

30. Sentence 7: **I quit my job over a year ago most** of my pay went for day care.

Which of the following is the best way to write the underlined portion of this sentence? If you think the original is the best way, choose option (1).

(1) ago most
(2) ago because most
(3) ago, and most
(4) ago, which most
(5) ago, but most

31. Sentences 8 and 9: **A local community college has helped to launch excellent careers for many former welfare recipients. I want to enroll.**

The most effective combination of sentences 8 and 9 would include which of the following groups of words?

(1) recipients, but I
(2) recipients, for I
(3) recipients, or I
(4) recipients, so I
(5) recipients, yet I

32. Sentences 10 and 11: **If Martin Peterson opened his eyes. He would see people who do not live well eager to get off welfare.**

Which of the following is the best way to write the underlined portion of these sentences? If you think the original is the best way, choose option (1).

(1) eyes. He
(2) eyes he
(3) eyes, he
(4) eyes, and he
(5) eyes which he

Part 2

<u>Directions</u>: This part of the Writing Skills Pretest is intended to see how well you write. You are asked to write a short paragraph on an assigned topic. To develop your paragraph you should take the following steps:

1. Read the topic carefully.

2. Use scratch paper to make notes about what you want to include in your paragraph.

3. Before you write your paragraph, decide how you will organize it.

4. Write your paragraph on a piece of lined paper.

5. Make changes in your paragraph that will improve it, including corrections in sentence structure, spelling, punctuation, capitalization, and usage.

TOPIC

In some places underage drinkers who have been arrested are required to do community service. Write a paragraph of about 50 words that gives your opinion for or against community service as a penalty for underage drinking.

Check your answers on page 225.

PRETEST SKILLS CHART

To study the writing skills covered by the items in Part 1 of the Pretest, refer to the following lessons in this book. The answers and explanations beginning on page 225 tell which part of each lesson pertains to each item.

The skills covered by Part 2 of the Pretest are covered in Unit 2 of this book.

Chapter 1	Subject-Verb Agreement	Item Number
Lesson 1	The Two Parts of Action Sentences	All items related to Chapter 1
Lesson 2	Finding Verbs and Subjects in Action Sentences	All items related to Chapter 1
Lesson 3	Subject-Verb Agreement in Action Sentences	13
Lesson 4	Subject-Verb Agreement in Describing Sentences	20
Lesson 5	Subject-Verb Agreement with Special Subjects	3, 10, 12
Lesson 6	Subject-Verb Agreement with Compound Subjects	7, 8
Lesson 7	Subject-Verb Agreement When the Subject Follows the Verb	4, 9, 15
Lesson 8	Subject-Verb Agreement with Interrupting Phrases	6, 21
Chapter 2	Verb Tenses	
Lesson 9	Past, Present, and Future Tenses	27
Lesson 10	Irregular Verbs	23
Lesson 11	The Continuous and Perfect Tenses	11
Lesson 12	Choosing the Correct Tense	17
Chapter 3	Pronouns	
Lesson 13	Subject and Object Pronouns	2
Lesson 14	Pronouns That End with -self or -selves	1
Lesson 15	Possessives	26
Lesson 16	Pronoun Agreement	18
Lesson 17	Avoiding Pronoun Shifts and Unclear References	14, 16
Chapter 4	Sentence Structure	
Lesson 18	Compound Sentence Parts	5, 28
Lesson 19	Compound Sentences	31
Lesson 20	Complex Sentences: Part 1	19, 29
Lesson 21	Complex Sentences: Part 2	22
Lesson 22	Correcting Run-On Sentences and Sentence Fragments	25, 30, 32
Lesson 23	Sentence Clarity	24

UNIT 1

Usage, Sentence Structure, and Mechanics

Both parts of the GED Writing Skills test require knowledge of English usage, sentence structure, and mechanics. The multiple-choice items in Part 1 test your ability to find and correct the kinds of errors often present in adults' writing—errors that can block a person's advancement at work or in school. The essay you write for Part 2 of the test can be effective only if it is mostly free of the same kinds of errors.

This unit covers usage skills, sentence-structure skills, and mechanical skills you'll need when you take the GED. They are the same skills you should use whenever you write. The unit gives you practice at finding and correcting errors and at writing original, error-free sentences.

Unit 1 Overview	
Chapter 1	Subject-Verb Agreement
Chapter 2	Verb Tenses
Chapter 3	Pronouns
Chapter 4	Sentence Structure

Chapter

1 SUBJECT-VERB AGREEMENT

The first lesson in this chapter covers the two-part structure of English sentences. The other lessons are about the verbs and subjects in sentences and the rules for their agreement with each other. The chapter gives you practice at finding and correcting subject-verb agreement errors of many types and at writing sentences without agreement errors.

The Two Parts of Action Sentences

Every sentence has two main parts. To show that, there is a line between the two parts of each of the following **action sentences**. (Think of them as action sentences because they tell what someone or something does.)

The **naming part** names who or what does something.

Crickets | chirp.
This carpenter | builds bookcases.
Active volcanoes | erupt sometimes.
My journal | holds my whole life.

The **action part** tells the action.

Notice that all the words in each sentence are in either the **naming part** or the **action part**.

The following steps will help you divide sentences into their two parts.

How to Find the Two Main Parts of an Action Sentence

STEP 1: To find the naming part, ask yourself: Which words in the sentence tell who or what does something?

STEP 2: To find the action part, ask yourself: Which words in the sentence tell what someone or something does?

Together, your two answers will contain all the words in the sentence. Use the two steps to find the two main parts of this sentence:

Some workers earn commissions.

STEP 1: To find the naming part, answer this question:
Which words in the sentence tell who or what does something?
ANSWER: **Some workers**

STEP 2: To find the action part, answer this question:
Which words in the sentence tell what someone or something does?
ANSWER: **earn commissions**

Here is the sentence with a line between its two parts:

Naming Part → Some workers | earn commissions. ← **Action Part**

Spotlight on Capitalization and Punctuation

| The first word in a sentence is **capitalized**. | Laborers work. Computers save time. Volcanoes spew lava. | When a sentence tells something, it ends with a **period**. |

EXERCISE 1

Part A. Draw a line between the naming part and the action part of each sentence.

Example: Old newspapers | burn easily.

1. Calculators multiply numbers quickly.

2. Liquids evaporate fast here.

3. Solid stone walls last for years.

4. Tourists travel for fun.

5. Gas stoves work for a long time.

6. Some subway trains stop here.

7. My metal files hold important papers.

8. Reporters gather the news.

9. I toss all night sometimes.

10. Some people suffer terrible pain.

Part B. Two lists of sentence parts follow. Write five sentences by joining each naming part together with an action part. Before you start, reread the Spotlight on page 13.

Naming Part	Action Part
~~amber traffic lights~~	drop morning newspapers there
car horns	~~flash at night~~
express buses	honk a lot
large cargo planes	roar overhead
loud police sirens	stop at that corner
some noisy delivery vans	wail all night long

Example: Amber traffic lights flash at night.

1. _____
2. _____
3. _____
4. _____
5. _____

Check your answers on page 228.

Lesson 2

Finding Verbs and Subjects in Action Sentences

In Lesson 1 you divided sentences into their two parts, the naming part and the action part. In this lesson you will find the two most important words in sentences. One of them is in the naming part of a sentence, and the other is in the action part.

Finding Verbs in Action Sentences

In each part of a sentence there is a core word. In the action part of a sentence, the core word tells the action. It is called the **verb**. Look at these five example sentences.

Winter | <u>comes</u>.
Pines | <u>drop</u> their dead needles.
Their branches | <u>droop</u> under snow.
Cold winds | <u>whistle</u> through their boughs.
People | <u>bundle</u> up.

The **verbs** are underlined twice.

> **Verb:**
> the word that tells the action in a sentence

Notice that in each sentence the verb is the word that tells what happens—the action. The following steps will help you find the verb in a sentence.

How to Find the Verb in an Action Sentence

STEP 1:   Find the two main parts of the sentence.

STEP 2:   To find the verb, ask yourself: Which word in the action part tells the action?

Use the two steps to find the verb in this sentence:

Tall ships sail on the Fourth of July.

STEP 1:   Find the two main parts of the sentence.

Naming Part   Tall ships | sail on the Fourth of July.   Action Part

STEP 2:   To find the verb, answer this question:
Which word in the action part tells the action?
ANSWER: **sail**

Here is the sentence with the verb underlined twice:

Tall ships <u>sail</u> on the Fourth of July.

EXERCISE 2a

In each sentence underline the verb twice.

Example: Kangaroos <u>live</u> in Australia.

1. Monkeys play.
2. Some dolphins perform.
3. Whales talk to each other.
4. Some parrots live in cages.
5. Most apes learn quickly.
6. Hippopotamuses stay under water a lot.
7. Bats hunt at night.
8. Some bees make honey.
9. These ants build underground nests.
10. Many dogs howl like wolves.

Check your answers on page 228.

Finding Subjects in Action Sentences

The core word in the naming part of a sentence is called the subject. It tells who or what does the action. Look at these four example sentences again.

The **subjects** are underlined once.

<u>Winter</u> | comes.
<u>Pines</u> | drop their dead needles.
Their <u>branches</u> | droop under snow.
Cold <u>winds</u> | whistle through their boughs.
<u>People</u> | bundle up.

> **Subject:** the word that tells who or what does the action in a sentence

Notice that in each sentence the subject is the word that tells who or what does the action. The following steps will help you find subjects.

How to Find the Subject in an Action Sentence

STEP 1: Find the verb in the sentence.

STEP 2: To find the subject, ask yourself: Who or what (say the verb)?

Use the two steps to find the subject in this sentence:

Tall ships sail on the Fourth of July.

STEP 1: Find the verb in the sentence.
THE VERB: **sail**

STEP 2: To find the subject, answer this question:
Who or what sail?
ANSWER: **ships**

Here is the sentence with the subject underlined once:

Tall <u>ships</u> sail on the Fourth of July.

EXERCISE 2b

Part A. In each sentence underline the verb twice and the subject once.

Example: <u>Kangaroos</u> <u>live</u> in Australia.

1. Monkeys play.

2. Some dolphins perform.

3. Whales talk to each other.

4. Some parrots live in cages.

5. Most apes learn quickly.

6. Hippopotamuses stay under water a lot.

7. Bats hunt at night.

8. Some bees make honey.

9. These ants build underground nests.

10. Many dogs howl like wolves.

Part B. Two lists of sentence parts follow. Write five sentences by joining each naming part together with an action part. Then, underline the verbs twice and the subjects once.

Naming Part	Action Part
~~all pitchers~~	cheer loudly at games
baseball fans	hit home runs frequently
catchers	make a lot of money
league teams	play against each other
professional baseball players	stay behind home plate
some batters	~~throw balls to batters~~

Example: All <u>pitchers</u> <u>throw</u> balls to batters.

1. _____

2. _____

3. _____

4. _____

5. _____

Check your answers on page 228.

Lesson 3

Subject-Verb Agreement in Action Sentences

In Lesson 2 you found verbs and subjects in action sentences. In this lesson you will edit action sentences so that their verbs and subjects agree.

Basic Rules for Subject-Verb Agreement

Subject-verb agreement concerns how many persons or things do the action in a sentence. When one person or thing does the action, the subject and verb are both **singular**. The subject and verb are both **plural** when two or more persons or things do the action. Look at the subjects and verbs in the following two sets of sentences:

These sentences have **singular** subjects and verbs.

Our <u>clerk</u> <u>files</u> every day.
This <u>office</u> <u>hires</u> ex-offenders.
<u>He</u> <u>works</u> here.

These singular verbs have an **s** ending.

These sentences have **plural** subjects and verbs.

Most <u>clerks</u> <u>file</u> sometimes.
Other <u>offices</u> <u>hire</u> ex-offenders.
<u>They</u> <u>work</u> here.

Plural verbs have **no** special ending.

Subjects and verbs agree when they follow one of the patterns shown in the following box:

Patterns for Subject-Verb Agreement

Singular subject   +   verb with an **s** ending
Plural subject   +   verb with **no** ending

Two exceptions to the pattern for singular verbs are explained later in this lesson.

A Test to Decide If a Subject Is Singular or Plural

If you aren't sure whether the subject in a sentence is singular or plural, try this test.

How to Use the He/She/It or They Test

- If you can replace the naming part of a sentence with **he**, **she**, or **it**, the subject is singular.

- If you can replace the naming part of a sentence with **they**, the subject is plural.

The following examples show how to use the test. A line divides each sentence into its two parts. In each sentence the subject is underlined once.

You can replace the naming part of this sentence with **he** or **she**. Therefore the subject, **doctor**, is singular.

He/She
~~The doctor~~ | sees forty patients a day.

You can replace the naming part of this sentence with **it**. Therefore the subject, **room**, is singular.

It
~~The waiting room~~ | holds only six people.

You can replace the naming part of this sentence with **they**. Therefore the subject, **patients**, is plural.

They
~~Some patients~~ | stand.

The subjects and verbs are underlined in the following sentences. In each blank write **singular** if one person or thing does the action in the sentence. Write **plural** if two or more persons or things do the action.

Example: _____plural_____ Many <u>cities</u> host tourists.

_____ 1. <u>Tourists</u> <u>travel</u> to Washington, D.C., all year long.

_____ 2. This <u>tourist</u> <u>prefers</u> monuments.

_____ 3. These <u>tourists</u> <u>like</u> museums.

_____ 4. Most <u>tourists</u> <u>visit</u> the White House.

_____ 5. Many <u>people</u> <u>enjoy</u> the zoo, too.

_____ 6. The underground <u>train</u> <u>gets</u> you there.

_____ 7. <u>Bells</u> <u>ring</u> near the entrance to the zoo.

_____ 8. Many <u>animals</u> <u>stay</u> outside in good weather.

_____ 9. Most <u>reptiles</u> <u>live</u> inside.

_____ 10. The <u>zoo</u> <u>houses</u> hundreds of animals.

Check your answers on page 228.

Editing for Subject-Verb Agreement in Action Sentences

The following steps will help you edit for subject-verb agreement in a sentence.

How to Edit for Subject-Verb Agreement

STEP 1: Find the verb and the subject in the sentence.

STEP 2: Ask yourself: Is the subject singular or plural?
(You can use the He/She/It or They Test to find the answer.)

STEP 3: Ask yourself: Does the verb agree with the subject?

STEP 4: If the verb does not agree, correct the sentence.

Use the steps to edit for subject-verb agreement in this sentence:

The hospital workers strikes every year.

STEP 1: Find the verb and the subject in the sentence.
THE VERB AND THE SUBJECT: **The hospital <u>workers</u> <u>strikes</u> every year.**

STEP 2: Ask yourself: Is the subject singular or plural?
ANSWER: ***Workers* is plural. (The hospital workers** can be replaced by **They**.)

STEP 3: Ask yourself: Does the verb agree with the subject?
ANSWER: ***Strikes* is singular, so it does *not* agree with *workers*.**

STEP 4: If the verb does not agree, correct the sentence.
strike

CORRECTION: **The hospital workers ~~strikes~~ every year.**

EXERCISE 3b

Edit the following sentences for subject-verb agreement. If a verb does not agree with a subject, change the verb. (Note: Some sentences do not need correction.)

require
Example: Trials ~~requires~~ several people.

1. A bailiff act as an usher in a courtroom.

2. Guards brings the defendant in and out.

3. One lawyer plead for the defendant.

4. Defense witnesses appear in most cases.

5. Another lawyer argues for the plaintiff.

6. Prosecution witnesses answer questions too.

7. Jurors listens to the case.

8. The judge rules according to laws.

9. A stenographer write down the whole conversation.

10. A clerk reads the verdict.

Check your answers on page 228.

Agreement with *I* and *You*

The word **I** is singular. The word **you** is singular when it refers to one person. The basic rules for subject-verb agreement do not apply to **I** and **you** (singular), as the table on page 21 shows. (The basic rules *do* apply to **he**, **she**, **it**, **we**, **you** [plural], and **they**.)

Patterns for Subject-Verb Agreement with *I* and *You*

	Singular Subjects	Plural Subjects
Even though **I** and **you** are singular, the verb has no **s** ending.	I work. You work. He work**s**. She work**s**. It work**s**.	We work. You work. They work.

Spotlight on Spelling: S Endings

When a word needs an **s** ending, you usually just add an **s**.
Examples:

file	turn	work
file**s**	turn**s**	work**s**

When a word ends in one of these ways, you need an **e** before the **s**:

ch	s	sh	x	z

Examples:

church**es**	bus**es**	dish**es**	box**es**	buzz**es**
watch**es**	miss**es**	wash**es**	mix**es**	fizz**es**

EXERCISE 3c

Part A. Edit the following sentences for subject-verb agreement. If a verb does not agree with a subject, change the verb. Before you start, reread the Spotlight above. (Note: Some sentences do not need correction.)

Example: Things ~~changes~~ *change* at work sometimes.

1. I hates my job now.

2. The new boss barks at the workers.

3. Some workers barks back at him.

4. The boss puts them on warning each time.

5. They complain to the union every week.

6. The union stays quiet about it.

7. Other bosses behaves better.

8. Your boss treat people right.

9. She mix with the workers easily.

10. You like her.

Part B. Complete each of the sentences. Be sure your verbs agree with the subjects that are provided.

Example: His son _____works out_____ every day.

1. I _____ every day.

2. You _____ every day.

3. The guards _____ every day.

4. My doctor _____ every day.

5. Her daughter _____ every day.

6. We _____ every day.

7. It _____ every day.

8. My friend _____ every day.

9. Her co-workers _____ every day.

10. Their friends _____ every day.

Check your answers on page 229.

Lesson 4

Subject-Verb Agreement in Describing Sentences

In Lesson 3 you edited action sentences for subject-verb agreement. In this lesson you will find verbs and subjects in describing sentences and edit for subject-verb agreement.

The Two Parts of Describing Sentences

Some sentences do not tell about an action. Instead, they describe one or more people or things.

Like action sentences, **describing sentences** have two main parts. There is a line between the two parts of the following describing sentences. The subjects and verbs are underlined.

The **naming part** tells who or what is described.

I | am an adult student.
Our classes | are usually interesting.
The picketers | look worn out.
This dessert | tastes very good.

The **describing part** tells something about the subject.

Finding Verbs and Subjects in Describing Sentences

No action occurs in a describing sentence. Therefore, to find the verb you can't ask which word tells the action. It is best to become familiar with the verbs that are common in describing sentences. That way you will recognize them when you see them. A list of frequently used verbs follows.

Verbs Common in Describing Sentences

appear	feel	remain	sound
be (am, are, is)	grow	seem	stay
become	look	smell	taste

The following steps will help you find the subject in a describing sentence.

How to Find the Subject in a Describing Sentence

STEP 1: Find the describing part—including the verb—of the sentence.

STEP 2: Ask yourself: Who or what (say the describing part of the sentence)?

Your answer to the question in the second step will be the subject. Use the two steps to find the subject in this sentence:

Tom stays depressed in winter.

STEP 1: Find the describing part—including the verb—of the sentence.
THE DESCRIBING PART: **stays depressed in winter**.
(The describing part includes **stays**, one of the verbs common in describing sentences.)

STEP 2: Ask yourself: Who or what stays depressed in winter?
ANSWER: **Tom**

Here is the sentence with the verb and the subject underlined:

Tom stays depressed in winter.

In each sentence underline the verb twice and the subject once.

Example: My <u>dreams</u> <u>are</u> often horrible.

1. One dream is a repeating dream.
2. I seem anxious at the beginning.
3. My wife looks upset.
4. We feel frightened by something.
5. The air becomes hot and steamy.
6. It smells awful.
7. Loud noises grow unbearable.
8. Objects appear evil.
9. My heart sounds like a bass drum.
10. I am suddenly awake with a scream.

Check your answers on page 229.

Editing for Subject-Verb Agreement in Describing Sentences

The patterns for subject-verb agreement in most describing sentences are the same as in action sentences.

Patterns for Subject-Verb Agreement

Singular subject	+	verb with an **s** ending
I or **you**	+	verb with **no** ending
Plural subject	+	verb with **no** ending

When the verb is a form of **be**, the agreement pattern is different.

Patterns for Subject-Verb Agreement with *Be*

Singular subject	+	**is**
I	+	**am**
You	+	**are**
Plural subject	+	**are**

Part A. Edit the following sentences for subject-verb agreement. If a verb does not agree with a subject, change the verb. (Note: Some sentences do not need correction.)

remains
Example: My hometown ~~remain~~ the same year after year.

1. I feels comfortable there.

2. The older people seems unchanged.

3. The brick houses look eternal.

4. Our wooden house appear a little worn.

5. The surrounding mountains grow more beautiful with time.

6. The air smell sweet with pine in those mountains.

7. The winds sound musical at night.

8. Spring water taste silver there.

9. I is at home in the mountains.

10. It stay the same there through all my changing.

Part B. Complete each of the following sentences. First, add the correct form of the verb in parentheses. Then add some describing words to complete each sentence.

Example: (am/are/is) My new apartment _____ is not very large _____.

1. (am/are/is) We _____.

2. (becomes/become) My youngest child _____.

3. (feels/feel) The union president _____.

4. (looks/look) You _____.

5. (am/are/is) The mayor _____.

6. (seems/seem) She _____.

7. (smells/smell) This kitchen _____.

8. (am/are/is) I _____.

9. (sounds/sound) The guitar _____.

10. (tastes/taste) The meals here _____.

Check your answers on page 229.

Subject-Verb Agreement with Special Subjects

In this lesson you will edit for subject-verb agreement in sentences that contain special subjects.

Singular Subjects That End with S

Most subjects that end with **s** are plural, but some are singular. Following are examples of sentences with subjects that end in **s**. The subjects and verbs are underlined. Notice the difference between the plural and the singular subjects.

The subjects in these sentences are **plural**.	Some <u>diseases</u> <u>are</u> easy to treat. These <u>courses</u> <u>are</u> hard for me.	The verbs in these sentences are **plural**.
The subjects in these sentences are **singular**.	<u>Mumps</u> <u>is</u> usually easy to treat. <u>Electronics</u> <u>is</u> hard for me.	The verbs in these sentences are **singular**.

Mumps is singular because it is the name of one disease. **Electronics** is singular because it is the name of one course or subject. Both words just happen to end in **s**, just as the singular words **bus** and **James** do. The **s** does not mean they are plural.

Here is a list of singular words that end in **s**. You should learn to recognize them.

Singular Words That End with S

aerobics	economics	mathematics	mumps
athletics	electronics	measles	news
checkers	gymnastics	molasses	politics

Spotlight on Special Agreement Patterns: *Have*

Have does not follow the regular agreement patterns for verbs. There are special agreement patterns for **have**, as shown here.

Singular subject +	**has**
I or **you** +	**have**
Plural subject +	**have**

Notice that the singular verb **has** ends with **s**. In that way, it is like other singular verbs.

Edit the following sentences for subject-verb agreement. If a verb does not agree with a subject, change the verb. Before you start, reread the Spotlight on page 26. (Note: Some sentences do not need correction.)

Example: The local news ~~are~~ *is* frightening sometimes.

1. Some exercises has benefits for the heart.

2. Aerobics are a popular type of such exercise.

3. Measles is usually a childhood disease.

4. Mumps cause swelling in glands near the ears.

5. Politics make strange bedfellows.

6. Some games has a lot of rules.

7. Checkers is a game like that.

8. Most topics catch my interest.

9. Gymnastics are my favorite sport.

10. Mathematics have many uses in my job.

Check your answers on page 229.

Plural Subjects That Name One Thing

We think of certain items as pairs: a pair of **scissors**, a pair of **sunglasses**, and a pair of **jeans**. When the names of those items are used as subjects, they are plural—even though they name only one object. Following are examples of sentences with such plural subjects. The subjects and verbs are underlined.

The subjects in these sentences name only one thing, but they are **plural**. The verbs are plural, too.

Her <u>scissors</u> <u>have</u> sharp blades.
My <u>sunglasses</u> <u>block</u> a lot of light.
Your new <u>jeans</u> <u>are</u> dirty.

Here is a list of plural subjects that name one thing. You should learn to recognize them.

Plural Words That Name One Thing				
glasses	pants	shorts	sunglasses	trunks
jeans	scissors	slacks	trousers	tweezers

Edit the following sentences for subject-verb agreement. If a verb does not agree with a subject, change the verb. You might want to review the agreement patterns for **have** in the Spotlight on page 26. (Note: Some sentences do not need correction.)

are
Example: My new slacks ~~is~~ too long.

1. Tweezers removes splinters easily most of the time.

2. His trousers clashes with his shirt.

3. My new glasses make me dizzy.

4. Your pants has a hole in the seat.

5. The scissors is part of my pocket knife.

6. My new swimming trunks are comfortable.

7. These jeans is too tight for you.

8. Her slacks are out of style.

9. Those sunglasses blocks out too much light.

10. Some shorts is just plain too short.

Check your answers on page 230.

Subjects That End in *-body*, *-one*, and *-thing*

Words that end in **-body**, **-one**, or **-thing** are singular although they may seem to be plural. Following are examples of sentences with such subjects. The subjects and verbs are underlined.

The subject in this sentence is **singular** and has a singular meaning. The verb is also singular.	<u>Someone</u> <u>is</u> at the door.
The subjects in these sentences are **singular** even though they have plural meanings. The verbs are also singular	<u>Anyone</u> <u>has</u> a chance at winning. <u>Everything</u> <u>goes</u> to his only surviving sister. <u>Nobody</u> <u>feels</u> up to it today.

A way to remember that such subjects are singular is to concentrate on their endings: **-body**, **-one**, and **-thing**. The meaning of each of those endings is singular. Become familiar with the words in the following list.

-body Endings	*-one* Endings	*-thing* Endings
anybody	anyone	anything
everybody	everyone	everything
nobody	no one	nothing
somebody	someone	something

EXERCISE 5c

Edit the following sentences for subject-verb agreement. If a verb does not agree with a subject, change the verb. Don't forget about the special agreement patterns for **have**, which are shown in the Spotlight on page 26. (Note: Some sentences do not need correction.)

$\qquad\qquad$ *needs*
Example: Everyone ~~need~~ some kind of income or financial support.

1. Nobody lives for free.

2. Everything cost something.

3. Someone have an income in every household.

4. Everyone knows the importance of financial support.

5. Everybody benefit from taxes.

Check your answers on page 230.

Subjects That Name Groups or Amounts

Subjects that name a group or an amount are usually singular. Following are examples of sentences whose subjects name groups or amounts. The subjects and verbs are underlined.

The **singular** subjects in these sentences name **groups**. They take singular verbs.	The <u>team</u> <u>plays</u> night games most of the time. The <u>club</u> <u>bowls</u> on Thursdays.
The **singular** subjects in these sentences name **amounts**. They take singular verbs.	Twenty-four <u>hours</u> <u>is</u> one day. Fifty <u>dollars</u> <u>buys</u> little food.

Even though a team or a club may have many members, it is still **one** group. Therefore, **team**, **club**, and other words that name groups are usually singular.

A similar rule applies to **hours**, **dollars**, and other measurement words. With numbers before them, each describes **one** amount, so they are singular.

Part A. Edit the following sentences for subject-verb agreement. If a verb does not agree with a subject, change the verb. (Note: Some sentences do not need correction.)

Example: Sixteen dollars ~~are~~ is all I have.

1. My family likes picnics in the summer.

2. Three years are a long time to wait.

3. The audience seem angry at the comedian.

4. The committee watch its spending closely.

5. A hundred dollars are not enough for rent.

6. Two cups is enough milk for tapioca.

7. My class have an excellent teacher.

8. Two tablespoons are a lot of hot sauce.

9. The whole staff comes here after work.

10. Twenty-six miles are the length of the marathon.

Part B. Complete each of the following sentences. First add the correct form of the verb in parentheses. Then add one or more words to complete each sentence.

Example: (practices/practice) My softball team ___practices on Thursdays___.

1. (looks/look) Molasses _____.

2. (has/have) Your shorts _____.

3. (pays/pay) Five hundred dollars _____.

4. (plays/play) The rock group _____.

5. (am/are/is) No one _____.

6. (costs/cost) These swimming trunks _____.

7. (am/are/is) One hundred yards _____.

8. (likes/like) My class _____.

9. (lasts/last) Chest colds _____.

10. (works/work) My scissors _____.

Check your answers on page 230.

Subject-Verb Agreement with Compound Subjects

In this lesson you will edit for subject-verb agreement in sentences with various types of compound subjects.

Compound Subjects with *and*

Some sentences have a **compound subject**. In such sentences there are at least two parts to the subject. Those parts are often connected by the word **and**. When **and** connects the parts, the verb is plural. It tells the action, or begins the description, of two or more persons or things.

Look at the following example sentences. In each, the parts of the compound subject and the verb are underlined.

In this sentence, two words name the things that are described.

The <u>street</u> and the <u>sidewalk</u> <u>are</u> wet.

The connecting word in each sentence is **and**. The verbs in both sentences are **plural**.

In this sentence, three words name the persons who do the action.

<u>Tom</u>, <u>his father</u>, and <u>I</u> <u>work</u> there.

EXERCISE 6a

Edit the following sentences for subject-verb agreement. Some have compound subjects. If a subject and verb do not agree, change the verb. (Note: Some sentences do not need correction.)

need

Example: Clarence and Lonny ~~needs~~ the literacy program.

1. The main library run a literacy program.

2. Clarence and Lonny are two of the students.

3. Julio, Katie, and Ron helps them with reading and math.

4. Clarence need a lot of help right now.

5. He and a co-worker is in line for the same promotion.

6. People takes written tests for promotions at their company.

7. Clarence have difficulty with reading.

8. Mathematics are also not easy for him.

9. Clarence and his co-worker are in competition with each other.

10. Clarence need high test scores.

Check your answers on page 230.

Compound Subjects with *Either . . . or* and *Neither . . . nor*

In some compound subjects, the parts are connected by the words *Either . . . or* or *Neither . . . nor*. One part, not both parts, of the subject does the action or is described. The verb agrees with the part of the subject that is closer to it.

The parts of the compound subject and the verb are underlined in each of the following example sentences.

The connecting words are **Either . . . or**.

Either the <u>sons</u> or the <u>father</u> <u>works</u> late.
Either the <u>father</u> or the <u>sons</u> <u>work</u> late.
Either <u>you</u> or <u>I</u> <u>am</u> late.

In all these sentences each verb agrees with the part of the subject closer to it.

The connecting words are **Neither . . . nor**.

Neither <u>Hector</u> nor the <u>Smiths</u> <u>are</u> here.
Neither the <u>Smiths</u> nor <u>Hector</u> <u>is</u> here.
Neither <u>he</u> nor <u>I</u> <u>am</u> sorry.

Spotlight on Capitalization, Punctuation, and Style

When **three or more** parts of a subject are connected by **and**, commas go between the parts. The last comma goes before the **and**.

A person's name is **capitalized**.

Rosa, Jorge, Kim, and I drive buses.
The pay, hours, and benefits seem good.
Promptness, courtesy, skill, and caution are important.

When I is part of a list of people in a sentence, it usually comes last.

EXERCISE 6b

Part A. Edit the following sentences for subject-verb agreement. Most have compound subjects. If a subject and verb do not agree, change the verb. (Note: Some sentences do not need correction.)

teaches
Example: Neither Julio nor Ron ~~teach~~ every evening.

1. Lonny is in the literacy program because of his children.

2. Either Julio or Ron help Lonny with math on Tuesday evenings.

3. Lonny help his wife with the same math at home later in the week.

4. Either Lonny or Latisha help their children with their homework.

5. Their son and daughters respects their parents for that.

6. Lonny and Latisha shows interest in their children that way.

7. Lonny, Latisha, and their children benefit from the literacy program.

8. Neither their son nor their daughters has much trouble with schoolwork.

9. The children are ahead of their parents in math now.

10. Neither Lonny nor Latisha are comfortable with that.

Part B. Combine each set of sentences by writing one sentence with a compound subject. Connect the parts of the subjects with **and**, **Either . . . or**, or **Neither . . . nor**. Be sure the subjects and verbs agree in the sentences you write. Before you start, reread the Spotlight on page 32.

Examples:

All of these are true: Jerry is here. Fernando is here. Hiro is here. I am here.

<u>Jerry, Fernando, Hiro, and I are here.</u>

Either of these is true: The bus comes late. The train comes late.

<u>Either the bus or the train comes late.</u>

Neither of these is true: He is happy. I am happy.

<u>Neither he nor I am happy.</u>

1. Both of these are true: Julio tutors people at the library. Ron tutors people at the library.

_____

2. Either of these is true: My son drives Julio to the library. I drive Julio to the library.

_____

3. All of these are true: Clarence benefits from their help. Lonny benefits from their help. Latisha benefits from their help.

_____

4. Either of these is true: Julio helps Lonny with math each night. Ron helps Lonny with math each night.

_____

5. Neither of these is true: Reading is easy for Clarence. Mathematics is easy for Clarence.

_____

6. Both of these are true: Lonny is better at math now. Latisha is better at math now.

_____

7. Either of these is true: Their son needs attention tonight. Their daughters need attention tonight.

_____

8. Both of these are true: Their son admires Lonny and Latisha. Their daughters admire Lonny and Latisha.

_____

9. All of these are true: Clarence has new skills. Lonny has new skills. Latisha has new skills.

_____

10. Neither of these is true: Julio takes the credit. Ron takes the credit.

_____

Check your answers on page 230.

Lesson 7

Subject-Verb Agreement
When the Subject Follows the Verb

In this lesson you will edit for subject-verb agreement in sentences that have the subject after the verb.

Sentences That Begin with *There* or *Here*

In many sentences that begin with **there** or **here**, the subject comes after the verb. The words **there** and **here** are neither singular nor plural. They have nothing to do with subject-verb agreement. To check agreement in such sentences, you need to look at the subject even though it follows the verb.

In the following example sentences, the verbs and subjects are underlined.

These sentences have **singular** subjects and verbs.

There <u>is</u> an easy <u>answer</u>.
There <u>goes</u> the <u>bus</u>.
Here <u>is</u> your <u>toolbox</u>.
Here <u>comes</u> <u>trouble</u>.

In all these sentences the subjects come **after** the verbs.

These sentences have **plural** subjects and verbs.

There <u>are</u> no easy <u>answers</u>.
There <u>go</u> the <u>lights</u>.
Here <u>are</u> your <u>tools</u>.
Here <u>come</u> the <u>children</u>.

Spotlight on Spelling: _Does_ and _Goes_

The singular forms of **do** and **go** are spelled with an **es** ending. The patterns for subject-verb agreement are the regular patterns, as shown here.

Singular subject + **does/goes**
I or **you**   + **do/go**
Plural subject   + **do/go**

Because the singular verbs **does** and **goes** end with **s**, they are like other singular verbs.

EXERCISE 7a

Edit the following sentences for subject-verb agreement. If a verb does not agree with a subject, change the verb. Before you start, reread the Spotlight above. (Note: Some sentences do not need correction.)

           come
Example: Here ~~comes~~ the new economy models.

1. There is several interesting new models.

2. There is some new features.

3. Here are my favorite design.

4. There are many improvements.

5. There is the old floor models.

6. Here are the sale price for the floor models.

7. Here come a hopeful couple.

8. There are their old wreck.

9. Here comes a tow truck.

10. There go one old floor model.

Check your answers on page 231.

Questions

In statements the subject usually comes before the verb. In many questions, that order is reversed. In a sense, such questions are statements turned around, as the following example shows.

| This sentence is a **statement**. | <u>John</u> <u>is</u> fine. | The subject comes **before** the verb. |
| This sentence is a **question**. | How <u>is</u> <u>John</u>? | The subject comes **after** the verb. |

The words **John is** in the statement change places in the question and become **is John**.

Usually when a form of **be** is the verb in a question, it comes before the subject. This reverse order for the subject and verb does not change how they agree. Notice the subject-verb agreement in the following examples. The verbs and subjects are underlined.

These questions have **singular** subjects and verbs.

<u>Is</u> <u>he</u> your brother?
<u>Am</u> <u>I</u> his keeper?
When <u>is</u> my <u>appointment</u>?
Where <u>is</u> <u>he</u>?
Who <u>is</u> your <u>boss</u>?

In all these questions the subjects follow the verbs, which are forms of **be**.

These questions have **plural** subjects and verbs.

<u>Are</u> <u>they</u> here?
<u>Are</u> <u>we</u> responsible?
How <u>are</u> your <u>parents</u>?
What <u>are</u> your favorite <u>foods</u>?
Why <u>are</u> <u>you</u> so early?

You need to be careful when you look for the subject in a question. The words **what** or **who** are often the subject of a question when the verb is *not* a form of **be**. In such cases, the verb usually follows the subject, as in a statement. When **what** or **who** is the subject, the verb is always singular. In these examples the subjects and verbs are underlined.

In these questions, **who** and **what** are the subjects.

<u>Who</u> <u>works</u> for him?
<u>What</u> <u>goes</u> on this line?

In both sentences the verb follows the subject and is singular.

EXERCISE 7b

Edit the following sentences for subject-verb agreement. If a verb does not agree with a subject, change the verb. (Note: Some sentences do not need correction.)

are
Example: Who ~~is~~ your co-workers?

1. What go with corned beef?

2. When is your morning break?

3. Where is your tools?

4. Why is the pliers broken?

5. How is Junior and his sister?

6. Is everything ready?

7. Who repair computers?

8. Who are your closest friends?

9. Are everyone at the office?

10. What is your new hours?

Check your answers on page 231.

Reverse-Order Statements

Like most questions, some statements have the subject and verb in reverse order. Such statements often begin with words that tell where or when something is. The order of the subject and verb does not affect how they agree.

The following examples show statements first in normal and then in reverse order. The verbs and subjects are underlined.

These statements are in **normal order**.

My <u>interview</u> <u>is</u> (in the morning.) ← These words tell **when**.

The <u>cabinets</u> <u>are</u> (below the sink.) ← These words tell **where**.

These words tell **when**. → (In the morning) <u>is</u> my <u>interview</u>.

These words tell **where**. → (Below the sink) <u>are</u> <u>cabinets</u>.

These statements are in **reverse order**.

When you check agreement in reverse-order sentences, it may help to say the sentences to yourself in normal order.

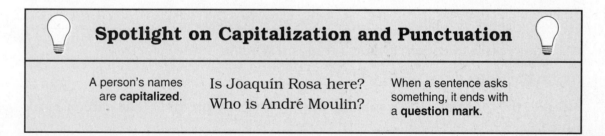

Spotlight on Capitalization and Punctuation

A person's names are **capitalized**.

Is Joaquín Rosa here?
Who is André Moulin?

When a sentence asks something, it ends with a **question mark**.

EXERCISE 7c

Part A. Edit the following sentences for subject-verb agreement. If a verb does not agree with a subject, change the verb. (Note: Some sentences do not need correction.)

Example: In the first few seconds ~~are~~ is the theme music.

1. Over there is more trees.

2. In the morning are my best hours.

3. On the top shelf is the cereals.

4. Below them are the sugar.

5. At 6:00 o'clock is the news.

6. In December comes the shortest days.

7. In June is the longest days.

8. After dinner comes the dessert.

9. Under the car seat is the ice scrapers.

10. In the trunk are the suitcases.

Part B. Complete the following sentences. Be sure the subject of your sentence agrees with the verb that is already there. Before you start, reread the Spotlight on page 37.

Example: Why is _____ *it so dark?* _____

1. There are _____

2. Here comes _____

3. When are _____

4. How is _____

5. Where are _____

Part C. Follow the directions to complete each sentence.

Example: Tell the time of the best TV movies.

Late at night _____ *are the best TV movies.* _____

1. Answer this question. (Name 3 things.): What is in the closet?

   In the closet _____

2. Ask the question that would get this answer: My brothers take care of him.

   Who_____ him?

3. Ask the question that would get this answer: John and Sylvia are fine.

   How_____

4. Tell the time of the heaviest traffic.

   During the morning rush hour _____

5. Tell the location of the most dust.

   Under the bed _____

Check your answers on page 231.

Subject-Verb Agreement with Interrupting Phrases

In this lesson you will edit for subject-verb agreement in sentences that have words between the subject and the verb.

Finding Subjects Separated from Verbs

In many sentences the subject and the verb are not next to each other. Often words that add information to a sentence come between the subject and the verb. The subjects and verbs are underlined in the following example sentences. Notice that words come between the subjects and the verbs in the second set of sentences.

<table>
<tr><td>In these sentences the subjects and verbs are next to each other.</td><td>These <u>numbers</u> <u>are</u> the page numbers.
The <u>supervisor</u> <u>is</u> out sick.
The <u>sides</u> <u>stand</u> an inch high.</td></tr>
<tr><td>In these sentences words come between the subjects and verbs.</td><td>The <u>numbers</u> at the top <u>are</u> the page numbers.
The <u>supervisor</u> of the shop <u>is</u> out sick.
The <u>sides</u> of the pan <u>stand</u> an inch high.</td></tr>
</table>

Editing for subject-verb agreement in sentences like the ones in the second set above above takes special care. The following example shows why that is so. Which verb is correct in this sentence?

The people on the bus (are/is) tired.

If **people** is the subject, it goes with the plural verb **are**. If **bus** is the subject, it goes with the singular verb **is**.

To decide which verb is correct, you must know which word is the subject.

ASK: Who or what are/is tired?
ANSWER: **The people are tired.**

People is the subject. The words **on the bus** come between the subject and the verb. The sentence is correct this way:

The people on the bus **are** tired.

Spotlight on Spelling: S Endings After Y

You need to add an **s** ending to a word that ends with **y**.

When a vowel (a, e, i, o, u) comes before the **y**, add an **s**:

bay	key	toy	guy
bay**s**	key**s**	toy**s**	guy**s**

When another letter comes before the **y**, change the **y** to **i** and add **es**:

baby	carry	sky	supply	try
bab**ies**	carr**ies**	sk**ies**	suppl**ies**	tr**ies**

EXERCISE 8a

Edit the following sentences for subject-verb agreement. If a verb does not agree with a subject, change the verb. Before you start, reread the Spotlight above. (Note: Some sentences do not need correction.)

                                             are
Example: The patrons of this barbershop ~~is~~ a mixed lot.

1. The short man near the windows carry a lot of money around.

2. The younger man with glasses is always with him.

3. Several stories around town casts suspicion on them.

4. One tale about some bad debts curl my hair.

5. The debtors in the story uses wheel chairs now.

6. Anyone with any brains stay away from Shorty.

7. The old man by the magazines has a different reputation.

8. Everybody within miles respect him.

9. People without power is his clients.

10. Anyone with problems get Poppy's ear.

Check your answers on page 231.

Identifying Interrupting Phrases

    Checking subject-verb agreement can be especially tricky in sentences when words come between the subject and verb.
    Which verb is correct in this sentence?

        This bag of groceries (are/is) heavy.

To find the subject, it doesn't help to ask "Who or what are/is heavy?" You can answer either way: **The bag is heavy** or **The groceries are heavy**. In sentences like this it is more helpful to find the words that come between the subject and the verb.

Words between a subject and a verb are often a **phrase**, a group of two or more words that go together. A **preposition**—a word like **at**, **of**, or **on**—begins some phrases. Look at the example sentence again:

This word is a preposition.

This bag **of** groceries (are/is) heavy.

These words are a phrase.

The word **groceries** is in the phrase that begins with **of**. A word in a phrase cannot be the subject of a sentence. Therefore, **bag** is the subject. The sentence is correct this way:

This bag of groceries **is** heavy.

A list of some common prepositions follows. You should learn to recognize them so that you can spot phrases, which will help you when you edit for subject-verb agreement.

Common Prepositions

about	before	for	onto
above	behind	from	outside
across	below	in	over
after	beside	inside	to
against	between	into	under
around	beyond	of	with
at	by	on	without

EXERCISE 8b

Edit the following sentences for subject-verb agreement. If a verb does not agree with a subject, change the verb. (Note: Some sentences do not need correction.)

tempts
Example: This plate of desserts ~~tempt~~ me.

1. Two pans of sliced turkey is in the oven.

2. Those pots of water has salt in them.

3. This pan of candied yams goes here.

4. A bowl of carrots add more color.

5. A large pot of greens are a must.

6. Two pounds of cranberries make enough sauce.

7. The bowls of dressing smell wonderful.

8. A mound of potatoes satisfy him.

9. That batch of cookies look fattening.

10. The loaves of bread is still warm.

Check your answers on page 232.

Phrases with Words That Replace *and*

In Lesson 6 you edited sentences with compound subjects. You saw that when parts of a subject are connected by the word **and**, the verb is plural. As a reminder, look at this example. The verb and the parts of the subject are underlined.

The word **and** connects the parts of the subject.   The <u>house</u> and the <u>furniture</u> <u>are</u> for sale.   The verb is **plural**.

This sentence can be written another way—without a compound subject. Compare the following sentence to the one you just read:

The subject is **house**.   These words replace **and**.

The <u>house</u>, (along with) the furniture, <u>is</u> for sale.

This is a phrase. The verb is singular to go with **house**.

It may seem that the subject in this sentence is plural because both the house and the furniture are for sale. It is not compound, however, because the word **and** is not used. Instead, the words **along with** are used. They begin a phrase that comes between the subject and the verb. The word **furniture** is in the phrase. Therefore, **furniture** cannot be part of the subject. The subject is **house**. It agrees with the singular verb **is**.

Compare the following sets of sentences. Look carefully at the subject-verb agreement in each sentence.

These subjects are compound. The parts of each subject are connected by **and**.

My <u>mother</u> **and** her <u>sisters</u> <u>go</u> to movies every weekend.   The verbs are **plural**.

<u>John</u> **and** the other <u>plumbers</u> <u>are</u> on strike.

Hard <u>work</u> **and** <u>skill</u> <u>make</u> a valuable employee.

My <u>son</u>, my <u>job</u>, **and** my <u>classes</u> <u>keep</u> me busy.

| These sentences have singular, not compound, subjects. | My <u>mother</u>, **along with** her sisters, <u>goes</u> to movies every weekend. | The verbs are **singular**. |
| | John, **as well as** the other plumbers, <u>is</u> on strike. | |

My <u>mother</u>, (**along with** her sisters,) <u>goes</u> to movies every weekend.

John, (**as well as** the other plumbers,) <u>is</u> on strike.

Hard <u>work</u>, (**in addition to** skill,) <u>makes</u> a valuable employee.

My <u>son</u>, (**together with** my job and my classes,) <u>keeps</u> me busy.

These are phrases. Each begins with words (the ones in dark type) that replace **and**.

It is a good idea to become familiar with the following words. They are often used to replace **and**. They begin phrases.

Words That Replace *and*

along with   in addition to
as well as   together with

Spotlight on Punctuation

Commas go before and after phrases that begin with **along with**, **as well as**, **in addition to**, or **together with** when they come between subjects and verbs.

This movie, along with its sequel, stars your idol.

The nurses, as well as some other workers, are on strike.

His latenesses, in addition to his attitude, cause problems.

The price, together with the tax, comes to $35.

EXERCISE 8c

Edit the following sentences for subject-verb agreement. Some sentences have compound subjects; some do not. If a verb does not agree with a subject, change the verb. (Note: Some sentences do not need correction.)

Example: My children, as well as my husband, ~~works~~ work all day.

1. A job, as well as a career, appeal to me now.

2. Medicine, along with law, is my interest.

3. My hopes, together with my fears, makes me nervous.

4. My children, together with my husband, encourages my hopes.

5. Jobs and careers is the focus of this fair.

6. A hospital, together with the junior college, sponsor an interesting program.

7. A paid job, along with free classes, are available at the hospital.

8. School, in addition to a job, means long hours.

9. Neither long hours nor hard work scare me.

10. The application and a pen is in front of me.

Check your answers on page 232.

Words That Can Be Singular or Plural as Subjects

When they are subjects, some words can be either singular or plural. They are often followed by a phrase that tells you whether the subject is singular or plural. The subjects and verbs are underlined in the following sentences.

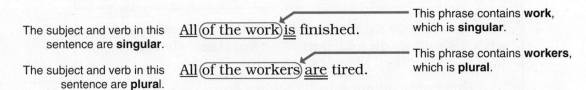

The subject and verb in this sentence are **singular**.   All (of the work) is finished.   This phrase contains **work**, which is **singular**.

The subject and verb in this sentence are **plural**.   All (of the workers) are tired.   This phrase contains **workers**, which is **plural**.

In the first sentence above, **all** is singular because it refers to **work**, which is singular. Therefore, the verb is singular: **is**. In the second sentence, **all** is plural because it refers to **workers**, which is plural. Therefore, the verb is plural: **are**.

Following are some words that can be singular or plural as subjects. You should learn to recognize them.

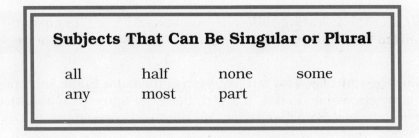

Subjects That Can Be Singular or Plural

all	half	none	some
any	most	part	

Part A. Edit the following sentences for subject-verb agreement. If a verb does not agree with a subject, change the verb. (Note: Some sentences do not need correction.)

Example: Only half of the battle ~~are~~ *is* won.

1. All of the tenants knows about the situation.

2. Part of our current problem come from a lack of tenant unity.

3. All of the tenants has strong opinions.

4. Most of the people favors some kind of action.

5. Any of our possible actions have drawbacks.

6. None of our plans is foolproof.

7. Some of the older tenants is afraid.

8. All of those tenants needs courage.

9. Most of the solution rest in their hands.

10. Most of my patience are gone.

Part B. Complete the following sentences. First add the correct form of the verb in parentheses. Then add some other words to complete the sentence.

Example: (am/are/is)   The used cars at that place _____ *are not too reliable.* _____

1. (walks/walk)   The man on crutches _____

2. (am/are/is)   Those cartons of milk_____

3. (suits/suit)   The salary, along with the benefits, _____

4. (needs/need)   All of the strikers _____

5. (has/have)   Some of those movies _____

Part C. Complete the following sentences. First add a phrase that begins with a preposition from the list on page 41. Then add the correct form of the verb in parentheses. Last add some other words to complete the sentence.

Example: (am/are/is)   The book _____ *on the table is mine.* _____

1. (goes/go)   A child _____

2. (weighs/weigh)   Some bags _____

3. (supports/support) The boss _____

4. (am/are/is)   Some _____

5. (makes/make)   Most_____

Part D. Complete the following sentences. First add a phrase that begins with words that replace **and**. (Use the list on page 43.) Then add the correct form of the verb in parentheses followed by some other words that complete the sentence. Before you begin, reread the Spotlight on page 43.

Example: (belongs/belong) The book, <u>as well as the pencil, belongs over here.</u>

    1. (goes/go)   This child _____

    2. (weighs/weigh)   Those bags_____

    3. (works/work)   The boss _____

    4. (am/are/is)   My sister _____

    5. (seems/seem)   Her friend _____

Check your answers on page 232.

GED PRACTICE 1

At the end of each chapter in this unit there is a GED Practice. GED Practice 1 introduces the two parts of the Writing Skills Test of the GED. Like the three other practices in this unit, it gives you a chance to apply the skills you are learning to items similar to those on the GED.

Part 1 of the Writing Skills Test

Part 1 of the Writing Skills Test is made up of 55 multiple-choice items. Most ask you to find and correct mistakes in short passages you read. Such items are presented in one of two ways. Look at the example on page 48. A key with the example points out special features of the passage and the items that follow it.

Both items are about subject-verb agreement. The correct answer to Item 1 is Choice (4); to Item 2, Choice (2).

Notice that the choices in each item are not only about subject-verb agreement. For example, Choice (2) in Item 1 is about capitalization of the first word in a sentence. The choices in most items on the GED offer a variety of correction possibilities.

For practice with multiple-choice items that cover the skills you have studied so far in this book, do Part 1 of GED Practice 1. It begins on page 50.

<u>Items 1 and 2</u> refer to the following paragraphs.

(b)   (1) There are two parts to the GED writing skills test. (2) There is 55 questions on the first part. (3) It takes about 75 minutes. (4) On the second part you have about 45 minutes to write a 200-word essay.

    (5) There is only one score for the Writing Skills Test. (6) It include both parts of the test.

(c)   (d)

1. Sentence 2: **There is 55 questions on the first part.**

(e)   What correction should be made to this sentence?

    (1) replace <u>There</u> with <u>It</u>
    (2) change <u>There</u> to <u>there</u>
    (3) replace <u>There</u> with <u>Here</u>
    (4) change <u>is</u> to <u>are</u>
(f)   (5) no correction is necessary

(c)   (g)

2. Sentence 6: **<u>It include</u> both parts of the test.**

(e)   Which of the following is the best way to write the underlined portion of this sentence? If you think the original is the best way, choose option (1).

(f)   (1) It include
    (2) It includes
    (3) it include
    (4) including
    (5) They includes

Key

(a)   This sentence tells which items refer to the passage that follows.

(b)   The sentences in the passage are numbered. Each paragraph is indented.

(c)   This part of the item tells which sentence the question is about.

(d)   This part of the item is an exact copy of a sentence from the passage. Here it is printed in dark type.

(e)   This is the question you must answer.

(f)   If there is nothing in the original sentence that needs correction, choose this option.

(g)   This part of the item is an exact copy of a sentence from the passage. Here it is printed in dark type. Part of the sentence is underlined.

Part 2 of the Writing Skills Test

On Part 2 of the Writing Skills Test you will write an essay. Before you finish with it, you will check it for mistakes.

The lessons you have been studying will help you find and correct mistakes you may make in your writing. You should make corrections as neatly as possible.

The following example shows ways to correct different kinds of mistakes. A key with the example describes ways to make corrections neatly.

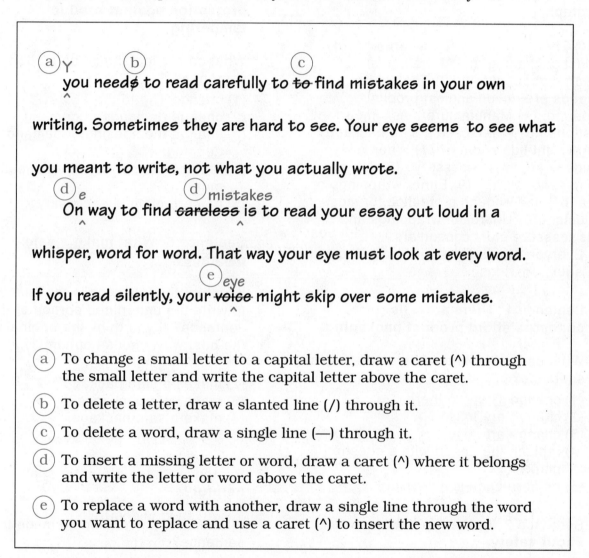

(a) To change a small letter to a capital letter, draw a caret (^) through the small letter and write the capital letter above the caret.

(b) To delete a letter, draw a slanted line (/) through it.

(c) To delete a word, draw a single line (—) through it.

(d) To insert a missing letter or word, draw a caret (^) where it belongs and write the letter or word above the caret.

(e) To replace a word with another, draw a single line through the word you want to replace and use a caret (^) to insert the new word.

Part 2 of GED Practice 1 begins on page 54. It gives you a chance to use the skills you have studied so far in this book to correct mistakes in paragraphs like those you might write in an essay.

Part 1

Directions: Choose the <u>one best answer</u> to each item.

<u>Items 1 through 7</u> refer to the following paragraph.

(1) There are a list of concerns about product packaging. (2) At the top is concerns about safety. (3) The public demands protection against product tampering. (4) Manufacturers ask important questions. (5) What make a safe package? (6) Are tight lids enough? (7) When are outside wrappings necessary? (8) Are a plastic seal helpful? (9) Either wrappings or a seal provide enough protection for most products. (10) Unbroken wrappings and seals reassure most consumers. (11) Everyone feels safer with more secure packaging

1. Sentence 1: **There are a list of concerns about product packaging.**

   What correction should be made to this sentence?
   (1) change <u>There</u> to <u>there</u>
   (2) change <u>are</u> to <u>is</u>
   (3) change <u>are</u> to <u>am</u>
   (4) replace the period with a question mark
   (5) no correction is necessary

2. Sentence 2: **At the top is concerns about safety.**

   What correction should be made to this sentence?
   (1) change <u>At</u> to <u>at</u>
   (2) remove the word <u>is</u>
   (3) change <u>is</u> to <u>am</u>
   (4) change <u>is</u> to <u>are</u>
   (5) no correction is necessary

3. Sentence 3: **The public demands protection against product tampering.**

   What correction should be made to this sentence?
   (1) change <u>The</u> to <u>the</u>
   (2) change <u>demands</u> to <u>demand</u>
   (3) change the spelling of <u>demands</u> to <u>demandes</u>
   (4) replace the period with a question mark
   (5) no correction is necessary

4. Sentence 5: **What <u>make a safe package?</u>**

   Which of the following is the best way to write the underlined portion of this sentence? If you think the original is the best way, choose option (1).
   (1) make a safe package?
   (2) makes a safe package?
   (3) make safe packages?
   (4) make a safe package.
   (5) makes a safe package.

5. Sentence 8: **Are a plastic seal helpful?**

   What correction should be made to this sentence?
   (1) change <u>Are</u> to <u>Is</u>
   (2) change <u>Are</u> to <u>is</u>
   (3) change <u>Are</u> to <u>are</u>
   (4) change <u>seal</u> to <u>seals</u>
   (5) no correction is necessary

6. Sentence 9: **Either wrappings or a seal provide** enough protection for most products.

Which of the following is the best way to write the underlined portion of this sentence? If you think the original is the best way, choose option (1).

(1) or a seal provide
(2) or a seal provides
(3) and a seal provide
(4) and seals provides
(5) nor a seal provides

7. Sentence 11: **Everyone feels safer with more secure packaging**

What correction should be made to this sentence?

(1) change Everyone to everyone
(2) change feels to feel
(3) insert a period after packaging
(4) insert a question mark after packaging
(5) no correction is necessary

Items 8 through 14 refer to the following paragraph.

(1) Packaged food and other items in a grocery store comes in various sizes. (2) Are the largest sizes always the most economical. (3) The labels on each shelf has the answer. (4) There is labels for every size of every product. (5) On those labels are unit prices. (6) A unit price tells the cost for a standard amount of a product in a particular package. (7) One-pound boxes of rice costs $.89 in a certain store. (8) Rice in large bags sells for $.84 per pound according to the unit price label. (9) Rice, along with most other foods, costs less in the larger size in that store. (10) You should read all unit price labels, though. (11) Some of the unit prices is lower for smaller packages in some stores at times.

8. Sentence 1: **Packaged food and other items in a grocery store comes in various sizes.**

What correction should be made to this sentence?

(1) change Packaged to packaged
(2) change the spelling of items to itemes
(3) change comes to come
(4) replace the period with a question mark
(5) no correction is necessary

9. Sentence 2: **Are the largest sizes always the most economical.**

Which of the following is the best way to write the underlined portion of this sentence? If you think the original is the best way, choose option (1).

(1) Are the largest sizes always the most economical.
(2) Is the largest sizes always the most economical.
(3) Are the largest size always the most economical.
(4) Are the largest sizes always the most economical?
(5) Is the largest sizes always the most economical?

10. Sentence 3: **The labels on each shelf has the answer.**

What correction should be made to this sentence?

(1) change The to the
(2) change the spelling of labels to labeles
(3) change has to have
(4) replace the period with a question mark
(5) no correction is necessary

11. Sentence 4: **There is labels for every size of every product.**

What correction should be made to this sentence?

(1) change There to there
(2) change is to are
(3) change is to am
(4) replace the period with a question mark
(5) no correction is necessary

12. Sentence 7: **One-pound boxes of rice costs $.89 in a certain store.**

What correction should be made to this sentence?

(1) change the spelling of boxes to boxs
(2) change the spelling of costs to costes
(3) change costs to cost
(4) replace the period with a question mark
(5) no correction is necessary

13. Sentence 9: **Rice, along with most other foods, costs less in the larger size in that store.**

Which of the following is the best way to write the underlined portion of this sentence? If you think the original is the best way, choose option (1).

(1) Rice, along with most other foods, costs
(2) Rice, along with most other foods, cost
(3) Rice along with most other foods cost
(4) Rice along with most other foods costs
(5) Rice, and most other foods, costs

14. Sentence 11: **Some of the unit prices is lower for smaller packages in some stores at times.**

What correction should be made to this sentence?

(1) change is to are
(2) change is to am
(3) change the spelling of packages to packags
(4) change the spelling of stores to stors
(5) no correction is necessary

Items 15 through 20 refer to the following paragraph.

(1) My work group gets special attention. (2) Everyone have classes three times a week. (3) Two hours is the length of each class. (4)   Writing math, and electronics are our courses. (5) Electronics are the most challenging course for us. (6) Either the students or the instructor brings problems to class. (7) The group searchs for solutions together. (8) The instructor, I and my co-workers enjoy our classes.

15. Sentence 2: **Everyone have classes three times a week.**

What correction should be made to this sentence?

(1) replace Everyone with Every one
(2) change have to has
(3) change the spelling of classes to classs
(4) replace the period with a question mark
(5) no correction is necessary

16. Sentence 3: **Two hours is the length of each class.**

Which of the following is the best way to write the underlined portion of this sentence? If you think the original is the best way, choose option (1).

(1) Two hours is
(2) Two hours are
(3) Two hour is
(4) Two hour are
(5) two hours is

17. Sentence 4: **Writing math, and electronics are our courses.**

Which of the following is the best way to write the underlined portion of this sentence? If you think the original is the best way, choose option (1).

(1) Writing math, and electronics are
(2) Writing math, and electronics is
(3) Writing, math, and electronics are
(4) Writing, math, and electronics is
(5) Writing, math and, electronics are

18. Sentence 5: **Electronics are the most challenging course for us.**

What correction should be made to this sentence?

(1) change Electronics to electronics
(2) change are to am
(3) change are to is
(4) replace the period with a question mark
(5) no correction is necessary

19. Sentence 7: **The group searchs for solutions together.**

What correction should be made to this sentence?

(1) change The to the
(2) change searchs to search
(3) change the spelling of searchs to searches
(4) replace the period with a question mark
(5) no correction is necessary

20. Sentence 8: **The instructor, I and my co-workers enjoy our classes.**

Which of the following is the best way to write the underlined portion of this sentence? If you think the original is the best way, choose option (1).

(1) The instructor, I and my co-workers enjoy
(2) The instructor, I and my co-workers enjoys
(3) The instructor, I, and my co-workers enjoy
(4) The instructor, my co-workers, and I enjoy
(5) The instructor, my co-workers and, I enjoy

Part 2

Directions: Edit the following paragraphs. The number of errors in each is shown.

- If any verb and subject do not agree, change the verb.
- Capitalize any word that should be capitalized.
- Correct errors in punctuation.
- Correct errors in spelling.

Paragraph 1 (3 errors)

Dogs guard property well. They barks warnings. My collie watch my house. she barks at strangers.

Paragraph 2 (3 errors)

Natural events causes homelessness sometimes. Erupting volcanoes destroy whole towns. earthquakes wreck houses and large apartment buildings. People is homeless because of wind, rain, and fire.

Paragraph 3 (6 errors)

The problem of poverty worry many people in this city. It is easy to see here. A lot of people begs on our streets. Some of them looks simply poor. There is others with mental illnesses. Either drugs or alcohol control the lives of many others. Is a solution possible in our society.

Paragraph 4 (6 errors)

I looks a lot better now. Aerobics keep me slim. My group exercises a half hour every day. Thirty minutes are a good workout. We wears sweat pants. The sweat pants is loose for easy movement. Everybody have a lot of fun in our group.

Paragraph 5 (7 errors)

Nobody grow as fast as my teenage son. He stretchs an inch taller every two months. His clothes and food costs a fortune. Either a bigger shirt or longer pants costs me $20 or more every month. My food bill is higher by $10 a week now. Sixty dollars eat quite a hole in my monthly income My money stretch less than my son.

Paragraph 6 (10 errors)

This city are more dangerous now than before. The television news report violence all the time. In the newspaper is more crime stories. There is murders every day. What cause all this crime. Is there an answer? You and I lives in fear. Nobody enjoy that. We need a solution

Check your answers on page 233.

GED PRACTICE 1 SKILLS CHART

To review the writing skills covered by the items in GED Practice 1, study the following lessons in Unit 1. The answers and explanations beginning on page 233 tell which part of each lesson pertains to each item.

Item numbers 21–55 refer to the numbering of the mistakes in Part 2 in the answers and explanations.

Chapter 1	Subject-Verb Agreement	Item Number
Lesson 1	The Two Parts of Action Sentences	7, 23, 25, 44, 46, 55
Lesson 3	Subject-Verb Agreement in Action Sentences	19, 21, 22, 24, 33, 36, 40, 45
Lesson 4	Subject-Verb Agreement in Describing Sentences	26, 47
Lesson 5	Subject-Verb Agreement with Special Subjects	3, 15, 16, 18, 34, 35, 37, 38, 39, 43, 48, 54
Lesson 6	Subject-Verb Agreement with Compound Subjects	6, 8, 17, 20, 31, 41, 42, 53
Lesson 7	Subject-Verb Agreement When the Subject Follows the Verb	1, 2, 4, 5, 9, 11, 30, 32, 49, 50, 51, 52
Lesson 8	Subject-Verb Agreement with Interrupting Phrases	10, 12, 13, 14, 27, 28, 29

2 VERB TENSES

This chapter shows how verbs, through their tenses, indicate time. It gives you practice at finding and correcting tense errors and at writing sentences that use tenses correctly.

The Simple Tenses

In Chapter 1 you found the verbs in action sentences and in describing sentences. In this lesson you will learn how verbs tell the time of a sentence.

To refresh your memory about what verbs are, look at the following example sentences. The verbs are underlined twice. Each agrees with the subject in its sentence.

Rick and Damon <u>are</u> at the restaurant already.
Cecile usually <u>orders</u> spaghetti.
Pizza with mushrooms and sausage <u>sounds</u> good to me.
Mark, like his two brothers, <u>drinks</u> a lot of beer.
On the table <u>are</u> napkins and cheese.
There <u>remain</u> many customers in line outside.
Neither Sam nor Sofia <u>wants</u> to sit under the plant.

Verbs Tell Time

In addition to agreeing with the subject in a sentence, a verb tells the time of the action in the sentence. It tells whether an action sentence or a describing sentence refers to the **past**, the **present**, or the **future**. The verbs in the following sentences illustrate how a verb shows time.

Someone <u>knock**ed**</u> on my door.   Most **past** time verbs end in **ed** or **d**.
Your jeans <u>fade**d**</u> in the wash.

Deliveries <u>come</u> before noon.   **Present** time verbs have no special ending or end in **s**.
The mail carrier <u>know**s**</u> me well.

She <u>**will** run</u> for public office.   **Future** time verbs follow **will**. They have no special ending.

Another word for "time" is **tense**. It is the word usually used to discuss the time a verb shows. In this lesson you will study the three basic verb tenses, the **simple tenses**. The simple past, present, and future tenses each have more than one use. A discussion of their uses comes later in this lesson.

Find the verb in each of the following sentences. Tell the time of each verb: past, present, or future.

Example: Vaughn always <u>puts</u> his taxes off.   _____present_____

1. He requests an extension every year.   _____

2. His brother Fred is just the opposite.   _____

3. He sets aside nine hours in early February.   _____

4. He sorts his canceled checks.   _____

5. He gets special tax forms from the library.   _____

6. Then he calls a toll-free number for tax advice.   _____

7. Last winter Fred mailed his taxes on February 12.   _____

8. His refund arrived on March 7.   _____

9. He will begin even earlier next year.   _____

10. Next year Vaughn will give Fred's method a try.   _____

Check your answers on page 236.

The Simple Past Tense

The simple past tense is used when a sentence
- states a fact that was true
- tells about a one-time event in the past
- tells about something that occurred regularly

The verbs, which are underlined in the following sentences, are in the simple past tense.

Years ago the library <u>charged</u> a nickel a day for overdue books.	This sentence states a fact that was true.
My mother once <u>owed</u> two dollars for a late book.	This sentence tells about a one-time event in the past.
After that she <u>returned</u> books on time.	This sentence tells about something that occurred regularly.

Spotlight on Spelling: *ed* and *d* Verb Endings

Following are most of the spelling rules for adding **d** and **ed** endings to verbs.

When a verb needs a past-tense ending, you usually add **ed**.

Examples:

explain	offer	work
explain**ed**	offer**ed**	work**ed**

When a verb ends in **e**, add **d**.

Examples:

experience	provide	receive	use
experience**d**	provide**d**	receive**d**	use**d**

When a verb ends in a consonant + **y**, change the **y** to **i** and add **ed**. (All the letters except **a**, **e**, **i**, **o**, and **u** are consonants.)

Examples:

bully	carry	cry	ferry
bull**ied**	carr**ied**	cr**ied**	ferr**ied**

When a verb ends in a stressed vowel + a consonant, double the consonant and add **ed**.
(The vowels are **a**, **e**, **i**, **o**, and **u**. A stressed vowel is one you emphasize when you say a word. For example, the second **e** in **prefer** is stressed: You say preFER; you don't say PREfer.)

Examples:

admit	annul	control	prefer
admit**ted**	annul**led**	control**led**	prefer**red**

The Simple Present Tense

The simple present tense is used when a sentence

- states a fact
- describes something that is true now
- tells about something that occurs regularly

The verbs in the following sentences, which are underlined, are in the simple present tense.

The fine for overdue books <u>is</u> ten cents per day.	This sentence states a fact.
This videotape <u>has</u> a review on the cover.	This sentence describes something that is true now.
The librarians <u>read</u> stories to children every Wednesday.	This sentence tells about something that occurs regularly.

The Simple Future Tense

The simple future tense is used when a sentence
- states a fact that will be true
- tells about an event that will happen
- tells about something that will occur regularly

The verbs in the following sentences, which are underlined, are in the simple future tense. Notice that a negative word, such as *not*, comes between *will* and *lead* in the last sentence. The word *not* is not part of the verb.

The overdue fine <u>will be</u> 15 cents a day starting Monday.	This sentence states a fact that will be true in the future.
My friend <u>will discuss</u> Nikki Giovanni's poetry next Tuesday.	This sentence tells about an event that will happen in the future.
She <u>will</u> not <u>lead</u> the book discussions every week, though.	This sentence tells about something that will occur regularly in the future.

The following chart summarizes uses of the simple present, past, and future tenses. (You need to use this chart to do Exercise 9b.)

Uses of the Simple Past, Present, and Future Tenses

Simple Past
- a. states a fact that was true
- b. tells about a one-time event in the past
- c. tells about something that occurred regularly

Simple Present
- d. states a fact
- e. describes something that is true now
- f. tells about something that occurs regularly

Simple Future
- g. states a fact that will be true
- h. tells about an event that will happen
- i. tells about something that will occur regularly

EXERCISE 9b

Part A. Find the verb in each of the following sentences. Tell each verb's tense and, using the appropriate letter from the **Uses** chart above, indicate its use.

Example: <u>simple present: d</u> There are several hundred diploma mills in this country.

_____ 1. These phony schools offer worthless degrees.

_____ 2. My friend Wesley passed the GED Tests last year.

_____ 3. Soon afterward he learned about a certain college from a well-known magazine.

_____ 4. The magazine printed an advertisement for the school every week.

_____ 5. It painted a glowing picture of the school.

_____ 6. Unfortunately Wesley swallowed the bait.

_____ 7. He wasted a lot of time and money on worthless courses.

_____ 8. He will never make the same mistake again. (Note: The negative word *never* comes between *will* and *make* in this sentence.)

_____ 9. Now he examines advertisements and catalogs very carefully.

_____ 10. He applies only to schools with accreditation.

_____ 11. He knows the ropes now.

_____ 12. This afternoon he will write to the American Council on Accreditation about the Hayes School.

Part B. Complete each of the following sentences by adding the correct simple tense of the verb in parentheses. Before you start, be sure to read what is in the Spotlight on page 58.

Example: (visit)   Yesterday my three-year-old _____visited_____ the dentist for the first time.

1. (refer)   Dr. Dreslin _____ me to a pharmacist for fluoride drops.

2. (stress)   He _____ the importance of fluoride.

3. (work)   Fluoride _____ well.

4. (prevent)   It _____ cavities.

5. (provide)   Many big cities now _____ fluoride in their water supplies.

6. (receive)   Over 115 million Americans _____ fluoride in their water every day.

7. (experience)   Children from communities with fluoridated water _____ 30–60 percent less tooth decay.

8. (use)   Unfortunately my family _____ well water without fluoride.

9. (fill)   I _____ the prescription tomorrow after work.

10. (take)   Starting the next day, Kenny _____ two drops of fluoride daily after brushing his teeth.

Part C. Complete the following sentences so that they tell about medical care. First, add the correct simple tense of the verb in parentheses. Then add some other words to complete the sentence. Before you start, reread the Spotlight on page 58.

Example: (shop)   Many people _____ *shop for doctors.* _____

1. (ask)   Before choosing a clinic now, I always _____

2. (need)   My family _____

3. (want)   We _____

4. (seem)   My last doctor always _____

5. (weary)   The waits in her office _____

6. (prefer)   She _____

7. (exceed)   Our medical costs _____

8. (resent)   I _____

9. (look)   A year ago I _____

10. (avoid)   In the future, I _____

Check your answers on page 236.

Lesson 10

Irregular Verbs

In Lesson 9 you learned the uses of the past tense. You learned that most past-tense verbs end in **ed** or **d**. Such verbs are called **regular verbs**. They follow a regular rule for forming the past tense: add **ed** or **d**.

Some verbs do not follow the "add **ed** or **d** rule" for forming the past tense. Such verbs are **irregular verbs**. The verbs, which are underlined in the following sentences, are all irregular. Note especially the forms they take in the simple past tense.

I always <u>sing</u> in the shower.
I <u>buy</u> a lot of songbooks.
Waterproof songbooks <u>sell</u> for $5.

The irregular verbs in these sentences are in the simple present tense.

Yesterday I <u>sang</u> in the shower.
Yesterday I <u>bought</u> a songbook.
Waterproof songbooks <u>sold</u> for $5.

The irregular verbs in these sentences are in the simple past tense.

Although irregular verbs do not follow the "add **ed** or **d** rule," many of them follow certain patterns for forming the simple past tense. The following chart shows some of those patterns.

Some Irregular-Verb Patterns

Characteristics	Simple Present	Simple Past
The **i** in the simple present tense becomes **a** in the simple past tense.	begin drink give ring sing swim	began drank gave rang sang swam
The **ow** in the simple present tense becomes **ew** in the simple past tense.	blow grow know throw	blew grew knew threw
The simple past tense ends in **o** + consonant + **e**.	break choose freeze speak steal tear write	broke chose froze spoke stole tore wrote
The **e** in the simple present tense becomes **o** in the simple past tense.	forget get	forgot got
These irregular verbs follow no pattern. You must memorize their simple-past-tense forms.	am, is are bring buy cost do eat feed fly go have hear hit lose pay put run see spend stand take tell wear	was were brought bought cost did ate fed flew went had heard hit lost paid put ran saw spent stood took told wore

Following are common mistakes in forming the simple past tense of some irregular verbs.

Incorrect	Correct
It <u>begun</u> to get dark.	It <u>began</u> to get dark.
Randy <u>brung</u> barbecued beans.	Randy <u>brought</u> barbecued beans.
They <u>done</u> a good job.	They <u>did</u> a good job.
I <u>drunk</u> all of it.	I <u>drank</u> all of it.
Elsie <u>gone</u> home for her show.	Elsie <u>went</u> home for her show.
She <u>seen</u> him on TV.	She <u>saw</u> him on TV.
We <u>swum</u> in the lake.	We <u>swam</u> in the lake.

EXERCISE 10

Part A. Complete each of the following sentences by adding the simple past tense of the verb in parentheses.

Example: (are) Before robots, some factory jobs _____*were*_____ dull and difficult.

1. (take) Metal plant workers _____ very hot metal out of huge furnaces.

2. (put) Other workers _____ metal parts into strong acid baths.

3. (have) Many auto workers _____ dangerous jobs, too.

4. (feed) Some workers _____ heavy steel pieces into giant presses all day.

5. (stand) Welders _____ in the middle of flying sparks.

6. (get) They frequently _____ burns on their arms and legs.

7. (buy) Factories _____ more and more robots for these jobs.

8. (bring) Computerized robots _____ greater safety to the workplace.

9. (lose) Some workers _____ their jobs to robots.

10. (go) Often these workers then _____ on to more interesting jobs.

Part B. Edit the following sentences to make sure the simple past tense is formed correctly. If the verb is in the wrong form, change it. (Note: Some sentences do not need correction.)

Example: The country and western singer ~~gone~~ *went* back to school to get his GED.

1. He done it for himself and his family.

2. He took his studies very seriously.

3. He even brung his review books with him on concert tours.

4. Last week he sung a song about it.

5. The song told about his pride.

6. The diploma give him more self-respect.

7. He begun every concert with that song.

8. I seen his show on my birthday.

9. My friend and I gone together.

10. She buyed the tickets as a surprise.

Part C. Complete the following sentences so that they tell about last year. First add the correct form of the verb in parentheses. Then add some other words to complete the sentence.

Example: (wear) Teenagers _____ *wore jeans jackets last year.* _____

1. (drink)   I _____

2. (write)   You _____

3. (hear)   We _____

4. (blow)   They _____

5. (know)   You _____

6. (speak)   My father _____

7. (spend)   Politicians _____

8. (run)   Computers _____

9. (steal)   A burglar _____

10. (be)   My parents _____

Check your answers on page 237.

The Continuous and Perfect Tenses

In Lesson 9 you learned about the three simple tenses and their uses. There are several tenses other than the simple tenses. Each has uses different from those of the simple tenses. In this lesson, you will study the continuous tense and the perfect tense.

The Past Continuous Tense

The past continuous tense is used when a sentence

- tells about an action that continued for a while
- tells about an action that continued while another action continued
- tells about an action that continued until something else happened

They <u>were studying</u> all morning.	This sentence tells about an action that continued for a while.
It <u>was snowing</u> the whole time the children <u>were playing</u> outside.	This sentence tells about an action that continued while another action continued.
He <u>was</u> skiing well until he <u>fell</u>.	This sentence tells about an action that continued until something else happened.

A verb in the past continuous tense is made up of two words. The helping verb, *was* or *were*, agrees with the subject. The main verb has an **ing** ending.

Notice that there are two verbs each in the last two example sentences above. Some of the example sentences in the other sections of this lesson also have two verbs. You will learn more about such sentences in Chapter 4.

The Present Continuous Tense

The present continuous tense is used when a sentence
- tells about an ongoing action
- tells about an action that is happening right now

I <u>am shopping</u> around for a computer. She <u>is working</u> at the factory.	These sentences tell about ongoing actions.
My children are <u>walking</u> home from school now.	This sentence tells about an action that is happening right now.

A verb in the present continuous tense is made up of two words. The helping verb—*am*, *are*, or *is*—agrees with the subject. The main verb has an **ing** ending.

The Future Continuous Tense

The future continuous tense is used when a sentence

- tells about an action that will continue for a while
- tells about an action that will continue while another action continues
- tells about an action that will continue until something else happens

They <u>will be studying</u> all morning.

This sentence tells about an action that will continue for a while.

He <u>will be studying</u> while you <u>are working</u>.

This sentence tells about an action that will continue while another action continues.

I <u>will be studying</u> when you <u>arrive</u>.

This sentence tells about an action that will continue until something else happens.

A verb in the future continuous tense is made up of three words: the helping verb, *will be*, and the main verb with an **ing** ending.

 # Spotlight on Spelling: *ing* Verb Endings

Following are most of the spelling rules for adding **ing** endings to verbs.

To form a continuous verb you usually just add **ing**.
Examples:

cry	explain	offer	work
cry**ing**	explain**ing**	offer**ing**	work**ing**

When a verb ends in a silent **e**, drop the **e** and add **ing**.
Examples:

experience	provide	receive	use
experienc**ing**	provid**ing**	receiv**ing**	us**ing**

When a verb ends in a stressed vowel + a consonant, double the consonant and add **ing**.
(The vowels are **a**, **e**, **i**, **o**, and **u**. A stressed vowel is one you emphasize when you say a word. For example, the second **e** in *prefer* is stressed: You say preFER; you don't say PREfer.)
Examples:

admit	annul	control	prefer
admit**ting**	annul**ling**	control**ling**	prefer**ring**

Part A. Complete each of the following sentences by adding the past continuous tense of the verb in parentheses. Before you start, reread the Spotlight on page 66.

Example: (go) Everything _____was going_____ better for him.

1. (work) He _____ his way up the ladder at the store.

2. (talk) His boss _____ about promoting him.

3. (find) His co-workers _____ him easier to work with.

4. (go) His wife _____ to A.A. meetings with him.

5. (try) All of us _____ to help him.

Part B. Complete each of the following sentences by adding the present continuous tense of the verb in parentheses. If needed, refer to the Spotlight on page 66.

Example: (choose) Today many men and women _____are choosing_____ careers in computer programming.

1. (take) I _____ a course in computer programming this semester.

2. (show) This month the instructor _____ us how to write coded instructions for a computer.

3. (learn) In addition, we _____ how to debug our programs.

4. (make) Right now I _____ a trial run of my program to find mistakes.

5. (plan) I _____ on working as a programmer for a large company.

Part C. Complete each of the following sentences by adding the future continuous tense of the verb in parentheses. You may refer to the Spotlight on page 66.

Example: (work) Freddy _____will be working_____ overtime every day this week.

1. (take) He _____ inventory.

2. (stay) Some of the other employees _____ late with him.

3. (earn) Everyone _____ overtime pay.

4. (complain) Some of Freddy's co-workers _____ all week about the late hours.

5. (gripe) No one _____ on payday, though.

Check your answers on page 237.

The Past Perfect Tense

The past perfect tense is used when a sentence tells about a past action completed before another past action.

They <u>had eaten</u> the tainted food before they <u>heard</u> the news.

This sentence tells about a past action completed before another past action.

A verb in the past perfect tense is made up of two words: the helping verb, *had*, and the past participle of the main verb. (A past participle is the form of a verb used with the perfect tenses. You will learn more about past participles following the discussion of the uses of the perfect tenses.)

The Present Perfect Tense

The present perfect tense is used when a sentence

- tells about an action that happened at an indefinite time in the past
- tells about an action that began in the past and continues in the present

He <u>has worked</u> as a cook before.

This sentence tells about an action that happened at an indefinite time in the past.

They <u>have worked</u> here since 1985.

This sentence tells about an action that began in the past and continues in the present.

A verb in the present perfect tense is made up of two words: the helping verb—*have* or *has*, whichever agrees with the subject—and the past participle of the main verb.

The Future Perfect Tense

The future perfect tense is used when a sentence tells about a future action that will be completed before another future action.

Your plane <u>will have arrived</u> before mine <u>does</u>.

This sentence tells about a future action that will be completed before another future action.

A verb in the future perfect tense is made up of three words: the helping verb, *will have*, and the past participle of the main verb.

Past Participles

Past participles are the forms of verbs used in the perfect tenses. Most verbs' past participles are identical to their past tenses. For example, both the past tense and the past participle of *study* are *studied*. However, the past participles of most irregular verbs—the kind you studied in Lesson 10—are different from their past tenses, as the following chart shows.

More Irregular-Verb Patterns

Characteristics	Simple Present	Simple Past	Past Participle
The **i** in the simple present tense becomes **a** in the simple past tense and **u** in the past participle.	begin	began	begun
	drink	drank	drunk
	ring	rang	rung
	sing	sang	sung
	swim	swam	swum
The **ow** in the simple present tense becomes **ew** in the simple past tense and **own** in the past participle.	blow	blew	blown
	grow	grew	grown
	know	knew	known
	throw	threw	thrown
The simple past tense ends in **o** + consonant + **e**. The past participle ending is the same as the simple past tense + **n**.	break	broke	broken
	choose	chose	chosen
	freeze	froze	frozen
	speak	spoke	spoken
	steal	stole	stolen
The **e** in the simple present tense becomes **o** in the simple past tense. The past participle is the same as the past tense, or may end with **ten**.	forget	forgot	forgot, forgotten
	get	got	got, gotten
The simple past tenses of these irregular verbs follow no pattern, but their past participles are the same as their simple past tenses.	bring	brought	brought
	buy	bought	bought
	cost	cost	cost
	feed	fed	fed
	have	had	had
	hear	heard	heard
	hit	hit	hit
	lose	lost	lost
	pay	paid	paid
	put	put	put
	spend	spent	spent
	stand	stood	stood
	tell	told	told
These irregular verbs follow no pattern. You must memorize their simple past-tense and past-participle forms.	am, is	was	been
	are	were	been
	do	did	done
	eat	ate	eaten
	fly	flew	flown
	go	went	gone
	give	gave	given
	run	ran	run
	see	saw	seen
	take	took	taken
	tear	tore	torn
	wear	wore	worn
	write	wrote	written

EXERCISE 11b

Part A. Complete each of the following sentences by adding the past perfect tense of the verb in parentheses.

Example: (go)   Everything _____had gone_____ well for him before he started drinking again.

1. (work)   He _____ his way up the ladder at the store.

2. (promote) His boss _____ him.

3. (regain)   His co-workers _____ respect for him.

4. (become)   His wife _____ happy with him again.

5. (be)   Everyone _____ proud of him.

Part B. Complete each of the following sentences by adding the present perfect tense of the verb in parentheses.

Example: (choose) Many men and women _____have chosen_____ careers in computer programming in the last twenty years.

1. (take)   They _____ courses in computer programming.

2. (learn)   They _____ how to write programs.

3. (hold)   Some _____ high paying jobs.

4. (continue) Each _____ to learn about computers.

5. (receive) Most _____ excellent job offers time and again.

Part C. Complete each of the following sentences by adding the future perfect tense of the verb in parentheses.

Example: (work) Freddy _____will have worked_____ 40 hours overtime by the end of this week.

1. (take)   He _____ inventory every day.

2. (work)   Some of the other employees _____ late with him.

3. (make)   Everyone _____ overtime pay.

4. (complain) Some of Freddy's co-workers _____ all week about the late hours.

5. (go)   All of them _____ home tired.

Check your answers on page 237.

Choosing the Correct Tense

In Lessons 9–11 you learned the forms and uses of nine verb tenses. This lesson summarizes and adds to what you have learned. It gives you practice in using correct tenses and contractions when you write or edit.

Clues to Tense: Time Words

The following chart summarizes what you have learned about the uses of tenses. It also gives examples of time words used with each tense.

Tenses: Uses and Related Time Words

Uses	Related Time Words
Used to write about the past:	
Simple Past	
• states a fact that was true	at that point, (a week/
• tells about a one-time event in the past	a while/three years) ago,
• tells about something that occurred regularly	in (1973, the past), last (Monday/month/ summer/time/year), recently, then, years ago, yesterday
Past Continuous	
• tells about an action that continued for a while	at that point, (a week/ a while/three years) ago,
• tells about an action that continued while another action continued	for (days/weeks/years), in (1973, the past), last (Monday/month/
• tells about an action that continued until something else happened	summer/time/year), recently, then, years ago, yesterday, while
Past Perfect	
• tells about a past action completed before another past action	after, before
Present Perfect	
• tells about an action that happened at an indefinite time in the past	at one time, before, in the past, up to now, yet
• tells about an action that began in the past and continues in the present	

continued on next page

Uses	Related Time Words

Uses **Related Time Words**

Used to write about the present:

Simple Present
- states a fact
- describes something that is true now
- tells about something that occurs regularly

always, daily/weekly, each (day/Sunday/week), every (day/Sunday/week), frequently, most of the time, never, nowadays, occasionally, often, regularly, sometimes, these days, usually

Present Continuous
- tells about an ongoing action
- tells about an action that is happening right now

at (the moment/present), at this time, currently, now, right now, these days, today

Used to write about the future:

Simple Future
- states a fact that will be true
- tells about an event that will happen
- tells about something that will occur regularly

in the future, next (time/week/year), some (day, time), tomorrow

Future Continuous
- tells about an action that will continue for a while
- tells about an action that will continue while another action continues
- tells about an action that will continue until something else happens

in the future, next (time/week/year), some (day, time), tomorrow

Future Perfect
- tells about a future action that will be completed before another future action

by the time, when

Time words in a sentence can often help you decide which tense of the verb to use. For example, the word *tomorrow* in each of the following sentences is a clue to use one of the future tenses.

Tomorrow I <u>will watch</u> a nature special on TV.

Tomorrow I <u>will be working</u>.

Clues to Tense in a Paragraph

Some sentences do not have time words to help you figure out what their tense should be. But because sentences are usually surrounded by a context that includes other sentences, there are usually clues to tense somewhere in that context.

The following three sentences are organized into a paragraph. Notice that a tense error in the second sentence has been corrected.

watched
(1) Yesterday I stayed home sick. (2) I ~~will watch~~ a nature special on television. (3) A friend brought me some magazines.

The verb in the second sentence should be in the simple past tense (*watched*), not in the simple future tense (*will watch*). The clues are in the first and third sentences. In the first sentence, the word *Yesterday* tells you that the action in the paragraph took place in the past. In the third sentence, the verb *brought* is in the simple past tense.

Can you find the two tense errors in the following paragraph?

(1) Last year I stay home. (2) Now I work every day. (3) My mother watches my twins for me. (4) I dropped them off before work at her apartment. (5) Then I pick them up at supper time.

The words *Last year* in the first sentence tell you that its verb should be in the simple past tense: *stayed*. The rest of the paragraph is about events that occur regularly. The word *Now* in the second sentence tells you that. It is a clue to switch to the simple present tense. The verb in the fourth sentence should not be in the past tense; it should be *drop*. Following is the same paragraph with the tense errors corrected.

ed
(1) Last year I stay home. (2) Now I work every day. (3) My mother watches my twins for me. (4) I drop~~ped~~ them off before work at her apartment. (5) I pick them up before supper time.

Contractions

Verbs or helping verbs in many tenses are often written with contractions. A contraction is a combined form of two words. Contractions join words by replacing one or more of their letters with an apostrophe (').

The following table gives examples of the contractions most often used with the verb tenses you have been studying.

Commonly Used Verb Contractions

COMPLETE FORM   CONTRACTION

Used with the Past Perfect Tense

I had cashed my paycheck.   **I'd** cashed my paycheck.
You had withdrawn money.   **You'd** withdrawn money.
He had been to the bank.   **He'd** been to the bank.
They had deposited money.   **They'd** deposited money.
Who had gone back to work?   **Who'd** gone back to work?
I **had not** gone back.   I **hadn't** gone back.
James **had not** cashed his check.   James **hadn't** cashed his check.
You **had not** withdrawn enough.   You **hadn't** withdrawn enough.

Used with the Present Perfect Tense

I have cashed my paycheck.   **I've** cashed my paycheck.
You have withdrawn money.   **You've** withdrawn money.
He has been to the bank.   **He's** been to the bank.
They have deposited money.   **They've** deposited money.
It has gotten late.   **It's** gotten late.
Who has gone back to work?   **Who's** gone back to work?
I **have not** gone back.   I **haven't** gone back.
James **has not** cashed his check.   James **hasn't** cashed his check
You **have not** withdrawn enough.   You **haven't** withdrawn enough.

Used with the Simple Present Tense

I am here.   **I'm** here.
You are there.   **You're** there.
He is there, too.   **He's** there, too.
We are away.   **We're** away.
They are away, too.   **They're** away, too.
I am not there.   **I'm** not there.
You are not here.   **You aren't/You're not** here.
She is not here, either.   **She isn't/She's not** here, either.
They are not away.   **They aren't/They're not** away.

Used with the Present Continuous Tense

I am cashing my paycheck.   **I'm** cashing my paycheck.
You are withdrawing money.   **You're** withdrawing money.
He is at the bank.   **He's** at the bank.
They are depositing money.   **They're** depositing money.
It is getting late.   **It's** getting late
Who is going back to work?   **Who's** going back to work?
I am not going back.   **I'm not** going back.
James **is not** cashing his check.   James **isn't** cashing his check.
You **are not** withdrawing.   You **aren't** withdrawing.

Used with the Simple Future Tense

I will operate tomorrow.   **I'll** operate tomorrow.
You will experience some pain.   **You'll** experience some pain.
She will give you pain killers.   **She'll** give you pain killers.
They will help.   **They'll** help.
We will do everything we can.   **We'll** do everything we can.
There **will not** be a problem.   There **won't** be a problem.

continued on next page

Used with the Future Continuous Tense
I will be cashing my paycheck.   **I'll** be cashing my paycheck.
You will be withdrawing money.   **You'll** be withdrawing money.
He will be waiting at the bank.   **He'll** be waiting at the bank.
They will be depositing money.   **They'll** be depositing money.
It will be getting late.   **It'll** be getting late.
Who will be going back to work?   **Who'll** be going back to work?
I will not be going back.   **I won't** be going back.
James **will not** be cashing his check.   James **won't** be cashing his check.
You **will not** be withdrawing.   You **won't** be withdrawing.

EXERCISE 12

Part A. Complete each of the following sentences by adding the correct tense of
the verb in parentheses. Use contractions wherever possible.

Example: (see)   Yesterday I _____*saw*_____ a flock of migrating birds.

1. (look)   Right now I _____ at this envelope.

   (receive)   I frequently _____ mail like this.

   (appear)   A message usually _____ on the envelope.

   (sound)   The messages often _____ like ones from
   the government.

2. (be)   My writing _____ usually full of spelling
   mistakes.

   (buy)   So, I _____ a new computer program
   last week.

   (correct)   The program _____ spelling mistakes.

   (load)   I _____ the program into my computer
   right now.

   (not have)   In the future my writing _____ spelling
   mistakes.

3. (change)   My brother _____ his mind about his future
   career frequently.

   (tell)   Once he _____ me he would become a chef.

   (talk)   For a while he _____ about being a stunt man.

   (decide)   Then he _____ acting was for him.

(announce) Last year he _____ that he wanted to get his

trucking license.

(talk) Now he _____ about a career with the

police department.

(fill) He _____ out his application right

this minute.

4. (hold) When Janice went to the consumer discount store last night,

it _____ its grand opening.

(drive) She _____ around the parking lot for fifteen

minutes before she found a space.

(leave) Shoppers were swarming into the new store like ants, and

satisfied customers _____ with carts

piled high.

(give) Some store employees were passing out flyers, and others

_____ balloons to the children.

(find) Janice _____ some good bargains inside.

(shop) She _____ there often in the future.

Part B. Edit the following letter to correct its tense errors. Use contractions
wherever possible. As an example, the first error is corrected.

Dear Gabby,

                    I was

A short time ago I'm buying groceries. I find an empty wallet under some

grapes in the fruit section. I was turning the wallet in at the check-out counter.

A little later a woman is claiming the wallet. The clerk points me out to her.

She marches up to me: "You steal my twenty-dollar bill! I tell the police about

this!"

Right now I waited for an apology. I will not returning lost items in the

future.

Do you think my decision is right?

Unjustly Accused

Check your answers on page 238.

GED PRACTICE 2

In GED Practice 1 you learned about the two kinds of items on the Writing Skills Test that ask you to find and correct mistakes in passages you read. There is a third GED item type—one that asks you to write part of a passage in a different way.

Look at the example on page 78. It includes a key that points out special features of the item.

The item is about verb tenses. The correct answer is Choice (2): it makes the tense of the new sentence the same as the tense of the originals. If Sentences 2 and 3 were combined, the new sentence would be the following:

Either Dave Magadan or Gregg Jefferies drove in two runs.

Part 1 of GED Practice 2 begins on page 79. It will give you practice with multiple-choice items that cover the skills you have studied so far in this book. Part 2 of the practice, beginning on page 81, will give you a chance to use those same skills to correct mistakes in paragraphs like those you might write in an essay.

<u>Item 1</u> refers to the following paragraph.

    (1) I missed part of the Mets game last night. (2) Dave Magadan drove in two runs. (3) Maybe it was Gregg Jefferies. (4) The New York Mets defeated San Francisco 6-4. (5) The win snapped the Giants' three-game winning streak.

(a)   (b)

1. Sentences 2 and 3: **Dave Magadan drove in two runs. Maybe it was Gregg Jefferies.**

(c)   If you combined sentences 2 and 3 beginning with

(d)   <u>Either Dave Magadan or Gregg Jefferies,</u>

(e)   the next word(s) should be

    (1) drives
    (2) drove
    (3) was driving
    (4) have driven
    (5) will have driven

<u>Key</u>

(a) This part of the item tells which sentence(s) to rewrite.

(b) This part of the item is an exact copy of the sentence(s) in the passage, printed in dark type. There are no errors in the sentences. The item merely asks you to write them in a different (and better) way.

(c) This part of the item tells you how to write the sentence(s) in a different way. (In this case, you are to *combine* the two sentences.)

(d) The underlined words show part of the rewritten sentence.

(e) This part of the item tells you what you should look for in choosing the correct option. As you look for the correct option, remember that the rewritten sentence must have the same meaning as the original(s).

GED PRACTICE 2

Part 1
Directions: Choose the <u>one best answer</u> to each item.

<u>Items 1 through 10</u> refer to the following paragraphs.

(1) On a rainy Thursday last fall, Sue Reilly takes a bike ride along a dirt road near the Massachusetts shore. (2) She looked back over her shoulder. (3) Maybe her front tire hit a stone. (4) Maybe her rear tire hit a stone. (5) The bike has flown into a ditch. (6) Sue will spend the next seven weeks on crutches. (7) Her injuries included cracked ribs, a broken leg, and scrapes over much of her body. (8) Fortunately, her head were fine. (9) Her bike helmet absorbed most of the shock. (10) The helmet probably was saving Sue's life.

(11) Over a thousand people die in bicycle accidents each year. (12) Most of those biking deaths resulted from head injuries. (13) According to one study, bike helmets are reducing the seriousness of head injuries by 85 percent. (14) Unfortunately, few bike riders wear helmets. (15) With education, perhaps the number of helmet-wearers will increase someday.

1. Sentence 1: **On a rainy Thursday last fall, Sue Reilly takes a bike ride along a dirt road near the Massachusetts shore.**

   What correction should be made to this sentence?

   (1) change <u>takes</u> to <u>take</u>
   (2) change <u>takes</u> to <u>was taking</u>
   (3) change <u>takes</u> to <u>were taking</u>
   (4) change <u>takes</u> to <u>will take</u>
   (5) change <u>takes</u> to <u>has taken</u>

2. Sentence 2: **<u>She looked</u> back over her shoulder.**

   Which of the following is the best way to write the underlined portion of this sentence? If you think the original is the best way, choose option (1).

   (1) She looked
   (2) She looks
   (3) She is looking
   (4) She'll look
   (5) She will have looked

3. Sentences 3 and 4: **Maybe her front tire hit a stone. Maybe her rear tire hit a stone.**

   If you combined sentences 3 and 4 beginning with

   <u>Either her front tire or her rear tire,</u>

   the next word should be

   (1) hit
   (2) hits
   (3) hitted
   (4) hat
   (5) was hitting

4. Sentence 5: **The bike has flown into a ditch.**

   What correction should be made to this sentence?

   (1) change <u>has flown</u> to <u>had flown</u>
   (2) change <u>has flown</u> to <u>was flying</u>
   (3) change <u>has flown</u> to <u>is flying</u>
   (4) change <u>has flown</u> to <u>flew</u>
   (5) no correction is necessary

5. Sentence 6: **Sue will spend the next seven weeks on crutches.**

   What correction should be made to this sentence?

   (1) change will spend to will spends
   (2) change will spend to spends
   (3) remove will
   (4) change will spend to spended
   (5) change will spend to spent

6. Sentence 8: **Fortunately, her head were fine.**

   Which of the following is the best way to write the underlined portion of this sentence? If you think the original is the best way, choose option (1).

   (1) her head were fine
   (2) her head was fine
   (3) her head are fine
   (4) her head had been fine
   (5) her head will be fine

7. Sentence 10: **The helmet probably was saving Sue's life.**

   What correction should be made to this sentence?

   (1) change was saving to were saving
   (2) change was saving to is saving
   (3) change was saving to saves
   (4) change was saving to saved
   (5) remove was

8. Sentence 12: **Most of those biking deaths resulted from head injuries.**

   What correction should be made to this sentence?

   (1) change resulted to result
   (2) change resulted to results
   (3) change resulted to were resulting
   (4) change resulted to are resulting
   (5) change resulted to is resulting

9. Sentence 13: **According to one study, bike helmets are reducing the seriousness of head injuries by 85 percent.**

   What correction should be made to this sentence?

   (1) change are reducing to were reducing
   (2) change are reducing to was reducing
   (3) change are reducing to is reducing
   (4) change are reducing to reduce
   (5) change are reducing to reduces

10. Sentence 15: **With education, perhaps the number of helmet-wearers will increase someday.**

    Which of the following is the best way to write the underlined portion of this sentence? If you think the original is the best way, choose option (1).

    (1) will increase
    (2) increased
    (3) had increased
    (4) increases
    (5) is increasing

Part 2

<u>Directions</u>: Edit the following passage. It contains 11 errors.

- If any verb and subject do not agree, change the verb.
- Correct errors in the use of verb tenses.
- Capitalize any word that should be capitalized.
- Correct errors in punctuation.
- Correct errors in spelling.

leonardo and tanisha are Melida's children. Since they were born, Melida spends every Mother's Day with them.

Last Mother's Day the sister and brother bring their mother breakfast in bed. On her tray was scrambled eggs, cereal, fresh fruit and, toast. There were also a vase of ragweed and dandelions. The children give their mother a cake, a bracelet, and a plant Melida smiled and thanks them.

Next Mother's Day Leonardo and Tanisha took Melida to a city park for a picnic.

Check your answers on page 238.

GED PRACTICE 2 SKILLS CHART

To review the writing skills covered by the items in GED Practice 2, study the following lessons in Unit 1. The answers and explanations beginning on page 238 tell which part of each lesson pertains to each item.

Item numbers 11–21 refer to the numbering of the mistakes in Part 2 in the answers and explanations.

Chapter 1	Subject-Verb Agreement	Item Number
Lesson 1	The Two Parts of Action Sentences	11, 19
Lesson 3	Subject-Verb Agreement in Action Sentences	9
Lesson 6	Subject-Verb Agreement with Compound Subjects	12, 16
Lesson 7	Subject-Verb Agreement When the Subject Follows the Verb	15, 17
Lesson 8	Subject-Verb Agreement with Interrupting Phrases	8

Chapter 2	Verb Tenses	
Lesson 9	The Simple Tenses	2, 7, 10, 20, 21
Lesson 10	Irregular Verbs	3, 4, 5, 6, 14, 18
Lesson 11	The Continuous and Perfect Tenses	1, 13
Lesson 12	Choosing the Correct Tense	(1–10, 13–15, 17–18, 20–21)

Chapter

3 PRONOUNS

The lessons in this chapter cover various types of pronouns. The chapter gives you practice in finding and correcting pronoun agreement errors of many types and in writing sentences without agreement errors. It gives you practice in finding and correcting pronoun shifts and in correcting sentences whose pronouns make unclear references.

Lesson 13

Subject and Object Pronouns

In Chapter 1 you learned that sentences have two main parts with a core word in each. The core word in the action or description part of a sentence is the verb. In the naming part the core word is the subject.

Nouns as Subjects

In many sentences the subject is a noun. **Nouns** name persons, places, or things. If the subject of a sentence *names* a person, a place, or a thing, it is a noun. The subject in the following sentence, which is a noun, is underlined.

> **Noun:**
> a word that names a person, place, or thing

The <u>cat</u> jumped onto the computer keyboard.

Cat is a noun because it names a thing.

 Spotlight on Capitalization of Nouns

Nouns that name particular persons, places, and things are capitalized. (In the following examples, notice that some nouns are made up of two words.)

These nouns are **capitalized** because they name particular persons, places, and things.	Anne Idaho	President Washington First Street	March
These nouns are **not capitalized** because they do not name particular persons, places, and things.	driver state	president street	month

---

The following exercise will help you review finding subjects in sentences. As you do it, notice that each subject is a noun.

The subject in each of the following sentences is a noun. Underline each once.

Example: The <u>chief</u> earned his GED years ago.

1. George dropped out of high school.
2. The young man soon realized his mistake.
3. Many jobs in law enforcement require a high school diploma.
4. That door slammed in his face.
5. The U.S. Navy accepted him.
6. George took correspondence courses.
7. His GED paved the way to college.
8. George's wife left high school at 15.
9. Ellen returned for her GED ten years later.
10. Her sister-in-law convinced her.

Check your answers on page 240.

Pronouns as Subjects

When the subject of a sentence is not a noun, it is usually a pronoun. **Pronouns** stand for and take the place of nouns. Like nouns, pronouns refer to persons, places, or things.

The following chart gives examples to show how pronouns stand for nouns.

Pronoun:
a word that takes the place of a noun

Examples of Nouns and the Pronouns That Stand for Them

Nouns	Pronouns
Terry	I (if I am Terry)
Felix	you (if you are Felix)
President Washington	he
Anne	she
March	it
Terry and Felix	we (if I am Terry)
David and Lena	you (if David and Lena are the people I am talking or writing to)
Idaho and Washington	they

When you use pronouns, you don't need to repeat nouns unnecessarily. Look at the following two sets of sentences. The naming part is underlined in each sentence. Which pair of sentences sounds better?

My brother works at a dry cleaning place. My brother is a presser.

My brother works at a dry cleaning place. He is a presser.

Most speakers would replace *My brother* with *He* in the second sentence. Notice that the whole naming part of the sentence, *My brother*, is replaced by *He*.

The following chart gives some examples of noun subjects replaced by pronoun subjects. Notice that when pronouns replace nouns, they replace the whole naming part of sentence.

Examples of Noun Subjects Replaced by Pronoun Subjects

Noun Subjects	Pronoun Subjects
Nate knows how to do word processing.	He knows how to do word processing.
Amy operates a robot in an auto factory.	She operates a robot in an auto factory.
The factory is a safer place to work now.	It is a safer place to work now.
Lenay, Michelle, Joe, and I work at the post office.	We work at the post office.
Lenay, Michelle, Joe, and Cal work at the post office.	They work at the post office.
Post offices, banks, and supermarkets have computers.	They have computers.
Computers have become part of our daily lives.	They have become part of our daily lives.

EXERCISE 13b

Rewrite the second sentence in each set. Replace the noun subject in each with a pronoun subject.

Example: John is looking for a state civil service position. John has already passed the test for the job he wants.

John is looking for a state civil service position. <u>He has already passed the test for the job he wants.</u>

1. David and Joe took a GED review class together. David and Joe told Maria about the class.

   David and Joe took a GED review class together. _____

   _____

2. Maria took the GED tests last month. Maria passed the test.

   Maria took the GED tests last month. _____

3. John, Jackie, and I received our GED diplomas last year. John, Jackie, and I got high scores on each of the tests.

   John, Jackie, and I received our GED diplomas last year. _____

   _____

4. David, Jackie, and Joe are applying to college. David, Jackie, and Joe hope to get associates degrees.

   David, Jackie, and Joe are applying to college. _____

   _____

5. John, Maria, and I are trying to get civil service jobs. John, Maria, and I want to get jobs in the state capital.

   John, Maria, and I are trying to get civil service jobs._____

   _____

Check your answers on page 240.

Pronouns as Objects

Not all nouns and pronouns in sentences are subjects. Some are objects. You learned in Lesson 2 that subjects do the action in action sentences. Objects receive the action in action sentences.

To understand better what *receive the action* means, look at the following pair of sentences.

> She helped my father.
>
> She helped him.

In both sentences the pronoun *She* is the subject. In the first sentence the noun *father* is the object; that is, *father* receives the action. In the second sentence the pronoun *him* is the object.

Most object pronouns have a different form from subject pronouns, as the following chart shows.

Subject and Object Pronouns

Subject Pronouns	Object Pronouns
I	me
you (singular)	you (singular)
he	him
she	her
it	it
we	us
you (plural)	you (plural)
they	them

Notice that both as subject and object *you* can be either singular or plural. The use of *yous* is always incorrect in written English.

Besides receiving action in a sentence, object pronouns have another common use. They often follow prepositions, such as those in the table of Common Prepositions on page 41. For example, the pronouns that could follow the preposition *with* in the following sentence are shown here.

Lloyd went with (me, you, him, her, it, us, them).

EXERCISE 13c

Edit the following sentences for the correct use of pronouns. (Note: Some sentences do not need correction.)

Example: Sheila asked ~~he~~ him.

1. Lou mentioned it.
2. Manuel told I.
3. I phoned he.
4. He called you.
5. You informed we.
6. Us told him.
7. We avoided she.
8. Brian notified she.
9. Sylvia advised they.
10. Secrets bother we.
11. I would recommend this career counselor to yous.
12. She helped I.
13. Without she I probably would never have known.
14. She helped all of we get back on the right track.
15. She gives good advice, so don't ignore she.

Check your answers on page 240.

Pronouns After Forms of *Be*

When the verb in a describing sentence is a form of *be*, a pronoun that follows the verb is a subject pronoun. The following sentences illustrate this.

> I am **he**.
> The caller was **she**.
> The culprit is **I**.
> The winners will be **they**.

It may sound formal to say "This is she" or "This is he" on the telephone, but it is correct. Because the verb in the sentence is a form of *be*, the pronoun after it should be a subject pronoun.

EXERCISE 13d

Edit the following sentences for the correct use of pronouns. (Note: Some sentences do not need correction.)

Example: That is ~~me~~ I with the hat in that picture.

1. The girl holding Milly is you.

2. The baby is her.

3. This is you with Gram and Grandpa.

4. It was her behind Grandpa.

5. It was him taking the pictures.

Check your answers on page 241.

Pronouns in Compound Subjects and Objects

As you learned in Lesson 6, some sentences have compound subjects. Such subjects have two parts. Some sentences also have compound objects. Their parts are usually joined by *and* or *or*.

This sentence has a **compound subject**.   **Sam and I** work at the gas station.

This sentence has a **compound object**.   The boss pays either **Sam or me** too little each week.

To decide whether to use a subject pronoun or an object pronoun in a compound, try the following test.

How to Choose the Correct Pronoun in a Compound

STEP 1:   Cover all the words in the compound that are not the pronoun.

STEP 2:   Read the sentence with just the pronoun part of the compound. If the sentence sounds correct, the pronoun is right. If it does not, change the pronoun.

Use the two steps to check the pronouns in these sentences.

> Malcolm and him work in the car repair shop.

> The former owners liked Malcolm and I.

STEP 1:   Cover all the words in the compound that are not the pronoun.
IN BOTH SENTENCES COVER: **Malcolm and**

STEP 2:   Read the sentences with just the pronoun part of each compound. If the sentences sound correct, the pronouns are right. If they do not sound correct, change the pronouns.

> SAY SENTENCE 1: **Him work(s) in the car repair shop.**
> SAY SENTENCE 2: **The former owners liked I.**

Neither sentence sounds correct, so the pronouns must be changed. The correct sentences follow.

> Malcolm and he work at the car repair shop.
> The former owners liked Malcolm and me.

EXERCISE 13e

Edit the following sentences for the correct use of pronouns. If a pronoun is incorrect, change it. (Note: Some sentences do not need correction.)

Example: Jeff, Dick, Luanne, and ~~me~~ work in different parts of the bakery.

1. Luanne sometimes helps Jeff and I make the baked goods downstairs.

2. You will be working upstairs with she and Dick.

3. Sometimes Luanne brings a coffee cake down to Jeff and I in the morning.

4. Her and I will soon be assigned to the front office.

5. Dick and me share an office.

6. There is another office next to us where John and Daphne do the bookkeeping.

7. There have been clashes between Daphne and he about the radio in their office.

8. She loves loud music.

9. The noise is too distracting for he.

10. Next Friday night Daphne and him are going bowling with Luanne and I.

Check your answers on page 241.

Lesson
14

Pronouns That End with *-self* or *-selves*

In some sentences the person who does and receives the action is the same. In such sentences, the object pronoun usually ends with *-self* or *-selves*. The following sentence gives an example.

You see yourself in the mirror.

The following chart shows the eight "-self/-selves" pronouns.

The "-self/-selves" Pronouns

The pronouns in these sentences are singular.

I see **myself**.
You see **yourself**.
He sees **himself**.
She sees **herself**.
It sees **itself**.

The pronouns in these sentences are plural.

We see **ourselves**.
You see **yourselves**.
They see **themselves**.

When you write, be sure to avoid the five common mistakes made with these pronouns.

MISTAKE 1: Do not use *hisself*. It is not a word.
    INCORRECT: He wants to do it **hisself**.
    CORRECT: He wants to do it **himself**.

MISTAKE 2: Do not use *ourself*. The correct form is *ourselves*.
    INCORRECT: We want to protect **ourself**.
    CORRECT: We want to protect **ourselves**.

MISTAKE 3: Do not use *theirself* or *theirselves*. They are not words.
    INCORRECT: They need to take responsibility for **theirself**.
                    They need to take responsibility for **theirselves**.
    CORRECT: They need to take responsibility for **themselves**.

MISTAKE 4: Do not use "-self/-selves" pronouns in compound subjects or objects.
           INCORRECT: George and **myself** are planning to be there.
                             It is important to him and **ourselves**.
           CORRECT: George and **I** are planning to be there.
                             It is important to him and **us**.

MISTAKE 5: Make sure "-self/-selves" pronouns agree (singular or plural) with the word they refer to.
           INCORRECT: The problems will not take care of **itself**.
           CORRECT: The problems will not take care of **themselves**.

Spotlight on Contractions

The table of Commonly Used Verb Contractions on page 74 contains many contractions formed by combining pronouns with verbs. It would be useful for you to review that table.

EXERCISE 14

Part A. Edit the following sentences for the correct use of pronouns. If a pronoun is incorrect, change it. (Note: Some sentences do not need correction.)

                          himself
Example: Dan is telling ~~hisself~~ there is nothing to be worried about.

1. Sitting alone, Arlene is humming a little tune to her.

2. Dan arrived by hisself.

3. He is making a nuisance of himself.

4. Did you hurt yourself when you tripped?

5. My husband and myself are fidgeting.

6. We are trying to keep our nervousness to ourself.

7. I have to remind me that I survived last week.

8. When I found me up in front of all those people, I nearly fainted.

9. The curtain seems to be opening by theirself.

10. Those kids should be proud of theirselves.

Part B. Add some words to complete each of the following sentences. Change the words in dark type to pronouns.

Example: _____I decided to put_____ ~~the television~~ *it* in the corner.

1. _____ for **Mr. Trinh, the landlord**.

2. **The woman in the apartment next door** _____.

3. _____ with **Mr. Fernandez**.

4. _____ on **you and me**.

5. Tina bought **Tina** _____.

6. _____ from Kathy and **Mark**.

7. Next month **Kathy and Shaleen** _____.

8. **You and I** _____.

9. _____ behind **the dripping faucet**.

10. _____ under **my windows**.

Part C. Rewrite each of the following sentences using contractions. Before you start, reread the Spotlight on page 91.

Example: ~~He has~~ *He's* used several power tools over the years.

1. She will need to wear safety glasses.

2. He will buy a power saw.

3. I am going to wear earplugs.

4. It is a noisy tool.

5. You have plugged in an extension cord.

Check your answers on page 241.

Lesson 15

Possessives

Possess means "own." A possessive word shows who or what owns something. To understand possessive pronouns, first look at possessive nouns.

Possessive Nouns

Possessive nouns always include apostrophes (') and sometimes *s*-endings. The following chart tells how to form possessive nouns and gives examples.

Forming Possessive Nouns

Rule	Examples	Examples in Sentences
To write the possessive form of a **singular** noun, add an apostrophe and an *s* at the end of the noun.	friend's bass's child's	This is my **friend's** petting zoo. The **bass's** tone is wonderful. Her **child's** swing set is broken.
To write the possessive form of a **plural** noun that ends in *s*, add only an apostrophe at the end of the noun.	friends' basses'	This is my two **friends'** petting zoo. Both **basses'** tones are wonderful.
To write the possessive form of a **plural** noun that does not end in *s*, add an apostrophe and an *s* at the end of the noun.	children's	The **children's** swing sets are broken.

EXERCISE 15a

Complete each of the following sentences by adding the possessive form of the noun in parentheses.

Example: (lizards) The _____lizards'_____ bowls are empty.

1. (mouse)   The _____ eyes are red.

2. (boys)   That must be the _____ room.

3. (doors)   Who broke these _____ hinges?

4. (window)   How was the front _____ sash damaged?

5. (men)   Do you see any _____ clothing around?

6. (women)   On that rack are _____ coats.

7. (rugs)   Those _____ patterns are traditional.

8. (chair)   This _____ cushion is lumpy.

9. (people)   Other _____ lives fascinate me.

10. (tooth)   One _____ color is not right.

Check your answers on page 241.

Possessive Pronouns

Pronouns show possession by changing forms, not by adding apostrophes. Possessive pronouns often appear with the noun that names the thing they possess. Sometimes they stand alone.

The following chart shows how possessive pronouns are formed and gives examples.

How Possessive Pronouns Are Formed

Subject Pronouns	Possessive Pronouns That Appear with Nouns	Possessive Pronouns That Stand Alone
I	my	mine
you (singular)	your (singular)	yours (singular)
he	his	his
she	her	hers
it	its	its (not often used)
we	our	ours
you (plural)	your (plural)	yours (plural)
they	their	theirs

Look at the following example sentences. In each, the possessive pronoun is in dark type.

In these sentences the possessive pronouns appear with the nouns that name the things they possess.

My prize is a necklace.
What is in **your** hand?
He wants **his** money now.
That is **her** ring.
Its stone is a ruby.
Those are **our** friends.
I will be late with **your** paychecks.
That's **their** problem.

In these sentences the possessive pronouns stand alone.

The necklace is **mine**.
These gloves are **yours**.
The money is **his**.
I am not **hers**.
This ruby is **its**. (correct, but awkward)
The decisions were **ours**.
Next week these jobs will be **yours**.
Last week the jobs were **theirs**.

Notice that in all the sentences the possessive pronouns have *no* apostrophes. Don't confuse possessive pronouns with contractions, such as *you're*, *they're*, and *it's*. Also, don't confuse *their* with *there*.

Edit the following sentences for the correct use of possessive pronouns. If a pronoun is incorrect, change it. (Note: Some sentences do not need correction.)

your
Example: The yard sale was ~~you're~~ idea.

1. The rug and it's owner are over there.

2. His hat once cost twenty dollars.

3. For twenty cents it can be your.

4. Our beautiful glass jug is for sale.

5. Its' handle is a bit chipped.

6. Hers sunglasses were a bargain.

7. They lenses are a little scratched.

8. The sneakers in the box of free items are mines.

9. There laces are missing.

10. Where are ours customers?

11. We received these notices in ours mail.

12. My sister entered the sweepstakes and now the stereo is her.

13. The prize red sports car behind the young man is his.

14. A happy couple said of their new home, "It's all ours now!"

15. I wish those prizes were mine and not they'res.

Check your answers on page 241.

Lesson 16

Pronoun Agreement

Now that you know about what pronouns are and do, you can learn to avoid common errors often made with pronouns.

Pronoun Agreement with Nouns

A pronoun has to agree in sex and number with the word it refers to. For example, if a possessive pronoun refers to a noun that names one male, the pronoun must be *his*. Look at the following examples.

In this sentence a **singular male pronoun** refers to a **singular male noun**.

The **boy** wanted **his** TV back.

In this sentence a **plural pronoun** refers to a **plural noun**.

The **girls** wanted **their** TV back.

When you were studying subject-verb agreement, you learned about some special nouns in Lesson 5:

- Singular nouns that end with *s*, such as *aerobics*, *economics*, and *mathematics*
- Singular nouns that name groups or amounts, such as *team* and *dollars*
- Plural nouns that name one thing, such as *glasses*, *pants*, and *scissors*

A pronoun that refers to a noun of those types must agree with it in number. Look at the following examples.

In each of these sentences a **singular pronoun** refers to a **singular noun**.

He took **mathematics** but found **it** hard.
I had **twenty dollars**, but **it** is gone now.

In this sentence a **plural pronoun** refers to a **plural noun**.

She lost the **scissors** but found **them** later.

EXERCISE 16a

Part A. Underline the correct pronoun to complete each of the following sentences. In one of the sentences you will also need to choose the correct verb.

Example: The oldest son was doing poorly on (his/their) tests.

1. The middle son was falling asleep at (his/her) job.

2. The youngest son was watching cartoons instead of playing with (his/their) friends.

3. The TV was on so much that (its/their) top was always warm.

4. The cats slept on the TV instead of getting (its/their) exercise.

5. The cats and the people in that house were adding fat to (his/their) waistlines.

6. The mother found that (she/they) herself (was/were) getting a headache from watching so much television.

7. The mother watched the boys and noticed that (she/they) fought more after watching fights on TV.

8. The boys often argued over the TV, and (his/their) arguments usually ended in blows.

9. The youngest boy was having tantrums because (he/they) wanted new toys.

10. After the TV was gone, the parents missed (it/them) more than the children did.

Part B. Edit the following sentences for pronouns. (Note: Some sentences do not need correction.)

Example: The team has ~~their~~ *its* own dugout.

1. I watch the news, but I find them disturbing.

2. The team almost lost their chance.

3. He does gymnastics because he enjoys them.

4. The audience showed their appreciation by clapping.

5. The jury reached its decision in record time.

6. Her father enjoyed politics, and she enjoys them too.

7. Those scissors need its blades sharpened.

8. The FBI headquarters closed their doors.

9. My family is going to have their reunion this summer.

10. Athletics has their place in the school day.

Check your answers on page 242.

Pronoun Agreement with Pronouns

As you read earlier in this lesson, a pronoun must agree in sex and number with the word it refers to. Sometimes a pronoun refers to another pronoun. Then the two pronouns must agree with each other.

Here is a chart of pronouns that often refer to other pronouns.

Pronouns That Refer to Other Pronouns		
Singular Pronouns	anybody	neither
	anyone	nobody
	anything	no one
	each	nothing
	either	one
	everybody	somebody
	everyone	someone
	everything	something
Plural Pronouns	both	many
	few	several
Pronouns That Can Be Singular or Plural	all	none
	any	some
	most	

The following examples illustrate agreement with these three kinds of pronouns.

In each of these sentences a **singular pronoun** refers to a **singular pronoun**.	**No one** brought **his** umbrella.* **Some** of the bread has lost **its** freshness.
In each of these sentences a **plural pronoun** refers to a **plural pronoun**.	**Both** have **their** drawbacks. **Some** of the rolls have lost **their** freshness.

Even though you did not read the word *pronoun* at the time, you learned about many of these pronouns in the Chapter 1 lessons on subject-verb agreement. The singular pronouns are discussed on page 29; the pronouns that can be singular or plural, on page 44. Do you remember why *Some* is singular when it refers to *bread* but plural when it refers to *rolls*? If not, you should review "Words That Can Be Singular or Plural as Subjects" on page 44 in Lesson 8.

 ### Spotlight on Agreement with Pronouns That End with *-body* or *-one*

The words *his*, *her*, or *his or her* are used to refer to pronouns that end with *-body* or *-one*. Use *his or her* when the pronoun refers to a person of either sex or people of both sexes.

Examples:

> Is there **nobody** in this boys' school who can volunteer **his** time?
> **Someone** has washed **her** dress in the slop sink.
> **Somebody** left **his or her** comb in my bathroom.
> **Everyone** should be at **his or her** work station before 8:00 A.M.

In the examples, notice the following:

- *Nobody* refers only to boys, so *his* agrees with it.
- *Someone* refers only to females, so *her* agrees with it.
- *Somebody* refers to a person of either sex, so *his or her* agrees with it.
- *Everyone* refers to people of both sexes, so *his or her* agrees with it.

---

* Note: It would not be correct to say *No one brought their umbrellas* because *no one* is singular.

Part A. Edit the following for correct agreement of pronouns. You will need to change the form of some verbs. (Note: Some sentences do not need correction.) Before you start, reread the Spotlight on page 98.

Example: Everything has ~~their~~ *its* cost.

1. Anybody can improve their diet.

2. Most of these fruits offer vitamins, but it can be high in calories.

3. All of these fruits have their share of calories.

4. Some of those canned fruits owe its sweetness to added sugar.

5. Nobody wants his or her favorite foods taken away.

6. Several of these vegetables lose its vitamins when peeled.

7. Some of those vegetables contain harmful chemicals in its peels.

8. Many like his or her food fried.

9. When most is fried, they become oily.

10. All of those vegetables keep more of its vitamins if cooked quickly in a little water.

Part B. Complete the following sentences by adding a pronoun to each blank. Before you start, be sure to reread the Spotlight on page 98.

Example: Everyone needs to think about __his or her__ eating habits.

1. That family has problems with _____ diet.

2. When butter is used to flavor vegetables, _____ adds calories and fat.

3. Spreads may be tasty on vegetables, but _____ are less healthy than lemon juice.

4. To reduce the calories in soup, refrigerate _____ and then skim the fat off.

5. Most of these dieters do not add sugar to _____ cereal or coffee.

6. Frying steaks adds fat to _____.

7. Removing the skin from a chicken reduces _____ calories.

8. To remove the grease from hamburgers, blot _____ with paper towels.

9. Anybody who uses a scale can keep a check on _____ weight.

10. Bran muffins may look blah, but _____ usually taste good.

Check your answers on page 242.

Avoiding Pronoun Shifts and Unclear References

Pronoun clarity is just as important as pronoun agreement. When you write, you need to be sure that the references you make with pronouns are clear.

Avoiding Pronoun Shifts Within Sentences

If you aren't careful when you use pronouns, you may shift from talking about one person or thing to talking about another. Switching from one pronoun to the pronoun *you* is one of the most common errors. In the first sentence in the pair that follows, such a pronoun shift occurs.

INCORRECT: *I* like walking because the exercise relaxes *you.*
CORRECT: *I* like walking because the exercise relaxes *me.*

The sentence is about the writer, so both pronouns in the sentence must refer to the writer. The pronouns must agree with each other. In the incorrect sentence, the writer shifts from talking about himself or herself to talking about you.

EXERCISE 17a

Edit each of the following sentences to correct pronoun shifts. You will need to change the form of some verbs.

Example: My cousin Nadine drank as a teenager because ~~one~~ *she* wanted to feel grown up.

1. She also used alcohol because you felt less shy after a drink or two.

2. I worried about her because you couldn't tell what she would do next.

3. I hoped she'd never mix alcohol with other drugs because you could die.

4. Now she wants to stop, but you are addicted after years of drinking.

5. Her family wants to help, and they are looking for a good treatment center.

Check your answers on page 242.

Avoiding Pronoun Shifts Within Paragraphs

Sometimes a pronoun shift occurs when you write more than one sentence on the same topic. Look at the following example.

INCORRECT:	**People** try drugs for many reasons. Often **they** don't want to be different from others in the group. Many times **they** are following adult examples. Usually **you** are curious about the effects.
CORRECT:	**People** try drugs for many reasons. Often **they** don't want to be different from others in the group. Many times **they** are following adult examples. Usually **they** are curious about the effects.

Throughout the incorrect paragraph above, *they* is used to refer to *people*, except in the last sentence where there is a shift to *you*. In the correct paragraph there is no shift from *they* to *you*.

Look at another example of a pronoun shift within a paragraph.

INCORRECT:	**Somebody** may take **his or her** first drink to relax. Then **they** find relaxing impossible without drinking.
CORRECT:	**Somebody** may take **his or her** first drink to relax. Then **he or she** finds relaxing impossible without drinking.
ALSO CORRECT:	**People** may take **their** first drink to relax. Then **they** find relaxing impossible without drinking.

In the incorrect paragraph there is a pronoun shift from singular pronouns, *somebody* and *his or her*, to the plural pronoun *they*. One way to correct the shift is to make all the pronouns in the paragraph singular. To do that, change *they* to *he or she*. Notice that the change from plural to singular pronouns in the second sentence requires a change in the form of the verb from *find* to *finds*.

Another way to correct the shift is to rewrite the paragraph using plural nouns and pronouns, as in the second correction above. Many writers use the plural to avoid using the sometimes awkward *he or she*.

EXERCISE 17b

Edit each of the following short paragraphs to correct the pronoun shifts. Make the pronouns in each Paragraph (a) singular and those in each Paragraph (b) plural. In some paragraphs you will need to change the form of some verbs and other words.

Example: (a) If someone wants to stop drinking, he or she should seek help.
                 he or she
       To find where to get help, ~~you~~ can try the yellow pages.
       people   *they*
     (b) If ~~someone~~ wants to stop drinking, ~~he or she~~ should seek help.
                       they
       To find where to get help, ~~you~~ can try the yellow pages.

1. (a) Someone may be trying to break his or her drug habit. They can receive one or more kinds of treatment.

   (b) Someone may be trying to break his or her drug habit. They can receive one or more kinds of treatment.

2. (a) A person may recognize the problems caused by his or her drug abuse. You can go to a clinic where doctors can help you get off drugs.

   (b) A person may recognize the problems caused by his or her drug abuse. You can go to a clinic where doctors can help you get off drugs.

3. (a) Another person may discover that he or she abuses drugs. They can go to a mental health center where counselors will help them deal with their problems.

   (b) Another person may discover that he or she abuses drugs. They can go to a mental health center where counselors will help them deal with their problems.

4. (a) A child can develop a drug problem. They sometimes live in halfway houses where they get treatment.

   (b) A child can develop a drug problem. They sometimes live in halfway houses where they get treatment.

5. (a) For someone to get help, he or she must recognize a problem. To get well, you must want to change.

   (b) For someone to get help, he or she must recognize a problem. To get well, you must want to change.

Check your answers on page 242.

Avoiding Unclear References

Sometimes it is not clear which word a pronoun refers to in the sentence. To make a sentence clear, it is often necessary to use nouns rather than pronouns.

A common error is using a pronoun that could refer to either of two nouns or pronouns.

INCORRECT: Louise brought home **two cats** for **her daughters** when **they** were young.

CORRECT: Louise brought home **two cats** for **her daughters** when the **girls** were young.

In the incorrect sentence above it is not clear whether the cats or the daughters were young. The correct sentence uses a noun, *girls*, instead of the pronoun *they*. The noun makes the sentence clear.

Another common error occurs when a pronoun does not clearly refer to anything in its context.

INCORRECT: I am a teacher. None of my sons or daughters chose **it** as a career.

CORRECT: I am a teacher. None of my sons or daughters chose **teaching** as a career.

In the incorrect example above it is not clear what *it* refers to. The correct sentence uses *teaching* instead of *it* to make the sentence clear.

EXERCISE 17c

Edit each of the following sentences to correct unclear references by pronouns.

Example: Gail has told her son and her daughters over and over, but ~~they~~ her children never listen.

1. When too much hair goes down the drain, it can cause a problem.

2. If you must wash your hair in the sink, clean it well afterward.

3. Wipe the hair out of the sink and throw it away.

4. Hair is clogging our sink, and we can't use it.

5. Gail's daughter is studying to be a plumber, and she likes it very much.

6. Gail told Josephine to go to her room.

7. In a shopping bag Josephine found a box; it contained a special powder.

8. When Josephine found the box in the bag, she looked at the bottom of it.

9. The label said to keep the powder out of children's reach, so it must be strong.

10. She poured the powder down the drain, and thirty minutes later it started working.

Check your answers on page 243.

Part 1 of GED Practice 3 begins below. It will give you practice with multiple-choice items that cover the skills you have studied so far in this book. Part 2 of the practice, beginning on page 107, will give you a chance to use those same skills to correct mistakes in paragraphs like those you might write in an essay.

PART 1

<u>Directions</u>: Choose the <u>one best answer</u> to each item.

<u>Items 1 through 15</u> refer to the following paragraphs.

(1) Bernard and their two friends, Jose and Anton, wanted to find jobs. (2) They weren't having much luck on your own.

(3) They paid a visit to a vocational counselor last month. (4) They got vocational interest questionnaires from the counselor. (5) The forms had questions about your abilities. (6) There are also questions about their interests.

(7) Both Jose and Anton had trouble with their. (8) Jose, who is a native of Mexico, reads Spanish. (9) He weren't able to read much English. (10) The counselor gives him a form in Spanish. (11) Anton haven't learned to read well yet. (12) The counselor provided an audiocassette tape for him. (13) He listened to the directions and followed it.

(14) No one spent more than an hour filling in their forms. (15) Each man scored his form hisself.

(16) The counselor met with each man. (17) She helped them match their interests and abilities with careers and discussed our plans for training. (18) By the end of three months, all three men had jobs.

1. Sentence 1: **Bernard and their two friends, Jose and Anton, wanted to find jobs.**

   What correction should be made to this sentence?

   (1) change <u>Bernard</u> to <u>bernard</u>
   (2) replace <u>their</u> with <u>his</u>
   (3) change <u>wanted</u> to <u>want</u>
   (4) change <u>wanted</u> to <u>wants</u>
   (5) no correction is necessary

2. Sentence 2: **They weren't having much luck on your own.**

   What correction should be made to this sentence?

   (1) change the spelling of <u>weren't</u> to <u>were'nt</u>
   (2) change <u>weren't</u> to <u>wasn't</u>
   (3) change <u>weren't</u> to <u>aren't</u>
   (4) replace <u>your</u> with <u>their</u>
   (5) replace <u>your</u> with <u>yours</u>

3. Sentence 3: **They paid a visit to a vocational counselor last month.**

What correction should be made to this sentence?

(1) change the spelling of <u>paid</u> to <u>payed</u>
(2) change the spelling of <u>paid</u> to <u>payd</u>
(3) change <u>paid</u> to <u>have paid</u>
(4) change <u>paid</u> to <u>had paid</u>
(5) no correction is necessary

4. Sentence 4: **They got vocational interest questionnaires from the counselor.**

If you rewrote sentence 4 beginning with <u>She gave</u>, the next word should be

(1) herself
(2) him
(3) them
(4) they
(5) their

5. Sentence 5: **The forms had questions about your abilities.**

What correction should be made to this sentence?

(1) change <u>had</u> to <u>has</u>
(2) change <u>had</u> to <u>have</u>
(3) replace <u>your</u> with <u>their</u>
(4) replace <u>your</u> with <u>yourself's</u>
(5) no correction is necessary

6. Sentence 6: **There are also questions about their interests.**

What correction should be made to this sentence?

(1) change <u>are</u> to <u>is</u>
(2) change <u>are</u> to <u>were</u>
(3) change <u>are</u> to <u>was</u>
(4) replace <u>their</u> with <u>your</u>
(5) no correction is necessary

7. Sentence 7: **Both Jose and Anton had trouble with their.**

What correction should be made to this sentence?

(1) change <u>had</u> to <u>has</u>
(2) change <u>had</u> to <u>have</u>
(3) change <u>their</u> to <u>theirs</u>
(4) change the spelling of <u>their</u> to <u>thier</u>
(5) replace <u>their</u> with <u>they're</u>

8. Sentence 9: **He weren't able to read much English.**

Which of the following is the best way to write the underlined portion of this sentence? If you think the original is the best way, choose option (1).

(1) He weren't
(2) He aren't
(3) He isn't
(4) They aren't
(5) They're not

9. Sentence 10: **The counselor <u>gives him</u> a form in Spanish.**

Which of the following is the best way to write the underlined portion of this sentence? If you think the original is the best way, choose option (1).

(1) gives him
(2) give him
(3) gave him
(4) gave himself
(5) given

10. Sentence 11: **Anton haven't learned to read well yet.**

What correction should be made to this sentence?

(1) change <u>haven't</u> to <u>hasn't</u>
(2) change the spelling of <u>haven't</u> to <u>have'nt</u>
(3) change <u>learned</u> to <u>learn</u>
(4) change <u>learned</u> to <u>learning</u>
(5) no correction is necessary

11. Sentence 12: **The counselor provided an audiocassette tape for him.**

What correction should be made to this sentence?

(1) change provided to provides
(2) change provided to will provide
(3) change him to them
(4) change him to himself
(5) no correction is necessary

12. Sentence 13: **He listened to the directions and followed it.**

What correction should be made to this sentence?

(1) change listened to listens
(2) change listened to listen
(3) change followed to follows
(4) replace it with them
(5) no correction is necessary

13. Sentence 14: **No one spent more than an hour filling in their forms.**

Which of the following is the best way to write the underlined portion of this sentence? If you think the original is the best way, choose option (1).

(1) their forms
(2) their form
(3) his forms
(4) his form
(5) his or her form

14. Sentence 15: **Each man scored his form hisself.**

What correction should be made to this sentence?

(1) change hisself to themself
(2) change hisself to themselves
(3) change hisself to theirselves
(4) change hisself to himself
(5) no correction is necessary

15. Sentence 17: **She helped them match their interests and abilities with careers and discussed our plans for training.**

What correction should be made to this sentence?

(1) change helped to will help
(2) change them to us
(3) change their to our
(4) change discussed to discusses
(5) change our to their

PART 2

Directions: Edit the following passage. It contains 15 errors.

- If any verb and subject do not agree, change the verb.
- Correct errors in the use of verb tenses.
- Correct errors in the use of pronouns.
- Capitalize any word that should be capitalized.
- Correct errors in punctuation.
- Correct errors in spelling.

Michael McVane is working at Finest Boat Companys main plant for over twenty-four years. He or she worked at the shipyard as a pipe fitter and later as a pipe shop superintendent. He died of cancer at age 58 on September 23, 1992. Breathing asbestos caused it.

This letter is from my children and myself. We wants to know why you're company didn't protect it's employees from asbestos. Those in charge cares only about theirselves. Its a shame. Yous taken him away from we. Everyone know that you are responsible.

Check your answers on page 243.

GED PRACTICE 3 SKILLS CHART

To review the writing skills covered by the items in GED Practice 3, study the following lessons in Unit 1. The answers and explanations beginning on page 244 tell which part of each lesson pertains to each item.

Item numbers 16–30 refer to the numbering of the mistakes in Part 2 in the answers and explanations.

4 SENTENCE STRUCTURE

The lessons in this chapter are about sentence structure. They give you practice at writing sentences with compound subjects, objects, and predicates; writing compound and complex sentences; finding and correcting run-on sentences and sentence fragments; and improving the clarity of sentences.

Lesson 18

Compound Sentence Parts

Writing that is choppy and repetitive is not effective writing. Reading such writing can be tedious. On the other hand, writing that is smooth can make reading it a pleasure. In this lesson you will practice writing smooth sentences by using compound sentence parts.

Compound Subjects

In Lesson 6 you learned that a sentence can have a compound subject, a subject with two or more parts. You also learned that the parts of a compound subject are often connected by the word *and*.

You can think of a sentence with a compound subject as the combination of two or more sentences. Look at the following example.

These two sentences are identical except for their subjects.	**The taco** was delicious. **The salad** was delicious.
This sentence combines the two sentences above by using a compound subject.	**The taco and the salad** were delicious.

The two sentences—the one about a taco and the other about a salad—are short and choppy. The second sentence repeats most of the words in the first. The sentence with the compound subject is smooth and does not repeat words.

When two sentences are combined by use of a compound subject with *and*, the subject, the verb, and sometimes other parts of the sentence are plural in the new sentence. Look at the following examples.

Was and **cook** become **were** and **cooks** in the combined sentence because that sentence is about two cooks.	Jon **was** a **cook**. Rodney **was** a **cook**. Jon and Rodney **were cooks**.
Cafeteria remains singular in the combined sentence because both cooks worked in the same cafeteria.	Jon worked in our **cafeteria**. Rodney worked in our **cafeteria**. Jon and Rodney worked in our **cafeteria**.

When you combine two or more sentences by writing a compound subject, it is sometimes necessary to use all the words from the naming part of each sentence in the combined sentence. Sometimes it is not. Words not usually repeated in compound subjects are words that do not name specific amounts, such as *a few*, *all*, *any*, *many*, *most*, *several*, and *some*. Repeated words are usually those that name specific amounts, such as *a*, *an*, *four*, and *the*. Look at the following examples.

When these three sentences are combined, the complete naming part of each is used in the combined sentence.

A hot dog was cooking on the grill.
Two hamburgers were cooking on the grill.
Ten chicken legs were cooking on the grill.
A hot dog, two hamburgers, and ten chicken legs were cooking on the grill.

When these three sentences are combined, the word **Some** is used only once in the combination.

Some hot dogs were cooking on the grill.
Some **hamburgers** were cooking on the grill.
Some **chicken legs** were cooking on the grill.
Some hot dogs, hamburgers, and chicken legs were cooking on the grill.

EXERCISE 18a

Combine the sentences in each of the following pairs.

Example: Karen was a student in the family literacy program.
Justina was a student in the family literacy program.

Karen and Justina were students in the family literacy program.

1. Many parents take part in the program.
   Many children take part in the program.

   _____

2. Several mothers are completing their high school educations.
   Several fathers are completing their high school educations.

   _____

3. Karen earned her high school degree after four months.
   Justina earned her high school degree after four months.

   _____

4. All of the parents are learning new skills.
   All of the children are learning new skills.

   _____

5. Most of the parents get library cards.
   Most of the children get library cards.

   _____

6. Mason Sr. likes doing his homework.
   Mason Jr. likes doing his homework.

   _____

7. Mason Sr. is a single parent.
   Milagros is a single parent.

   _____

8. Mason Sr. doesn't want his child to think it's OK to quit school.
   Milagros doesn't want her child to think it's OK to quit school.

   _____

9. Mason Sr. learns how to help his son do homework.
   Milagros learns how to help her son do homework.

   _____

10. Several libraries are sponsors of the literacy program.
    A women's support group is a sponsor of the literacy program.

    _____

Check your answers on page 245.

Compound Objects

In Lesson 13 you learned that the words that receive the action in action sentences are objects. Some action sentences have compound objects. You can think of a sentence with a compound object as the combination of two or more sentences. Look at the following example.

<table>
<tr><td>These two sentences are identical except for their objects.</td><td>The beans burned **my tongue**.
The beans burned **my fingers**.</td></tr>
<tr><td>This sentence combines the two sentences above by using a compound object.</td><td>The beans burned **my tongue and fingers**.</td></tr>
</table>

The sentence with the compound object is smooth and does not repeat words. Notice that the word *my* is not repeated in the compound object. The possessive pronoun *my* is understood to "own" both *tongue* and *fingers*.

 Spotlight on Punctuation

When **three or more** parts of an object are connected by **and**, commas go between the parts. The last comma goes before the **and**.

Examples:

   I drove Rosa, Jorge, and Kim to the ball game.
   My job required promptness, courtesy, and skill.

Combine the sentences in each of the following sets. Before you start, be sure to reread the Spotlight on page 111.

Example: He burned the hot dog. He burned the hamburger. He burned the chicken legs.

He burned the hot dog, the hamburger, and the chicken legs.

1. She bought few steaks. She bought few chops.

   _____

2. I ate a lot of corn. I ate a lot of salad. I ate a lot of coleslaw.

   _____

3. We had some pretzels. We had some chips. We had some carrot sticks.

   _____

4. I bought two drinks. I bought a burger. I bought two hot dogs.

   _____

5. We visited my mean cousin. We visited my grumpy grandmother. We visited my spoiled nephew.

   _____

6. We played a little volleyball. We played a little softball. We played a little football.

   _____

7. The children lost my volleyball. The children lost my softball. The children lost my football.

   _____

8. My husband had too much sun. My husband had too much soda. My husband had too much cake.

   _____

9. We picked some blackberries. We picked some raspberries. We picked some blueberries.

   _____

10. I got a bee sting. I got a sunburn. I got a scratch.

   _____

Check your answers on page 245.

Compound Predicates

In Lessons 1 and 4 you learned about the action parts and the description parts of sentences. Those parts of sentences can be called predicates. In any sentence, the predicate is made up of all the words that do not belong to the naming part of the sentence.

> **Predicate**:
> the action part or describing part of a sentence

Some sentences have compound predicates. You can think of a sentence with a compound predicate as the combination of two or more sentences. Look at the following example.

These two sentences are identical except for their predicates.

The beans **burned my tongue**.
The beans **filled my stomach**.

This sentence combines the two sentences above by using a compound predicate.

The beans **burned my tongue and filled my stomach**.

The sentence with the compound predicate is smoother than the two separate sentences. Notice that the verbs in the compound predicate are both in the past tense. The same tense is used for the verbs in a compound predicate when the actions occur at the same time.

EXERCISE 18c

Combine the sentences in each of the following pairs.

Example: Exercise strengthens your heart.
Exercise improves your sleep.

Exercise strengthens your heart and improves your sleep.

1. Suki rides an exercise bike.
   Suki uses a treadmill.

2. Ross quit swimming.
   Ross started jogging.

3. Warm up lightly before a workout.
   Stretch slowly before a workout.

4. Ronald plays basketball at lunch time.
   Ronald runs after work.

5. One day while jogging he became exhausted.
   One day while jogging he felt dizzy.

6. His doctor examined him.
   His doctor suggested indoor exercise.

   _____

7. Yesterday the secretaries left for lunch early.
   Yesterday the secretaries arrived at the rink ten minutes later.

   _____

8. By skating every lunch hour they burn up calories.
   By skating every lunch hour they save money.

   _____

9. After dinner Georgina shoots baskets.
   After dinner Georgina jumps rope.

   _____

10. She gets thirsty.
    She stops for a sip of water now and then.

    _____

Check your answers on page 245.

Using Parallel Structures in Compounds

The parts of a compound subject, object, or predicate must have parallel structures. That is, similar ideas must be worded in similar ways. Look at the following examples.

INCORRECT: Fatigue, stress, and **being hungry** cause Aaron's headaches.
             He likes bowling, fishing, and **hikes**.
             After work he snacks a little, chats for a while, and **relaxing**.

CORRECT: Fatigue, stress, and **hunger** cause Aaron's headaches.
             He likes bowling, fishing, and **hiking**.
             After work he snacks a little, chats for a while, and **relaxes**.

The first incorrect sentence has a compound subject. The words *being hungry* are not parallel to *fatigue* and *stress*. The correct sentence uses *hunger* to make all three parts of the compound parallel.

The second incorrect sentence has a compound object. The word *hikes* is not parallel to *bowling* and *fishing*, which both end with *-ing*. The correct sentence uses *hiking* to make all three parts of the compound parallel.

The third incorrect sentence has a compound predicate. The word *relaxing* is not parallel to *snacks* and *chats*, which are verbs. The correct sentence uses *relaxes* to make all three parts of the compound parallel.

Part A. Edit the following sentences to correct errors in parallel structure.

Example: Carla is orderly, thorough, and ~~a quiet person~~. *quiet*

1. She felt both disappointed and relief when she didn't get the job as business office clerk.

2. She tells me her hopes, her dreams, and what she fears.

3. Accepting money, making out receipts, and to help people fill out papers are not tasks she wants.

4. She is kind, patient, and a shy person.

5. What the pay is, the duties, and the hours of a medical records clerk are more up her alley.

6. She noticed a job listing, requesting an application, and completed it.

7. I know that she will like the job and is good at it.

8. A medical records clerk must be good at both filing and a good typist.

9. Filing and to type don't interest Imogene.

10. She likes to meet people, answering questions, and to help others.

Part B. Combine the sentences in each of the following groups. Before you start, be sure to reread the Spotlight on page 111.

Example: Ellen decided to go to a San Francisco 49ers football game.
Francine decided to go to a San Francisco 49ers football game.
Shirley decided to go to a San Francisco 49ers football game.

   Ellen, Francine, and Shirley decided to go to a San Francisco 49ers football game.

1. Ellen had no money. Francine had no money. Shirley had no money.

_____

2. Francine drove to the bank. Francine dropped Shirley off at the door. Francine parked the car in the lot.

_____

3. Shirley pressed the door handle. Shirley pulled the door handle. Shirley twisted the door handle.

_____

4. She scratched her head. She raised her eyebrows. She looked at her watch calendar.

_____

5. The bank closed an hour ago. The bank won't open again until Monday.

   _____

6. She could call a friend. She could borrow some money.

   _____

7. She pulled out her wallet. She pulled out her change purse. She pulled out her checkbook.

   _____

8. She found her bank card. She put it in the slot. She typed in her code. She requested some cash.

   _____

9. The bank's computer received her message. The bank's computer read her message. The bank's computer acted on her message.

   _____

10. The computer pushed the bills through an opening. The computer returned her card through another opening. The computer ejected her receipt through a third opening.

   _____

Check your answers on page 246.

Lesson
19

Compound Sentences

A long sentence often sounds better than two short choppy ones. A long sentence may also show how its ideas are related better than two short sentences can.

Effective long sentences can often be made by combining two related short sentences into a compound sentence. The parts of compound sentences are joined by the use of a comma and connecting words like *and* or *but*. Look at the following examples.

These **two short sentences** are related because the careers students pick are the ones they write about.	Students in Mr. Tucker's class pick a career. They write about it.
This **compound sentence** joins the two short sentences above with a comma + **and**. The combination makes the relationship between the ideas clearer than the separate short sentences do.	Students in Mr. Tucker's class pick a career, **and** they write about it.

These **two short sentences** are related because the idea in the second is in contrast to the idea in the first.

Homework in many classes is boring. Assignments are interesting in Mr. Tucker's class.

This **compound sentence** joins the two short sentences above with a comma + **but**. The combination makes the contrast between the ideas clearer than the separate short sentences do.

Homework in many classes is boring, **but** assignments are interesting in Mr. Tucker's class.

Notice that the verbs in each compound sentence above are in the same tense. In the first, the actions occur at the same time; in the second, both parts of the sentence state facts.

Compound sentences are different from sentences with compound predicates. In a compound sentence, each part of the sentence has a subject and a verb. The subjects are usually different from each other. In a sentence with a compound predicate, there is only one subject in the whole sentence. To see the difference, look at the following examples.

This sentence has a **compound predicate**. The subject of the sentence is **I**. The two parts of the predicate are connected by the word **but** with no comma.

I drive a bus on weekends **but** do construction work during the week.

This sentence is a **compound sentence**. The subject of the first part of the sentence is **I**. The subject of the second part is **friend**. The two parts are connected by a comma + **but**.

I wrote about an occupation I would enjoy, **but** my friend explored an occupation he wasn't even interested in learning about.

If you are not sure whether a sentence is compound or not, split it in two. If the two parts—without the connecting word or the comma, if there is one—are complete sentences by themselves, their combined form is a compound sentence. In that case, a comma is necessary between the two parts of the sentence. The following shows how you would test the examples above by this method.

To find out if this is a compound sentence, split it into two parts leaving out the comma and the word **but**.

I wrote about an occupation I would enjoy, but my friend explored an occupation he wasn't even interested in learning about.

The result is two complete sentences. Therefore, the long sentence above is a compound sentence.

I wrote about an occupation I would enjoy. My friend explored an occupation he wasn't even interested in learning about.

To find out if this is a compound sentence, split it into two parts leaving out the word **but**.

I drive a bus on weekends but do construction work during the week.

The result is only one sentence and part of another sentence. Therefore, the long sentence above is not a compound sentence.

I drive a bus on weekends. do construction work during the week.

The chart on page 118 shows seven common connecting words used in compound sentences. Each connecting word shows a certain relationship between the compound sentence's two ideas.

Connecting Words Used in Compound Sentences

Word	Used to Show	Example
and	similarity between ideas	I know you, and you know me.
but	contrast between ideas	I was there, but he didn't see me.
for	cause	He is hungry, for dinner is late.
nor	no choice between ideas	He hasn't any, nor do I.
or	choice between ideas	You bring it, or I will.
so	effect	He showed up, so I left.
yet	contrast between ideas	I want to learn, yet she won't help me.

EXERCISE 19

Part A. Edit the following sentences for proper use of commas. Strike out any comma that doesn't belong. Insert commas that are needed. (Note: Some sentences do not need correction.)

Example: She applied for/ and got the job.

1. She will enjoy using the register but she may not like bagging.

2. She won't have to punch in prices, for the scanner takes care of that.

3. She slides the item over a small window and a laser beam reads the bar code.

4. Computers can read the name, and price of the item.

5. She will not have to deduct coupons, or food stamps.

6. Weighing vegetables, and approving checks are handled by the computer.

7. She, or the customer puts the groceries into bags.

8. Customers are served faster and better with fewer cashiers.

9. Computers also keep track of popular items, and sold-out stock.

10. Computers can tell whether an ad, or a special offer raised sales.

Part B. Use the connecting word in parentheses to join the sentences in each of the following pairs.

Example: (and) Our teacher wants us to understand different careers.
I think that will be very useful to all of us.

Our teacher wants us to understand different careers,

and I think that will be very useful to all of us.

1. (and) Some students explored medical careers.
Others looked at careers as hair stylists.

_____

2. (and) Dottie found some facts about her career in pamphlets.
Raj found information for her in library books.

_____

3. (and) She wrote a list of words that describe her.
Raj found words that describe a hair stylist.

_____

4. (and) Dottie examined the want ads.
Raj looked for ads in store windows.

_____

5. (and) Dottie looked in the telephone book for the names of hair salons.
Raj wrote down their phone numbers for her.

_____

6. (but) She may call a hair salon.
Raj thinks she should write a letter.

_____

7. (so) Dottie wants job applications mailed to her.
She made up some labels with her name and address on them.

_____

8. (so) Dottie is not a certified beautician.
Raj encouraged her to get certification.

_____

9. (for) She filled in applications without making spelling errors.
Employers look at writing skills.

_____

10. (so) Dottie's friend Bonnie is a certified stylist.
Bonnie told Dottie about certification requirements.

_____

Part C. Use one of the following connecting words to join the sentences in each of the following pairs: *and*, *but*, *for*, *nor*, *or*, *so*, or *yet*.

Example: He wasn't absent.
He went on the field trip yesterday.

<u>He wasn't absent, for he went on the field trip yesterday.</u>

1. We will be studying the types of writing people in certain careers do.
Some of us will write papers about our findings.

_____

2. Shana will write a letter to an editor.
Celestine will write a report to a supervisor.

_____

3. Celestine will visit a workplace.
He will find out some things he hadn't known.

_____

4. I try to capture the moods of an office.
Others notice the decor.

_____

5. Writing character sketches of workers was not easy.
It taught them a lot.

_____

6. Justin wrote a description of a particular job.
The teacher told him her feelings about his writing.

_____

7. Mary prepared an advertisement for a job opening.
Elizabeth listed the job's requirements.

_____

8. Conrad didn't like his original application.
Regina helped him make corrections.

_____

9. Gloria will prepare a report for your boss.
You may prepare it.

_____

10. Felix has never actually worked at a job like this.
He's doing very well.

_____

Check your answers on page 246.

Complex Sentences: Part 1

In Lesson 19 you wrote long sentences by combining related short sentences into compound sentences. Related short sentences can also be combined into complex sentences.

A complex sentence, like a compound sentence, has two parts and is smoother than two short sentences. Like the parts of compound sentences, each part of a complex sentence has its own subject. The difference between a compound and a complex sentence is this:

- When a compound sentence is split into its two parts, the result is two complete sentences each of which can stand alone.
- When a complex sentence is split into its two parts, the result is one complete sentence and a sentence part that depends on that complete sentence for meaning.

The following examples show the difference between compound and complex sentences.

This is a **compound sentence**.	I needed advice, so I spoke to a friend.
When it is split into its two parts (leaving out the comma and the word **so**), the result is two complete sentences.	I needed advice. I spoke to a friend.
This is a **complex sentence**.	I spoke to a friend who usually gives good advice.
When it is split into its two parts, the result is one complete sentence (the first part of the complex sentence) and a sentence part that depends on that complete sentence for meaning (the second part of the complex sentence).	I spoke to a friend. who usually gives good advice.
This is also a **complex sentence**.	I spoke to a friend when I needed advice.
When it is split into its two parts, the result is one complete sentence (the first part of the complex sentence) and a sentence part that depends on that complete sentence for meaning (the second part of the complex sentence).	I spoke to a friend when I needed advice.

In the following sections of this lesson you will learn about one type of complex sentence. You will learn about another kind in Lesson 21.

Complex Sentences with *That, Which, Who, Whom,* and *Whose*

Sometimes one of two related short sentences describes a noun in the other sentence. Such sentences can often be joined into a complex sentence using the connecting word *that, which, who, whom,* or *whose*. In the complex sentence, the connecting word directly follows the noun described. Look at the following examples.

The second of these two short sentences describes the **book** in the first sentence. The sentences can be combined using the connecting word **that**.	We studied the book. The book teaches business writing. We studied the book **that** teaches business writing.
The second of these two short sentences tells more about the **man** in the first sentence. The sentences can be combined using the connecting word **who**.	The man taught us today. The man wrote our textbook. The man **who** wrote our textbook taught us today.

The connecting words *that, which, who, whom,* and *whose* are pronouns. You learned in Lesson 13 that pronouns take the place of nouns. In the complex sentences above, the pronouns *that* and *who* replace the noun subjects *book* and *man* in the second short sentence in each pair. Notice that in the combined sentences, the pronouns *that* and *who* directly follow the words they relate to.

EXERCISE 20a

Use the pronoun in parentheses to join the sentences in each of the following pairs.

Example: (that) Do you see the car? It is parked over there.

Do you see the car that is parked over there?

1. (who) That space is for people. The people are physically disabled.

   _____

2. (who) A man has a "Disabled Person" sign in his car window. He is not disabled.

   _____

3. (that) I saw him dash into the music store. The music store is across the street.

   _____

4. (who) A man doesn't deserve that parking space. He isn't disabled.

   _____

5. (who) He probably bought his sign from the woman. The woman sells them from her red van at the weekend flea market.

   _____

6. (who) I wish someone would put the woman out of business. She sells the signs.

   _____

7. (that) A sign does not rightfully belong to an able-bodied person. The sign lets handicapped motorists park in reserved spaces.

_____

8. (who) People need spaces close to the store. People use canes, walkers, or wheelchairs.

_____

9. (that) The police have computerized information. The information identifies handicapped drivers.

_____

10. (that) The police are able to identify and ticket cars. The cars don't belong in reserved parking spaces.

_____

Check your answers on page 247.

The Uses of *That, Which, Who, Whom,* and *Whose*

Each of these five connecting pronouns has a particular function. The examples below illustrate those functions. An arrow shows the word the pronoun in each sentence refers to.

The pronoun **that** can be either a subject or an object pronoun. It refers to one or more animals, places, or things.	The dogs **that** live in your building are barking.
	The city **that** you live in has "No barking" laws.
	The apartment **that** has the most dogs is mine.
The pronoun **which** can be either a subject or an object pronoun. It refers to one or more animals, places, or things.	My male dog, **which** is my oldest, is named Rumpole.
	Your city, **which** is old, has some strange laws on its books.
	Her apartment, **which** we saw, has been renovated.
The pronoun **who** is a subject pronoun. It refers to one or more people—male or female.	The man **who** lives in your building is walking his dogs.
	The woman **who** lives there doesn't walk her dogs enough.
	The children **who** live near her walk dogs to earn money.

The pronoun **whom** is an object pronoun. It refers to one or more people—male or female.

The man **whom** I met was not my father after all.

The woman **whom** we employed has not shown up yet.

The children **whom** she teaches are brain damaged.

The pronoun **whose** is possessive. It refers to one or more people, animals, places, or things.

A woman **whose** dog barks a lot moved into my building.

Some dogs **whose** tails curl are pugs.

Kennels **whose** cages are clean are good for boarding dogs.

Dogs' dishes **whose** bases are broad don't tip over.

EXERCISE 20b

Complete each of the following sentences by adding to it the word *that* or *who*.

Example: The nurse attaches wires ___that___ measure a patient's heartbeat.

1. A computer sounds a signal _____ warns when something goes wrong.

2. Any nurse _____ is at the desk hurries to the patient's room.

3. The computer has a program _____ records the event.

4. The doctors _____ make morning rounds study the computer's printout.

5. Blood tests _____ are required are done by computer.

6. A certain patient _____ lives in a small town is too far from the hospital to travel to it regularly.

7. She is a young woman _____ has a pacemaker.

8. The pacemaker is a device _____ keeps her heart beating steadily.

9. The woman uses a box _____ picks up signals from the pacemaker and sends them to the hospital over the phone.

10. At the hospital a computer _____ records and stores her pacemaker's signals helps doctors assess her condition.

Check your answers on page 247.

Using *That* and *Which*

Using *that* and *which* correctly takes thought.

That is used when the sentence part it introduces is essential to the meaning of the complex sentence. The information in that sentence part must be so essential that if it were removed, the meaning of the complex sentence would change or would become unclear.

Which is used when the sentence part it introduces contains information that is "additional" but is not essential to the meaning of the complex sentence. The information is so unnecessary that it can be removed without affecting the meaning of the complex sentence.

The words **that diagnose illness** are essential to the meaning of the sentence. Without them, it would not be clear what kinds of computer programs the corpsmen use. Notice that there is no comma before **that**.	Medical corpsmen use computer programs **that** diagnose illness.
The words **which is in Texas** are not essential to the meaning of the sentence. The sentence could be understood without them. Notice the commas around the sentence part introduced by **which**.	Corpus Christi, **which** is in Texas, is a large, modern city.

When **that** introduces a sentence part, no commas are used. When *which* introduces a sentence part, commas are needed before and after that part. (The commas are a further clue that the information between them is not essential to the meaning of the complex sentence.)

EXERCISE 20c

Combine the sentences in each of the following pairs by using *who*, *that*, or *which*.

Example: Medical problems arise frequently on submarines.
Medical problems include depression.

Medical problems, which include depression, arise frequently

on submarines.

1. Submariners might be interviewed by a computer.
   Submariners seem depressed.

   _____

2. The computer might begin by asking how the person feels.
   The computer is programmed to ask several questions.

   _____

3. Many patients find talking to a computer easier than talking to a doctor.
   A computer doesn't pass judgment.

   _____

4. A question is less threatening if it appears on a computer screen.
   A question would usually bother a person.

   _____

5. Computers are often better than doctors at predicting suicide attempts.
   Computers have modernized methods of suicide prevention.

   _____

Check your answers on page 247.

Using *Who*, *Whom*, and *Whose*

When you need to decide whether to use *who*, *whom*, or *whose* in a complex sentence, you can do a simple test. Just split the complex sentence in two. Substitute *he*, *him*, or *his* for *who*, *whom*, or *whose*. If *he* (or another subject pronoun) fits, the pronoun in the complex sentence should be *who*. If *him* (or another object pronoun) fits, the pronoun in the complex sentence should be *whom*. If *his* (or another possessive pronoun) fits, the pronoun in the complex sentence should be *whose*. It is usually easiest to turn questions into statements to do this test. Look at the following examples.

Who is correct in this complex sentence because when the sentence is split, **he** would be used.

Joe is the man **who** always runs for a county office.
Joe is the man.
He always runs for a county office.

Whom is correct in this complex sentence because when the sentence is split, **him** would be used.

Joe is the man **whom** you met.
Joe is the man.
You met **him**.

Whose is correct in this complex sentence because when the sentence is split, **his** would be used.

Joe is the one **whose** wife is an invalid.
Joe is the one.
His wife is an invalid.

Don't confuse the possessive pronoun *whose* with the contraction *who's*, which means *who is*.

EXERCISE 20d

Part A. Complete each of the following sentences by adding the word *who*, *whom*, *who's*, or *whose*.

Example: Is this the person ____*whom*____ you were calling?

1. Is this the person _____ ordered the pizza?

2. A man _____ you know asked to borrow some money from me.

3. The women _____ group usually meets on Thursdays will meet on Saturday for a picnic.

4. No one _____ is here today was in Montreal last year.

5. Each person _____ you contact will get a month's free service.

6. I wonder _____ going to claim the prizes.

7. A person _____ a regular jogger needs shoes with extra shock absorption.

8. A runner, _____ feet may hit the ground with a force of 400 pounds or more, needs good shoes.

9. Runners _____ shoes lack cushioning can damage their feet.

10. Are you the person _____ is missing a pair of red sneakers?

Part B. Combine the sentences in each of the following pairs by using *that*, *which*, *who*, *whom*, or *whose*.

Example: Taxes pay for maintenance. Maintenance includes the care of roads and sidewalks.

Taxes pay for maintenance, which includes the care of

roads and sidewalks.

1. The new town library cost a lot to build. The new town library opened last year.

_____

2. The sewers were expensive. They put the sewers in this year.

_____

3. The workers are paid overtime. They plow the roads in the middle of the night.

_____

4. The three blizzards created plenty of overtime work. We had the three blizzards in February.

_____

5. Without the snowplows, people would be out of luck. Their houses are in the country.

_____

6. Many of those people are the same ones. The same ones lost their jobs when the factory closed.

_____

7. Many senior citizens are going to vote against the budget. The senior citizens live on limited incomes.

   _____

8. Some people resent paying for our children's schooling. Their children are grown and gone.

   _____

9. Unfortunately our children cannot vote. Our children deserve good schools.

   _____

10. The newspaper editor will publish my letter. The newspaper editor received my letter.

   _____

Check your answers on page 248.

Lesson 21

Complex Sentences: Part 2

In Lesson 20 you learned about one kind of complex sentence. In this lesson you will learn about another kind.

Remember that a complex sentence has two parts. Split into its two parts, one part would be a complete sentence. The other would be a sentence part that depends on the complete sentence for meaning.

A time relationship exists between the two parts of many complex sentences. The connecting word in such sentences makes that relationship clear. Look at the following examples. The connecting words are in dark type.

In these complex sentences **after** is the connecting word. It shows that first the meeting ended and that the members went out for coffee afterward.	**After** the meeting was over, some of the members went out for coffee. Some of the members went out for coffee **after** the meeting was over.
In these complex sentences **when** is the connecting word. It shows that the two actions in each sentence occurred at the same time.	Everyone listened **when** he told his story at the meeting. **When** he told his story at the meeting, everyone listened.

By splitting the sentences above, you can see their parts.

This part of the first and second complex sentences depends on the other part for meaning.	After the meeting was over
This part of the same complex sentences is a complete sentence.	Some of the members went out for coffee.

This part of the third and fourth complex sentences is a complete sentence.

Everyone listened.

This part of the same complex sentences depends on the other part for meaning.

when he told his story at the meeting.

Notice two things about the four complex sentences above:

- Their parts can come in either order. The part that is a complete sentence can come at the beginning of the sentence or at the end.
- When the dependent part comes at the beginning, it is followed by a comma. When it is at the end, there is no comma.

In addition to time, several other relationships can be expressed between the two parts of a complex sentence. Connecting words make each type of relationship clear. The following table shows connecting words used in complex sentences.

Connecting Words Used in Some Complex Sentences

Used to Show	Word	Examples
a time relationship	after	**After** we met, we fell in love.
	as	We met **as** we were getting on a bus.
	before	We were in love **before** we knew each other well.
	once	**Once** we knew that, we got married.
	until	We should have waited **until** we knew each other.
	when	**When** I think back, I feel sad.
	whenever	**Whenever** I feel sad, I cry.
	while	Everything was fine **while** we were still in love.
a space relationship	wherever	**Wherever** I go, I'll like it better than this place.
a cause/effect relationship	as	**As** you are tired, you should lie down.
	because	You should sleep **because** you look exhausted.
	since	**Since** her car was in the garage, she took a taxi.
the purpose	in order that	He called **in order that** I not forget our date.
	so that	**So that** I remember, I'll make a note.
a condition	although	**Although** you feel well, you are not healthy.
	even though	You are at risk **even though** you smoke little.
	although	It can be done, **although** it won't be easy.
	if	**If** you want to stop, you can.
	unless	You can't stop **unless** you really want to.

Spotlight on Tenses in Complex Sentences

Sometimes the verbs in the two parts of a complex sentence must be in different tenses to show the time relationship of events.

Examples:

Although there **will be** enough seats at the park concert, he **wants** to take his lawn chair.

> *Will be* is in the simple future tense because the action will occur later.
>
> *Wants* is in the simple present tense because it describes something that is true now.

She **was sleeping** when a pain in her finger **woke** her.

> *Was sleeping* is in the past continuous tense because it tells about an action that continued until something else happened.
>
> *Woke* is in the simple past tense because it tells about a one-time event in the past.

After Pam **had cooked** breakfast for her children, she **went** to a clinic.

> *Had cooked* is in the past perfect tense because it tells about a past action that was completed before another past action occurred. The other past action—*went*—is in the simple past tense.
>
> NOTE: When two actions occurred at almost the same time in the past, use the same past tense for both. Example: When the doctor **saw** her finger, he **whistled**. (Both verbs are in the simple past tense.)

EXERCISE 21

Part A. Underline the connecting word in each of the following sentences. Wherever a comma is needed to separate the two parts of a sentence, insert it.

Example: <u>When</u> people like their jobs, they usually do better work.

1. It is still interesting to think about other types of jobs after you have chosen a career.

2. Most people try more than one job before they settle into a career.

3. When you are learning things about different types of jobs you also learn things about yourself.

4. Whenever my friend finds out something about a job he tells everyone what he has learned.

5. He visits a lot of job sites so that he can talk to people about their work.

6. Because he wants to find a career he listens carefully.

7. He doesn't mind when people ask him to make an appointment.

8. Unless he has other things to do he reads about jobs.

9. If he does his research carefully he will probably get all the information he needs.

10. He would probably make a good TV reporter even though he isn't sure about that job choice yet.

Part B. Combine each of the sentence pairs using one of the connecting words from the table on page 129. Make sure to use commas where they are needed.

Example: Priscilla gave Arnie political posters to put up.
            He felt they would be noticed.

        <u>Priscilla gave Arnie political posters to put up wherever</u>

        <u>he felt they would be noticed.</u>

1. The budget passes. The town has to vote on it.

   _____

2. The budget would increase taxes. One large group of citizens wants it voted down.

   _____

3. Another group wants the budget approved. It would result in a higher bill at tax time.

   _____

4. Taxes are not raised. Several teachers will be fired.

   _____

5. The town collects the money for their salaries. They cannot be kept.

   _____

6. Cuts are made in the budget. The largest cuts are made in education.

   _____

7. I go. I hear people talking about how tight money is.

   _____

8. Priscilla will vote. Arnie watches the children.

   _____

9. She comes home. Arnie will go to the polling place.

   _____

10. Tomorrow's newspaper hits the stands. I want to see the headline.

   _____

Part C. Complete each of the following sentences by adding the correct tense of the verb in parentheses. Before you start, reread the Spotlight on page 130.

Example: (turn)   The doctor saw Pam's finger after it ____had turned____ blue.

1. (examine)   After the doctor _____ the finger, he ordered an X-ray.

2. (show)   When the X-ray returned, he _____ it to her.

3. (see)   When he held the X-ray up to the light, they _____ no broken bones.

4. (hope)   Pam was disappointed because she _____ for an easy answer.

5. (have)   The doctor asked Pam if she _____ arthritis.

6. (explain)   After Pam _____ last year's injury, he changed his theory.

7. (hurt)   I remember when Pam _____ that finger last year.

8. (slam)   After she _____ it in a car door, she bandaged it herself.

9. (become)   Even after the finger _____ swollen and blue, she refused to see a doctor.

10. (receive)   Because she has had an examination this time, she _____ a bill for $250 soon.

Part D. A list of dependent sentence parts follows. Use each once to complete the sentences below.

> ~~although computers cannot replace doctors~~
> before a patient comes to a doctor's office
> although doctors used to rely mainly on their own experience
> once the doctor tells the computer the symptoms
> before a doctor decides how to treat the symptoms
> just as you might keep boxes in a storehouse
> whenever the doctor needs to know their names
> because an unusual problem has just come up
> when doctors and computers work together
> if Mr. Jones comes in for a yearly checkup
> even though he may not admit it

Example: __Although computers cannot replace doctors,__ computers can assist them.

1. _____ doctors are less likely to forget important details.

2. _____ the physician can get his or her records from the computer.

3. The computer holds records in a data base _____

_____

4. _____ the doctor can get a computer report of all past physicals.

5. _____ Mr. Jones sometimes forgets the names of his medications.

6. _____ he can get a report from the computer.

7. Another patient may go to the doctor _____

_____

8. _____ it can scan thousands of patient records.

9. _____ they can now share knowledge with each other by computer.

10. _____ he or she can check treatments used by other doctors.

Check your answers on page 248.

Correcting Run-On Sentences and Sentence Fragments

The knowledge you have about compound sentence parts, compound sentences, and complex sentences can help you to avoid or correct two common errors in sentence structure: run-on sentences and sentence fragments.

Correcting Run-On Sentences

Run-on sentences combine two related sentences incorrectly. One sentence runs on into another without proper punctuation or connecting words. Most run-on sentences can be corrected in one of several ways. An example follows.

INCORRECT: Magic took a pair of sneakers to the sales desk he handed the sales clerk the money to pay for them.

The incorrect "sentence" runs two complete sentences together. The first begins with *Magic took*... The second begins with *he handed*... Following are four ways to correct it.

CORRECTION 1: Magic took a pair of sneakers to the sales desk. He handed the sales clerk the money to pay for them.

CORRECTION 2: Magic took a pair of sneakers to the sales desk and handed the sales clerk the money to pay for them.

CORRECTION 3: Magic took a pair of sneakers to the sales desk, and he handed the sales clerk the money to pay for them.

CORRECTION 4: When Magic took a pair of sneakers to the sales desk, he handed the sales clerk the money to pay for them.

The first correction splits the run-on sentence into two complete sentences. Each ends with a period.

The second correction changes the run-on sentence to a sentence with a compound part—in this case, a compound predicate. The first part of the predicate is *took a pair of sneakers to the sales desk*. The second part is *handed the sales clerk the money to pay for them*. The two parts of the compound predicate are joined by the connecting word *and*. (You studied compound sentence parts in Lesson 18.)

The third correction turns the run-on sentence into a compound sentence by using a comma and the connecting word *and*. Each part of the compound sentence is a complete sentence. The first part is *Magic took a pair of sneakers to the sales desk*. Omitting the comma and the word *and*, the second part is *he handed the sales clerk the money to pay for them*. (You studied compound sentences in Lesson 19.)

The fourth correction changes the run-on sentence into a complex sentence by using a comma and the connecting word *When*, which shows the time relationship between the two parts of the sentence. The first part of the complex sentence is *When Magic took a pair of sneakers to the sales desk*. For its meaning it depends on the second part, *he handed the sales clerk the money to pay for them*. (You studied this kind of complex sentence in Lesson 21.)

EXERCISE 22a

Using one of the correction methods illustrated above, correct each of the following run-on sentences. Use each of the four methods illustrated above at least once.

Example: Customers drive up to a window outside the bank the drive-in teller helps them.

   Customers drive up to a window outside the bank, and the

   drive-in teller helps them.

1. The sidewalks outside the bank are clean the inside of the bank is just as tidy.

2. The heat was smothering on the day of my visit the cool air inside the bank brought me back to life.

_____

3. The rug in the bank is burnt orange the curtains are the same shade.

_____

4. Ten tellers stand behind windows several other workers sit at desks.

_____

5. Personal bankers help people with new accounts they help with other bank business.

_____

6. Only one security guard stands inside the bank lobby another sits in a control room.

_____

7. Most of the time it is very quiet traffic noises come in through an open door.

_____

8. The vault is in the basement people keep their personal belongings in safe deposit boxes there.

_____

9. Behind two doors is an office with a fireplace the bank's executive officer works there.

_____

10. My first job here will be at a teller's window I plan to sit at the desk near the fireplace someday.

_____

Check your answers on page 249.

Correcting Sentence Fragments

Sentence fragments are parts of sentences—not complete sentences—that incorrectly stand alone. Most sentence fragments can be corrected in several ways. Examples of three methods of correction follow.

INCORRECT: We bought Pam a card. Because she had broken her finger.

The second "sentence" above is a sentence fragment. Following are three ways to correct it.

CORRECTION 1:   We bought Pam a card. She had broken her finger.

CORRECTION 2:   We bought Pam a card because she had broken her finger.

CORRECTION 3:   We bought Pam a card. We wanted to cheer her up after she had broken her finger.

The first correction turns the sentence fragment into a complete sentence by removing the connecting word *Because*.

The second correction joins the two sentences into a complex sentence. The sentence fragment becomes the dependent sentence part in the complex sentence. (You studied this kind of complex sentence in Lesson 21.)

Deleting the word *Because*, the third correction adds words to the fragment to make it a complete sentence—in this case, a complex sentence.

EXERCISE 22b

Using one of the correction methods illustrated above, correct the sentence fragment in each of the following sets. Use each of the three methods illustrated above at least once.

Example: Last year I found a baby-sitter. Through an advertisement on a bulletin board.

<u>Last year I found a baby-sitter through an advertisement on a</u>

<u>bulletin board.</u>

1. Pam is a licensed day-care provider. Who takes care of eight children in her home.

   _____

2. She gives play materials to the children. When they are with her.

   _____

3. I read a newspaper article. That suggested tips on choosing day care.

   _____

4. Go to a center you can visit any time. Even if you don't make an appointment.

   _____

5. Many people prefer to hire a child care provider. Who has a license.

   _____

6. I had a goal. A safe place for my children.

   _____

7. The state checks on the safety of homes. That provide care for children.

   _____

8. There are a couple of things I don't want to see. When I visit a day-care center.

_____

9. There should be good discipline. But no spanking.

_____

10. Pam serves the children healthy snacks. Cheese, apples, carrots, and crackers.

_____

Check your answers on page 250.

Choosing the Right Connector

When you use a compound or a complex sentence to correct a run-on sentence or a sentence fragment, it is important to use the right connecting word. It should make the relationship between the two parts of the sentence clear. The same is true when you write a compound or complex sentence.

The wrong connecting word can confuse a reader. The connecting words in the following sentences make the sentences confusing.

INCORRECT: Raj wanted to interview a famous actor, **but** he telephoned an actors' agent.

He preferred to interview a star **since** he would probably have to settle for a local actor.

The first example above uses the connecting word *but*, which announces a contrast between the two parts of a sentence. Since there is no contrast between the ideas in this sentence, *but* is not a good connector to use.

The second example above uses the connecting word *since*, which shows a cause-effect relationship between the two parts of a sentence. Since there is no cause-effect relationship in this sentence, *since* is not a good connector to use.

In contrast, the connecting words in the following sentences make the relationships between the two ideas in each clear.

CORRECT: Raj wanted to interview a famous actor, **so** he telephoned an actors' agent.

He preferred to interview a star **even though** he would probably have to settle for a local actor.

The first example above is a compound sentence. The connecting word *so* is right for this cause-effect sentence. The first part of the sentence contains the cause. The word *so* introduces the effect in the second part.

The second example above is a complex sentence. The connecting words *even though* are right for this sentence because the second part of the sentence explains a condition that affects the outcome of the first part.

Edit the following sentences to make the connecting word in each right for the sentence. (Note: Some sentences do not need correction.)

and

Example: Eric enjoys using tools, ~~yet~~ he is good at fixing things.

1. Last week he repaired our door, or I fixed the broken window.

2. He works as a handyman in an apartment complex, and he is not satisfied with his job.

3. He would rather run his own business because he needs to learn how.

4. Because his friends encouraged him to stay in school, he dropped out.

5. Now he wants to improve his writing skills, yet he has come back.

6. A handyman mainly uses tools, but he must also be able to speak and write clearly.

7. Because a customer requests a written estimate, Eric may have some trouble.

8. Last week he agreed to paint a customer's house, and he is unsure about how to write a contract.

9. He will work on his own, but he will work with a partner.

10. Since he would love to start his own business now, it will have to wait until he finishes his schooling.

Check your answers on page 250.

Choosing Between a Compound and a Complex Sentence

A common error is to write a compound sentence when a complex sentence would make the relationship between the parts of the sentence clearer.

The following compound sentence does not make the relationship between its parts clear.

UNCLEAR: Actors have questions about their lines, **and** they often write on their scripts.

Does the sentence mean that actors perform two unrelated activities—have questions and write on their scripts? It seems to, but that was probably not the writer's intention.

The meaning of the sentence is clearer with a connecting word that makes it a complex sentence.

CLEAR: **When** actors have questions about their lines, they often write on their scripts.

With complex sentences, the more important idea should be stated in the sentence part that could stand alone. The less important idea should follow the connecting word in the dependent part of the sentence.

UNCLEAR: Even though he finished the application, it was long.

CLEAR: He finished the application even though it was long.

EXERCISE 22d

Part A. Edit the following sentences for clarity. If the relationship between the ideas in a compound sentence or two sentences could be made clearer in a complex sentence, rewrite the sentence(s).

Example: Karen's apartment was burglarized, ~~and~~ *when* she was on vacation in Hawaii.

1. She returned from Hawaii, so she found her door open.

2. The police gave her ideas for making her apartment more secure. The police came to her apartment.

3. She could replace her flimsy window locks, and the burglars easily broke one of Karen's.

4. She could make her apartment look lived in, and she used a timer on her lights.

5. She leaves, and she could turn on a radio.

6. A neighbor could pick up her mail, but an overflowing mailbox is an invitation to a burglar.

Part B. Edit the following sentences for clarity. Make sure less important ideas follow the connecting word in the dependent part of a sentence. (Note: Some sentences do not need correction.)

Example: Computers help save lives because they are often used in emergency rooms.

Because computers help save lives, they are often used in

emergency rooms.

1. Since Richard rushed him to the hospital, his baby had a high fever.

_____

2. The doctor needed to make a blood test since he drew blood from the boy's arm.

_____

3. In order that it was rushed to the laboratory, it could be tested immediately.

_____

4. The blood arrived when the lab worker analyzed it by computer.

_____

5. Since the computer had a built-in printer, the results were available quickly.

_____

6. The doctor gave the boy a shot unless he would become sicker.

_____

Check your answers on page 251.

Separating Unrelated Sentence Parts

Another common error is to write compound or complex sentences with ideas that are not related. Doing so makes the meaning of the ideas unclear.

UNCLEAR: Many people do not realize how much writing some jobs require, **and** Raj listed the types of writing an actor must do.

The connection between the ideas in the two parts of the compound sentence above is not close. One part is about something people don't realize. The other is about a list Raj wrote. To make these ideas clearer, split the sentence into two separate sentences.

CLEAR: Many people do not realize how much writing some jobs require. Raj listed the types of writing an actor must do.

EXERCISE 22e

Edit the following sentences for clarity. As needed to make ideas clearer, split sentences into two separate sentences. (Note: Some sentences do not need correction.)

Example: The police officers saw a car pass through a red light, and running lights is illegal.

1. The police car's siren didn't work well, but the driver had asked for a new siren.

2. They sped up, and they were traveling way over the speed limit.

3. They used the computer on the dashboard since it measured other cars' speeds.

4. The computer did its job, and the other car was going 80 miles per hour.

5. They finally caught the driver, and one of them arrested her.

Check your answers on page 251.

Sentence Clarity

In Lessons 19–22 you learned to combine sentence parts to make sentences smooth and to make the relationships between ideas in a sentence clear. This lesson covers some other issues having to do with sentence clarity.

One-Word Adjectives

In Lesson 13 you learned that a noun is a word that names a person, place, or thing. In vivid or lively writing, nouns rarely stand alone. They are usually described. In a sentence any word or group of words that describes a noun serves as an adjective. Adjectives answer these questions about nouns: How many/ much? What kind of? Which one? Adjectives sometimes describe pronouns, too.

> **Adjective:** a word that describes a noun

Compare the following pair of sentences. Notice how much more vivid the description in the second is than that in the first. The adjectives are in dark type.

Some is an adjective that tells how many crackers I ate. **Stale** is an adjective that tells what kind of crackers I ate.

I ate crackers.

I ate **some stale** crackers.

A one-word adjective usually appears in one of three places in a sentence. In the following sentences the adjectives are in dark type. Arrows point to the nouns they describe.

An adjective may appear just before the noun it describes.

The **weary** men went home.

In a describing sentence, an adjective may appear after the verb.

The men were **weary**.

Sometimes, but rarely, an adjective appears after the noun it describes.

The two men, **weary** after their work, went home.

Underline the adjective in each of the following sentences. Draw an arrow to the noun it describes.

Example: The guest drank <u>decaffeinated</u> coffee.

1. Have you tried bran cereal in yogurt?

2. The melons feel soft.

3. Someone brought blueberry muffins.

4. The muffins were tasty.

5. Herman likes pork sausages.

6. The sausages taste spicy.

7. Lulu put purple flowers on the table.

8. The lilacs smell sweet.

9. Grandma, happy as ever, played with her grandchildren.

10. The noisy family began to eat.

Check your answers on page 251.

Adjective Phrases

In Lesson 8 you learned about phrases that begin with prepositions. (You may want to refer to the table of Common Prepositions on page 41.) Such phrases often function as adjectives. That is, they can describe nouns. Adjective phrases almost always appear right after the nouns they describe.

In the following sentences the adjective phrases are in dark type. Arrows point to the nouns they describe.

Under your candidate's name is an adjective phrases that describes the lever.

Did you pull the lever **under your candidate's name**?

With an open mind is an adjective phrase that describes the candidate.

A candidate **with an open mind** is my preference.

Writers sometimes confuse their readers by placing an adjective phrase too far away from the noun it describes, as the following example shows.

INCORRECT: I watched a show about frogs **on television**.

The sentence above is incorrect unless the show was only about frogs that appear on TV, like Kermit.

CORRECT: I watched a show **on television** about frogs.

In the correct sentence above, the adjective phrase *on television* appears directly after *show*, the word it describes. In this sentence, the show is on television, not the frogs.

Another kind of phrase also functions as an adjective. The first word in such a phrase ends with *-ing*, as the following example shows.

Walking by our house, John fell.

The phrase describes *John*, the noun that follows it. Notice that there is a comma after the phrase.

 ## Spotlight on Commas with Adjective Phrases

Whenever an adjective phrase begins a sentence, follow it with a comma.

Example:

   Having been born prematurely, Sadie was a tiny baby.

When an adjective phrase appears in the middle of a sentence, set it off by commas if it does not contain information essential to the meaning of the sentence.

Example:

   This baby, having been born prematurely, is tiny.

EXERCISE 23b

Part A. Write each sentence so that the adjective phrase in parentheses describes the noun it should.

Example: (with red hair)   The girl hardly ever speaks.

   The girl with red hair hardly ever speaks.

  1. (next to the window)   She just sits and rocks in the chair.

  _____

  2. (with a recorded voice)   The girl is using a computer to teach her new words.

  _____

  3. (on the keyboard)   The child sat at the computer and pushed a key.

  _____

  4. (of a dog)   A picture appeared on the screen.

  _____

5. (on the recording) The girl heard a voice say "dog."

_____

Part B. Add an adjective phrase to each sentence.

Example: I would like that fish _____ below the price sign. _____

1. I don't like to eat fish _____

2. My wife enjoys fish _____

3. The customer _____ seems to be
   buying ingredients for stew.

4. He has just bought a pound _____

5. He is pointing at the sign _____

Part C. Rewrite each of the following sentences to correct the placement of the adjective phrases. Use commas where they are needed. (Note: Some sentences do not need correction.)

Example: Licking the curtains of the house next door, we saw the flames.

We saw the flames licking the curtains of the house next door.

1. Charles dialed 911 running to his phone.

_____

2. He reported a fire speaking too quickly.

_____

3. Forgetting that the street had been renamed, he gave the old address.

_____

4. The operator listened to a recording of Charles's message turning on the message repeater.

_____

5. Changing the old street name to its new name, a computer told the operator where the call was from.

_____

6. The operator called for the Fire Department pushing a button next to his terminal.

_____

7. The firefighters put on their siren speeding to the scene.

_____

8. They quickly put out the fire arriving within minutes.

_____

9. The neighbor had fallen asleep on her couch having forgotten a lighted candle.

_____

10. Using computers, 911 dispatchers help save more lives than ever before.

_____

Part D. Write each sentence so that the adjective phrase in parentheses describes the noun it should. Use commas where they are needed.

Example: (having been blind since birth)
        Sadie learned to read Braille when she was very small.

    Having been blind since birth, Sadie learned to read Braille when

    she was very small.

1. (memorizing the feel of the raised dots)
   She learned to read with her fingertips.

   _____

2. (waiting for her Braille books to arrive in the mail)
   She sometimes grew impatient.

   _____

3. (lining her room)
   The Braille books taught her a lot, but she wanted to read other books.

   _____

4. (itching to read her friends' comics)
   Sadie told her parents how she felt.

   _____

5. (hearing about the Optaconer)
   Her father decided to look into it.

   _____

6. (containing a tiny TV camera)
   A small computerized tool is moved across a line of print.

   _____

7. (changing the computer pictures into vibrations)
   The device allows the holder to read print.

   _____

8. (opening a gift beside her bed)
   Sadie found an Optaconer inside.

   _____

9. (holding the device in one hand and feeling the pattern with the other)
   She showed her folks how it worked.

   _____

10. (hugging her parents)
    She told them how happy they had made her.

    _____

Check your answers on page 251.

Sentence Parts That Function as Adjectives

In Lesson 20 you studied sentence parts that begin with the words *that,
which, who, whom,* and *whose.* Those sentence parts function as adjectives in
a sentence. They describe nouns. Like phrases, such sentence parts should be
placed right after the noun they describe. If they are not, the result can
sometimes be funny, as in the following sentence.

INCORRECT: The father gave the ice cream to his little boy **that was topped
               with sprinkles**.

The sentence above is incorrect unless the boy, not the ice cream, was
topped with sprinkles. The following sentence corrects the probable mistake.

CORRECT: The father gave the ice cream **that was topped with sprinkles**
               to his little boy.

EXERCISE 23c

Rewrite the following sentences to place correctly the sentence parts that serve
as adjectives. Use a comma or commas where needed. (Note: Some sentences
do not need correction.)

Example: I showed the booklet to my uncle that you gave me.

    I showed the booklet that you gave me to my uncle.

1. I wanted to share the tips about prevention of accidents that occur at
   home.

   _____

2. He really needs to heed the tips about safety in garages that are on the last
   page.

   _____

3. Uncle Bert always smokes the special pipe in the garage that he received
   for his birthday.

   _____

4. Garages are not good places for lighting up cigarettes, cigars, or pipes which often contain gasoline.

   _____

5. During cookouts, Uncle Bert often leaves the grill to chat with friends that he has just lit.

   _____

6. A fire is a bad idea that is unattended.

   _____

7. Uncle Bert's habit is putting the barbecue near the lawn mower that bothers me even more.

   _____

8. He should keep the barbecue away from materials that could catch on fire.

   _____

9. The garden tools should be put in the shed and garage that are usually lying all over his yard.

   _____

10. The clippers belong on a wall hook that have those sharp blades.

    _____

Check your answers on page 252

Part 1 of GED Practice 4 begins below. It will give you practice with multiple-choice items that cover the skills you have studied so far in this book.

Part 2 of the practice, beginning on page 151, will give you a chance to use those same skills to correct mistakes in paragraphs like those you might write in an essay.

Part 1

Directions: Choose the <u>one best answer</u> to each item.

<u>Items 1 through 12</u> refer to the following paragraphs.

(1) Until recently, there has been three basic ways to send a message to another person. (2) You can mail a letter, send a telegram, or by making a telephone call. (3) Although mailing a letter is slow the other person receives a piece of paper. (4) The paper is called a hard copy. (5) It bears the message. (6) Telegrams are delivered as hard copies, but their messages must be brief. (7) A telephone call is extremely fast but there is no hard copy of the message.

(8) The newest way to send messages combines the benefits of the mail, a telegram, and the telephone it is called electronic mail. (9) Electronic mail is as fast as a phone call, and provides a hard copy like a letter or a telegram.

(10) One device that sends hard copies by electronic mail were a facsimile machine, or "fax." (11) When you insert a letter into a fax machine. (12) The machine changes the letter's words, numbers, drawings, or photographs into electronic signals.

(13) Those signals pass through telephone lines to another fax machine that changes them back into hard copy. (14) Sometimes computers are attached to fax machines that tell the user how to work the machines.

1. Sentence 1: **Until recently, there has been three basic ways to send a message to another person.**

   What correction should be made to this sentence?

   (1) change the spelling of <u>there</u> to <u>their</u>
   (2) change the spelling of <u>there</u> to <u>they're</u>
   (3) change <u>has</u> to <u>have</u>
   (4) replace <u>ways to</u> with <u>ways. To</u>
   (5) no correction is necessary

2. Sentence 2: **You can <u>mail a letter, send a telegram, or by making</u> a telephone call.**

   Which of the following is the best way to write the underlined portion of this sentence? If you think the original is the best way, choose option (1).

   (1) mail a letter, send a telegram, or by making
   (2) mail a letter send a telegram, or by making
   (3) mail a letter, sending a telegram, or making
   (4) mail a letter, send a telegram, or made
   (5) mail a letter, send a telegram, or make

3. Sentence 3: **Although mailing a letter is slow the other person receives a piece of paper.**

What correction should be made to this sentence?

(1) replace Although with Since
(2) change is to was
(3) insert a comma after slow
(4) change receives to receive
(5) no correction is necessary

4. Sentences 4 and 5: **The paper is called a hard copy. It bears the message.**

The most effective combination of sentences 4 and 5 would include which of the following groups of words?

(1) It is called
(2) a hard copy bearing
(3) that bears the message
(4) which bears the message
(5) and it bears the message

5. Sentence 6: **Telegrams are delivered as hard copies, but their messages must be brief.**

Which of the following is the best way to write the underlined portion of this sentence? If you think the original is the best way, choose option (1).

(1) copies, but
(2) copies but
(3) copies, so
(4) copies because
(5) copies. Their

6. Sentence 7: **A telephone call is extremely fast but there is no hard copy of the message.**

What correction should be made to this sentence?

(1) change call is to call are
(2) insert a comma after fast
(3) insert a comma after but
(4) replace but with so
(5) change there is to there was

7. Sentence 8: **The newest way to send messages combines the benefits of the mail, a telegram, and the telephone it is called electronic mail.**

Which of the following is the best way to write the underlined portion of this sentence? If you think the original is the best way, choose option (1).

(1) telephone it
(2) telephone because it
(3) telephone unless it
(4) telephone. It
(5) telephone, it

8. Sentence 9: **Electronic mail is as fast as a phone call, and provides a hard copy like a letter or a telegram.**

Which of the following is the best way to write the underlined portion of this sentence? If you think the original is the best way, choose option (1).

(1) call, and
(2) call and
(3) call, or
(4) call that
(5) call, which

9. Sentence 10: **One device that sends hard copies by electronic mail were a facsimile machine, or "fax."**

What correction should be made to this sentence?

(1) change that to who
(2) change sends to sent
(3) insert commas after device and mail
(4) change were to is
(5) no correction is necessary

10. Sentences 11 and 12: **When you insert a letter into a fax <u>machine. The</u> machine changes the letter's words, numbers, drawings, or photographs into electronic signals.**

Which of the following is the best way to write the underlined portion of these sentences? If you think the original is the best way, choose option (1).

(1) machine. The
(2) machine the
(3) machine, the
(4) machine, and the
(5) machine which

11. Sentence 13: **Those signals pass through telephone lines to another fax machine that changes them back into hard copy.**

What correction should be made to this sentence?

(1) change <u>pass</u> to <u>passed</u>
(2) replace <u>that</u> with <u>which</u>
(3) replace <u>them</u> with <u>the signals</u>
(4) replace <u>them</u> with <u>the telephone lines</u>
(5) no correction is necessary

12. Sentence 14: **<u>Sometimes computers are attached to fax machines that</u> tell the user how to work the machines.**

Which of the following is the best way to write the underlined portion of the sentence? If you think the original is the best way, choose option (1).

(1) Sometimes computers are attached to fax machines that
(2) Sometimes computers are attached to fax machines, which
(3) Sometimes computers are attached to fax machines who
(4) Sometimes fax machines are attached to computers that
(5) Sometimes fax machines are attached to computers even though they

Part 2

Directions: Edit the following passage. It contains 13 errors.

- If any verb and subject do not agree, change the verb.
- Correct errors in the use of verb tenses.
- Correct errors in the use of pronouns.
- Correct errors with compound and complex sentences.
- Correct sentence fragments.
- Correct run-on sentences.
- Rewrite for clarity, as necessary.
- Capitalize any word that should be capitalized.
- Correct errors in punctuation.
- Correct errors in spelling.

Stress may be the key element in half of all illnesses. Studies suggests that your stress level affects your nervous system heart function and hormone levels. Researchers believe that stress may affect your recovery from an illness.

A group of adult students recently meets at a stress clinic they shared ideas about how to handle stress. When the pressure gets too great so Thelma likes to go somewhere private and yell or cry. Louise likes to close her eyes, and imagine yourself in a pleasant setting. If a situation upset Arnold he often talked it out with a sympathetic friend he sometimes writes his complaint that he does'nt send in a letter.

Check your answers on page 252.

GED PRACTICE 4 SKILLS CHART

To review the writing skills covered by the items in GED Practice 4, study the following lessons in Unit 1. The answers and explanations beginning on page 253 tell which part of each lesson pertains to each item.

Item numbers 13–25 refer to the numbering of the mistakes in Part 2 in the answers and explanations.

UNIT 2

Writing

Part 2 of the GED Writing Skills Test is the essay-writing section of the test. You will write approximately 200 words on an assigned topic in about 45 minutes. For your essay to receive a good score, it will have three main traits:

- It will be well organized.
- Each of its key points will be supported effectively.
- It will be written so that your ideas are clear to the reader.

Writing an essay with these traits takes skill and practice. As you work through this unit, you will write frequently in order to build the skills you need to write an essay. Your chief goal will be to write paragraphs that have the traits a well-written essay has.

Unit 2 Overview	
Chapter 1	Beginning to Write
Chapter 2	The Writing Process
Chapter 3	Writing Paragraphs

Chapter

1 BEGINNING TO WRITE

If you do not write regularly, the task of writing can seem very difficult. You may experience a kind of "block" that makes it almost impossible to get anything down on paper.

This chapter gives you practice at unlocking your ideas and writing them down. The first three lessons introduce activities you can do to begin writing regularly. The last two lessons suggest ways to explore your ideas and surroundings for topics to write about.

Lesson 24

Free Writing

Free writing is writing for the fun of it. It's writing anything you want without concern for rules. Its benefit is that it gets your writing juices flowing.

To get a better idea about what free writing is, look at the following three examples. You may notice that they contain misspellings and other mistakes, but that's all right since free writing is done without concern for rules.

EXAMPLE 1: A woman decided to write down the first word she thought of. She would think about that word and then write the next word that came to mind. She would continue in that way until she had written ten words. This is what she wrote:

1. pie   2. apple   3. cinamin

4. spice   5. butter   6. cow

7. colestorall   8. blood   9. heart

10. diet

EXAMPLE 2: Four people played a sentence-completion game. One person wrote the beginning of a sentence. Each of the others wrote a completion for the sentence. This is what they wrote:

My favorite exercise   is jogging.

My favorite exercise   is exercise I watch other people do.

My favorite exercise   show come on durin my morning snack.

EXAMPLE 3:   A middle-aged person wrote about sitting down in a small
              classroom desk:

> The desk I have to sit in has the writing part attach to the chair and
> the space between them is narrower than I am. So when I start to slide
> into the chair I push the whole desk. I just keep going til I hit a wall then I
> can squeeze myslef in.

Free writing gives you practice at coming up with ideas and getting them down on paper. You can write anything you want. You can write about whatever you want. You don't have to avoid a word because you aren't sure how to spell it. Spell it as best you can. You don't have to think about subject-verb agreement, punctuation, or any such thing. Just relax and write whatever comes to mind. Take as much or as little time as you like. Write as much or as little as you want. Have fun doing it.

Free writing is not something that should be assigned. To help you get started, the following exercise suggests some free-writing activities you can do.

EXERCISE 24

Part A. Make a list of the next five words that come to mind when you think about each of the following words.

Example: clock   ___time___   ___late___   ___hurry___   ___run___   ___puff___

1. pork   _____   _____   _____   _____   _____

2. autumn   _____   _____   _____   _____   _____

3. snowball _____   _____   _____   _____   _____

4. incense _____   _____   _____   _____   _____

5. justice _____   _____   _____   _____   _____

Part B. Complete each of the following sentences.

1. If I _____

2. That liar _____

3. Before you were born, _____

4. Once a week _____

5. Too much of that will _____

Part C. Look around where you are sitting right now. Pick out something you see and do one of the following:

(a) Describe it in writing.

(b) Write about something it reminds you of.

_____

_____

_____

_____

_____

Part D. Play this story-writing game with a group:

One person writes the first sentence of a story at the top of a page and folds the paper so that the sentence can't be seen. The second person adds a sentence to the story, folds the paper, and passes it on. Each person adds a sentence in the same way. The last person writes the sentence that ends the story. Then someone unfolds the paper and reads the story to the group.

Part E. Think of a free-writing activity you would like to do and do it. Write whatever you want. Write a little or a lot, as you prefer. Take as much time as you like. Do this each day until you go on to Lesson 2.

There are no entries for this exercise in the answer section.

Lesson 25

Fast Writing

A special kind of free writing is called **fast writing**. It is *like* the free writing you have done in that you write whatever you want without concern for rules. It is *different from* free writing in that you time yourself. You write as much as you can in a certain amount of time.

To do fast writing, just follow these simple rules:

Rules for Fast Writing

RULE 1: Think of a topic to write about.

RULE 2: Decide how many minutes you will write.

RULE 3: Time yourself and start writing.

RULE 4: Stop writing when the time is up, even if you are in the middle of a sentence.

Following are two examples of fast writing done by different people. Each one wrote for half a minute. After they wrote, they recorded the time and the number of words they wrote.

You may notice some errors in the two people's writing. As with free writing, errors don't matter. Writing fast matters.

EXAMPLE 1: An unhappy worker wrote this:

> My boss drives me crazy. He tell me to do something. I start then he changes his mind and tells me to
>
> Time: <u>1/2 minute</u>   Words: <u>22</u>

EXAMPLE 2: Someone who didn't know what to write about wrote this:

> I hate to do fast writing because I can never think of anything to write about I can never think of anything to write
>
> Time: <u>1/2 minute</u>   Words: <u>24</u>

Fast writing can help you increase your writing skills in several ways:

- **Fast writing builds writing speed and output.**

  The more comfortable you get with fast writing, the faster you will be able to write. As your speed increases, the number of words you write in a certain amount of time will increase. You will see your improvement if you record the amount of time and the number of words for each of your fast writings.

- **Fast writing gives you practice at thinking of things to write.**

  By doing fast writing, you learn to come up with topics to write about and things to say about them. That is a skill you need for most kinds of writing.

- **Fast writing can help you overcome blocks to writing.**

  Fast writing can give you a feeling of success because it enables you to put something down on paper. You probably know how frustrating it feels when it seems impossible to think of something to write. Fast writing allows you to avoid that problem altogether because you can write anything that comes to mind, even nonsense. That success can help you feel more confident as you approach other writing tasks.

The important thing in fast writing is to keep your pen or pencil moving. Don't stop. If you run short of things to say, just write the same words over again.

Like free writing, fast writing should not be assigned. To help you get started, some fast-writing activities are suggested in the following exercise.

Part A. Write at least a half minute on each of the following fast-writing topics, longer if you like. Record the amount of time and the number of words you write.

1. Write about a relative of yours.

    _____

    _____

    _____

    _____

    _____

                           Time: _____   Words: _____

2. Write about a car, train, or bus you use.

    _____

    _____

    _____

    _____

    _____

                           Time: _____   Words: _____

3. Write about a television show.

    _____

    _____

    _____

    _____

    _____

                           Time: _____   Words: _____

Part B. Do some fast writing every day on any topic you choose. You may want to ask someone to suggest topics for you. For a few days, do short fast writings—about a half minute each. When you feel comfortable, do some one-minute writings. Later, write for one-and-a-half minutes. Continue to increase the amount of time until you are writing for five or ten minutes.

There are no entries for this exercise in the answer section.

Journal Writing

Many people like to keep a **journal**, or diary. In it they may write about things they do, think, or feel. They may write about events and people around them.

People keep journals for different reasons. Two examples from different kinds of journals follow.

EXAMPLE 1: Some people like to keep an orderly record of important things that happen in their lives. Reading back through such a journal is something like looking through a photo album. Events long forgotten come to life again. This is an example of an entry from that kind of journal. The writer prefers to write rather brief notes.

Monday, December 7, 1992

Jamal got his license today. Nervous. Kept pacing before we went. Drove around to impress his friends. So far, no tickets or accidents.

EXAMPLE 2: Other people write private things in their journals. They confide in their journals the way they might confide in a close friend. They may get things off their chests in their journals. This entry comes from that sort of journal.

Monday, Dec. 7, 1992, at home. 6:30 A.M. Snow. Cold.

They offered me the job for more money than I even hoped for. I accepted it and I start on January 4. But I m worried and nervous. I m afraid I wont be able to handle it. I told them my experience is limited, but they acted like they thought I was being modest. I did better on their test than I thought I had. I wonder if they marked it wrong. I m afraid I ll fall on my face. I m afraid they ll think I lied to them. I m so nervous about failing that I might just make myself fail.

Journal writing can help you with writing in general.

- **Journal writing can help you become more comfortable with writing.**
  One of your goals as you prepare for the GED is to write without getting yourself tied up in knots. Practice makes writing easier for most people. Anyone who keeps a journal regularly benefits from a good deal of valuable practice at writing.

- **Journal writing can help you improve the quality of your writing.**
  As you work through this unit, you will pick up a lot of tips for improving your writing. You can apply these tips in your journal writing. That way you'll develop good habits that will affect all your writing.

Most people think of their journals as private. If you keep your journal private, you will probably feel freer to write whatever you want in it. You can show or read parts of your journal to someone else only if you want to.

A group of people who are all keeping journals sometimes read portions of their journals to each other. By doing so they share ideas about the kinds of things that can go in a journal. They also encourage each other in their journal writing.

EXERCISE 26

Begin keeping a journal. (If you already keep one, continue to write in it regularly.) Set aside a special notebook or buy a diary. Try to write in it every day. Experiment with writing different kinds of things in your journal. Eventually you'll find out what kinds of things you like to write about most.

There are no entries for this exercise in the answer section.

Writing Discovery Questions

You've done some free writing, including fast writing; you've been keeping a journal. Because of those activities you've had the experience of choosing topics to write about. You may have found that after you choose a topic, it is difficult to decide what to write about it.

Writing **discovery questions** can help you explore a topic and choose what to write about it. Discovery questions begin with these words: **who**, **what**, **when**, **where**, **why**, and **how**.

Suppose you know that you want to write about your neighborhood, but you don't know exactly what you want to write. You can begin by writing discovery questions.

EXAMPLE: Someone who wanted to write about her neighborhood started by writing these discovery questions.

> Topic: My Neighborhood
>
> Who are my neighbors?
> What does my neighborhood look like?
> When did my family move here?
> Where is my neighborhood?
> Why do I like my neighborhood?
> How do the neighbors get along with each other?

None of the questions gave her an idea she liked, so she wrote some more discovery questions.

<u>Who</u> controls things in my neighborhood?

<u>What</u> is the biggest problem my neighborhood faces?

<u>When</u> were the houses here built?

<u>Where</u> do the people in my neighborhood work?

<u>Why</u> do so many people live in my neighborhood?

<u>How</u> well does the city serve my neighborhood?

When you use discovery questions, you can continue writing questions until one of them suggests what you would like to write about your topic.

EXERCISE 27

Part A. Choose a topic you would like to write about. Then write a set of discovery questions about that topic. Write additional sets of questions until one of the questions suggests something you'd like to write. If you don't want to choose your own topic, use one of these:

a food	a friend	an interview
a job	a movie	a park

Topic: _____

Who _____?

What _____?

When _____?

Where _____?

Why _____?

How _____?

Part B. Do some free writing on your topic or write about it in your journal.

There are no entries for this exercise in the answer section.

Making Observations

When you do free writing or write in your journal, you may want to describe something—an object, an event, a person, or a feeling. The best descriptions are usually detailed. Details can make a description vivid or lively.

Compare the following two sentences. The second one has more details than the first and is more vivid.

My sister was sitting on a chair.
My teenage sister was slumped in a smelly, thread-bare overstuffed chair.

To write vivid descriptions you need to include details. If you observe something carefully, you will notice details about it. Pay attention to the information you get from each of your five senses: hearing, sight, smell, taste, and touch. For example, think about what your senses could allow you to notice when you sip a glass of iced lemonade:

hearing: the clicking and cracking of ice cubes

sight: a light yellow color; water droplets on the outside of the glass

smell: lemon

taste: both sweet and sour

touch: the chill and wetness of the glass

To sharpen your powers of observation, practice paying attention to information you get from each of your five senses. Make detailed notes.

You might like to make a chart of your observations like this one made by an office worker.

Observations of an Event: A walk to a coffee shop in winter		
hearing:	car horns	bus noises
sight:	my breath	people bundled up
smell:	doughnuts	exhaust fumes
taste:	coffee	doughnut filling
touch:	wool scarf on my neck	cold nose

Part A. Imagine that you have observed the object and the event named below. Fill in each chart with at least two observations for each sense.

Observations of an Event: An abandoned house
hearing:
sight:
smell:
taste:
touch:

Observations of an Event: A walk through a fair or circus
hearing:
sight:
smell:
taste:
touch:

Part B. Each of the following descriptions relates to an observation made by one of the senses. In the blank by each sentence, tell which sense made the observation.

Observation   **Sense**

Example: He banged his elbow as he fell.   _touch_

1. There was clanging under the hood and then the car sputtered to a stop.

_____

2. She wrinkled her nose and tried to hold her breath when she opened the garbage can.

_____

3. The breeze that blew off the lake felt cool.

_____

4. The sour grapefruit caused his saliva to flow.

_____

5. Except for the color of their clothes, the twins were dressed just alike.

_____

Part C. The next time you do free writing or write in your journal, describe something. First make an observation chart. (You can use one of the charts you made in Part A of this exercise if you want to.) Then write a description that includes some of the information from the chart.

Check your answers to Part B of this exercise on page 254.

Chapter
2 THE WRITING PROCESS

When you take the GED, you will write an essay. By writing it, you will communicate your ideas to someone other than yourself. Writing to communicate ideas is different from free writing, fast writing, and journal writing. What you write for someone else to read must be so clear that your reader can easily understand it.

It is helpful to follow a process when you write to communicate. A process allows you to approach writing in a logical, step-by-step fashion. In this chapter you will use a writing process to develop a well-written paragraph. You will also learn about the elements in and structure of good paragraphs.

Introduction to the Writing Process

You follow all kinds of processes in your daily life. One simple example is the process you follow when you have guests to dinner. After you decide what to cook, you buy the food. Then you cook it. Finally, you serve the meal. Obviously you can't do all of these things at once. You can't do them out of order, either.

It's the same with writing. You can't do everything at once, and you have to do things in order. Once you have chosen a topic, using the writing process helps you express your ideas effectively.

This chart shows the steps in the writing process. In Lessons 31–35 you will use these steps to write a paragraph.

Steps in the Writing Process

STEP 1: Brainstorm for ideas.   Jot down ideas about your topic.

STEP 2: Organize your ideas.   Using the notes you made in Step 1, choose the ideas you want to include in your paragraph and put them in order. Cross out ideas you don't want to use.

STEP 3: Write the paragraph.   Following the organization you planned in Step 2, write your ideas in a paragraph.

STEP 4: Revise the paragraph.   If necessary, make changes in your paragraph so that your ideas are presented as clearly and effectively as possible.

STEP 5: Edit the paragraph.   Correct any errors you made in usage, sentence structure, or mechanics.

The following example shows how one writer used the five steps of the writing process.

EXAMPLE: A woman wanted a job as a classroom aide in an elementary school. One of the directions on the application form said this: "In a few sentences, tell why you are suited for this position." She used the writing process to write a paragraph for that part of her job application.

STEP 1: The woman decided to write about experiences of hers that prepared her to be an aide. She brainstormed for ideas and jotted down the following notes:

My Experiences

5 children   Girl Scout leader

baby-sit   tutor

class trip monitor

STEP 2: The woman organized her ideas. She thought about what she had jotted down and decided not to include baby-sitting. She also decided to number her experiences in time order. This is how she organized her notes:

My Experiences

(1) 5 children   (3) Girl Scout leader

~~baby-sit~~   (4) tutor

(2) class trip monitor

STEP 3: The woman wrote her ideas in a paragraph. Using the organization she planned in Step 2, she mentioned her experiences in time order. Her paragraph follows. (She made some errors when she wrote, but she knew she could correct them later.)

I have raise five children of my own. I was a monitor when there class took field trips. I became a Girl Scout leader for four years. I help some of the children in my neighborhood with their school work.

STEP 4: The woman revised her paragraph. When she read over what she had written, she noticed that all of the sentences began with *I*. She wanted to change that and to make a few other improvements in her writing. Her revision follows. (It still has errors to be corrected later.)

I have raise five children of my own. When there class took field trips, I volunteer to be a monitor. I served as a Girl Scout leader for four years now I tutor some of the children in my neighborhood.

STEP 5:   The woman edited her paragraph. She looked for mistakes and corrected them. This shows how she edited her writing:

I have raise̬ five children of my own. When ther̶e̶ class̬ took field

trips, I volunteer̬ to be a monitor. I served as a Girl Scout leader

for four years̬.̬ n̶o̶w̶ I tutor some of the children in my

neighborhood.

When you use the writing process, don't try to do everything all at once. At each step in the process, concentrate on only the things that are important at that stage.

In later lessons you will get a lot of practice with each step of the writing process. Just to try the process out, do the following exercise.

EXERCISE 29

Make up a situation that would require you to write a short note (three or four sentences) to your child's or your own teacher. After you decide on the topic for your note, use the five steps of the writing process to write the note.

STEP 1:   Brainstorm for ideas: Jot down ideas for your note.

_____

_____

_____

STEP 2:   Organize your ideas: Using the notes you made in Step 1, choose the ideas you want to include in your note and put them in order. Cross out ideas you don't want to use.

STEP 3:   Write the note: Following the organization you planned in Step 2, write your ideas in a paragraph.

_____

_____

_____

_____

_____

_____

_____

_____

STEP 4: Revise your note. If necessary, make changes in your note so that your ideas are presented as clearly and effectively as possible. (For this exercise write your note over, making changes as you do so.)

_____

_____

_____

_____

_____

_____

_____

_____

STEP 5: Edit your note: Correct any errors you made in usage, sentence structure, or mechanics. (For this exercise write your note over, making changes as you do so.)

_____

_____

_____

_____

_____

_____

_____

_____

_____

There are no entries for this exercise in the answer section.

Lesson
30

The Parts of a Paragraph

In Lessons 31–35 you will concentrate on using the five steps of the writing process to develop a good paragraph. This lesson looks at what a good paragraph is. An understanding of the makeup of a good paragraph will help you write good paragraphs of your own.

The Topic of a Paragraph

A paragraph is a set of related sentences. The topic of a paragraph is what all the sentences in the paragraph tell about. The topics of most paragraphs are not difficult to figure out. Paragraphs typically contain many clues to their topics. Clues to a paragraph's topic include words that are repeated throughout the paragraph.

A graduate of an adult training program wrote the following paragraph for his town's newspaper. Notice the repeated words in the paragraph. Use them to help you figure out what the paragraph's topic is.

> Seventy adults received high school diplomas during ceremonies at JFK Middle School on Friday. Forty of the adult graduates had completed the Middletown Adult High School Diploma Program. The other thirty graduates received their diplomas after having passed the Tests of General Educational Development (the GED).

The topic of this paragraph is *adult graduates who received high school diplomas*. All of the sentences tell about adult graduates who have successfully completed their educational programs. Three words repeated throughout the paragraph—*adult(s)*, *graduates*, and *diploma(s)*—provide clues to the topic.

Topic Sentences

A paragraph's **topic sentence** tells what the paragraph is about. In other words, it tells what the paragraph's topic is. It often states the most important point the paragraph makes about the topic. A paragraph's topic sentence is usually the first sentence in the paragraph.

The paragraph about adult graduates that you read is reprinted below. Its topic sentence is underlined.

> <u>Seventy adults received high school diplomas during ceremonies at JFK Middle School on Friday</u>. Forty of the adult graduates had completed the Middletown Adult High School Diploma Program. The other thirty graduates received their diplomas after having passed the Tests of General Educational Development (the GED).

Notice that even though the topic sentence does not contain the word *graduates*, it is clear that it refers to adult graduates, the topic of the paragraph. The second and third sentences support the topic sentence by telling more about the seventy adults who received their diplomas.

Sometimes a paragraph's topic sentence is at the end of the paragraph. Look at the following rewritten paragraph about the seventy adult graduates. Its topic sentence is underlined.

Forty adult graduates have recently completed the Middletown Adult High School Diploma Program. Another thirty adults have just passed the Tests of General Educational Development (the GED). <u>All seventy adults received high school diplomas during ceremonies at JFK Middle School on Friday</u>.

In this paragraph the first two sentences support and lead up to the topic sentence at the end of the paragraph. The first and second sentences describe two groups of people who have something in common: all are recent adult graduates. The final sentence reveals the main point about the two groups and states the topic of the paragraph: adult graduates who received high school diplomas.

How to Find the Topic and the Topic Sentence of a Paragraph

STEP 1: To find the topic of a paragraph, ask yourself: What do all the sentences tell about?

STEP 2: To find the topic sentence in the paragraph, ask yourself: Which sentence tells what the whole paragraph is about? (The sentence may contain the most important point about the topic.)

Use these steps to find the topic and topic sentence of the following paragraph.

A computer program tells a computer how to perform certain tasks. A program for a bank's computer instructs the computer in handling people's accounts. A program for an airline's computer tells the computer how to make flight reservations and to print out tickets.

STEP 1: To find the topic of a paragraph, answer this question: What do all the sentences tell about? ANSWER: **computer programs**

STEP 2: To find the topic sentence in the paragraph, answer this question: Which sentence tells what the whole paragraph is about? (The sentence may contain the most important point about the topic.) ANSWER: **A computer program tells a computer how to perform certain tasks**.

Read the following three paragraphs and answer the questions about each.

1.   During his 29 years at the Mosther container factory, James Whitmore worked in almost every phase of the operation. He started out as an assembler and progressed steadily through the ranks. Eventually, he supervised entire work crews.

    a. What is the topic of the paragraph? _____

    b. Which sentence is the topic sentence? _____

_____

2.   The lack of a diploma can prevent a capable worker from finding a job. James Whitmore, for example, found that his experience counted for very little when he was forced to look for a new job. As soon as employers discovered that he had no high school diploma, they tossed his application aside. Many job applicants with solid experience face the same difficulty every day.

    a. What is the topic of the paragraph? _____

    b. Which sentence is the topic sentence? _____

_____

3.   The auditorium was steamy because the audience of 650 people filled every seat and lined the walls. People's programs became hand-held fans that fluttered throughout the 90-minute ceremony. The room was hotter and more crowded than the graduates' families and friends had expected.

    a. What is the topic of the paragraph? _____

    b. Which sentence is the topic sentence? _____

_____

Check your answers on page 254.

Supporting Sentences

A paragraph is like a file folder. The topic sentence is the label on the folder. The supporting sentences are the contents of the folder.

A paragraph with sentences that do not support the topic sentence is like a file folder with the wrong contents. Sentences that don't support the topic sentence don't belong in the paragraph.

The following paragraph comes from a letter someone sent to the editor of a small-town newspaper. Its "supporting sentences" are not good because they do not support the topic sentence, the first sentence.

Many parking tickets handed out in this town are undeserved. I see the police on Main Street every day passing out tickets like candy. Last Monday I was ticketed one morning, and my husband was ticketed later the same day. We spent more on those tickets than on food last week.

According to the topic sentence, the topic of the paragraph is *undeserved parking tickets*. Yet the sentences that follow the topic sentence do not give examples of undeserved tickets. Instead, they complain about the volume and cost of traffic tickets.

The following paragraph's supporting sentences are good. They provide examples of parking tickets that most people would agree are undeserved.

Many parking tickets handed out in this town are undeserved. I know several people who have been given tickets after having put money into broken meters. I have also seen dozens of cars ticketed on weekends outside my shop, even though the "No Parking on Weekends" sign was taken down months ago.

EXERCISE 30b

Part A. Read each of the following pairs of paragraphs. Each paragraph's topic sentence is underlined. Choose the paragraph in each pair that has good supporting sentences.

1. (a)   <u>Someone has been playing practical jokes on me</u>. I used to pull a lot of pranks when I was a kid. Some of those pranks got me into trouble. My wife doesn't think practical jokes are very funny.

   (b)   <u>Someone has been playing practical jokes on me</u>. This morning I found my locker wrapped in aluminum foil. My uniform was covered with flour. Later I found a plastic frog in my coffee cup.

2. (a)   <u>Computers handle many tasks in post offices</u>. Computerized scales weigh packages and calculate postage. Other computers read zip codes and sort mail.

   (b)   <u>Computers handle many tasks in post offices</u>. Computers often assist postal workers, but others have replaced employees altogether. Employees' jobs in many industries are threatened by computerization.

3. (a)   <u>I have decided to disable the alarm on my car because it doesn't seem to scare thieves away</u>. Since I installed it, my windshield has been broken, and the lock on the passenger door has been jimmied. I even found my trunk wide open and empty one morning.

   (b)   When I forget where I've parked my car, I set the alarm off briefly so I can find it. Several car stereos have been stolen on my block. No one has ever tried to break into my car. <u>So I have decided to disable the alarm on my car</u>.

Part B. Read each of the following paragraphs, whose topic sentences are underlined. Tell which sentences in each paragraph support the topic sentence well. (Each paragraph has two or more sentences that do not belong in the paragraph.)

1.   (1) <u>My little girl is lying about her homework</u>. (2) She can't look me in the eye when she says she's done it. (3) Next year she will be in third grade. (4) Her teacher told me she often turns in no homework or only partially completed assignments. (5) My son is too young for homework.

2.   (1) <u>Pipe fitting is a good career</u>. (2) My husband is a pipe fitter. (3) Many pipe fitters are unemployed. (4) The pay is good. (5) Pipe fitters do not have particularly dangerous jobs.

3.   (1) <u>There are several things you can do to prepare for a test</u>. (2) You can review your notes. (3) You can explain the significance of the chapter headings in your textbook to a fellow student. (4) You should check your answers before handing in your test. (5) Be sure to write your answers legibly.

4.   (1) <u>I would like to see a law that bans smoking in all public places</u>. (2) The U.S. Constitution protects the right to smoke. (3) Some employers forbid workers to smoke at home. (4) Passive smoking can be harmful to nonsmokers' health. (5) Parents have no way to protect children from the bad example set by smokers who puff in public.

Part C. For each of the following topic sentences write at least three good supporting sentences.

1. My dog is sick.

_____

_____

_____

2. It is worthwhile to read a daily newspaper.

_____

_____

_____

3. Dental assistants have good jobs.

_____

_____

_____

Check your answers to Parts A and B of this exercise on page 255.

Brainstorming for Ideas

This lesson and the four that follow it will allow you to take a close look at how to use the five steps of the writing process.

You learned in Lesson 29 that the first step of the writing process is to brainstorm for ideas—to jot down ideas about the topic you plan to write about. Brainstorming helps you find out what you already know about your topic. It helps you write well-organized paragraphs.

While you are brainstorming for ideas, you should not judge the ideas that come to mind. You should put down every idea you can think of. (You make judgments about your brainstormed ideas in Step 2 of the writing process.)

To get the ideas flowing when you brainstorm, you can ask yourself discovery questions like those you wrote in Lesson 27. You probably remember that discovery questions begin with *who, what, when, where, why,* or *how.* If you are writing a description of something—an object, an event, a person, or a feeling—it also helps to note observations your five senses make, as you practiced doing in Lesson 28.

This lesson explores two popular ways to make notes when you brainstorm.

Jotting Notes

One way to make notes when you brainstorm is simply to jot your ideas down without any particular pattern or plan.

A woman decided to write about one of her childhood birthdays. Here are the notes she jotted while she brainstormed for ideas. (She made some spelling errors, but she knew spelling is not important when you brainstorm.)

<u>My Seventh Birthday</u>

age seven	got wrong doll	Raggedy Ann
upset	disappointed	let down
held back tears— tried to smile	raining when I woke up	special breakfast— waffles with strawberries
pink party dress	pile of presents	hoped for Crying Katie
soda tastes bitter with cake	cut the cake	cousins there
coarse paper tablecloth	sound of noisemakers	smell of melting wax
feel proud	blow out candles	excitement

Notice that the woman included details from all five senses. She may have asked herself discovery questions as she brainstormed. Her notes are not jotted in any special order. The most important point is that she put down everything she remembered about her seventh birthday.

In Exercise 33 you will write a paragraph about one of your birthdays. You may decide to write about a childhood birthday. To prepare to do so, brainstorm for ideas about an early birthday you remember. Jot down at least 10 ideas that come to mind.

_____

_____

_____

_____

_____

There are no entries for this exercise in the answer section.

Clustering

Another way to make notes when you brainstorm is to cluster them in categories. Clustering makes your notes easier to organize during Step 2 of the writing process. It is especially useful if you have some notion about how the paragraph you plan to write will be organized.

To cluster, write your topic in the center of a piece of paper and draw a circle or box around it. Then write your ideas down on "stems" around the topic. Put related ideas near each other.

If the woman who planned to write about her seventh birthday had clustered her notes, they might have looked like this:

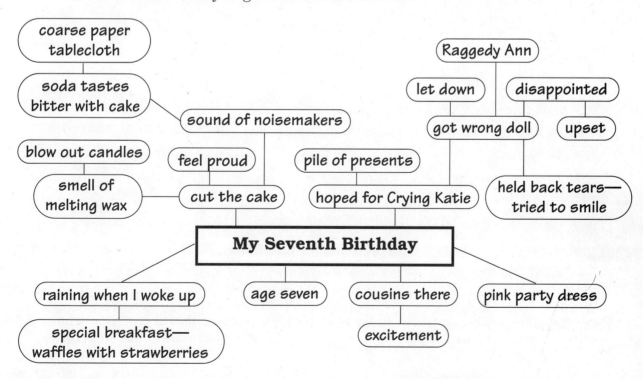

The cluster shows the beginnings of organization for the paragraph. Two early-morning events are in a group in the bottom left corner of the cluster. Events having to do with the birthday cake are in another group in the top left corner of the cluster. Ideas about getting the wrong doll are at the top right corner of the cluster. Four seemingly unrelated ideas are at the bottom right corner of the cluster.

It may seem right now that clustering is a little harder than simply jotting notes. Once you've had some practice with clustering, you may find that you prefer it to jotting notes.

EXERCISE 31b

To try clustering, brainstorm for ideas about a birthday you have had as an adult. In Exercise 33 you may decide to write about that birthday instead of a childhood birthday. Cluster at least 10 ideas that come to mind.

There are no entries for this exercise in the answer section.

Lesson 32

Organizing Ideas

After you have brainstormed for ideas on a topic, you need to judge and organize your notes. You need to decide how your paragraph will begin, in what order to arrange your supporting sentences, and how your paragraph will end.

This lesson will introduce two ways to organize notes from a brainstorm: mapping and numbering.

Mapping

Just as a world map shows where countries are in relation to each other, a map of ideas shows how they relate to each other.

When you map, judge the ideas you brainstormed. Cross out repetitions and ideas that are not to the point. Keep the ideas that should go into your paragraph. Arrange the ideas you keep in categories with titles. Then decide on an order in which to write about your ideas.

The following steps tell how to create a map.

How to Create a Map of Brainstorm Notes

STEP 1: Think about all the words in your jotted list. Cross out words that you don't need.

STEP 2: Arrange the remaining words in categories with titles.

STEP 3: Decide which idea should come first, and choose an order for the remaining ideas.

Following are the notes jotted by the woman writing a paragraph about her seventh birthday. She has crossed out the ideas she decided not to use.

My Seventh Birthday

~~age seven~~	got wrong doll	Raggedy Ann
~~upset~~	disappointed	~~let down~~
held back tears— tried to smile	~~raining when I woke up~~	~~special breakfast— waffles with strawberries~~
pink party dress	pile of presents	hoped for Crying Katie
~~soda tastes bitter with cake~~	cut the cake	cousins there
~~coarse paper tablecloth~~	~~sound of noisemakers~~	~~smell of melting wax~~
feel proud	blow out candles	excitement

The woman made the following map of the remaining ideas—those she planned to use in her paragraph. She organized her ideas in time order. She organized her map into three time categories: *Before Cake*, *During Cake*, and *After Cake*.

My Seventh Birthday

Before Cake: pink party dress
                           cousins there
                           excitement

During Cake: blow out candles
                           cut the cake
                           feel proud

After Cake: pile of presents
                           hoped for Crying Katie
                           got wrong doll
                           Raggedy Ann
                           disappointed
                           held back tears—tried to smile

As you become experienced at making maps, you will be able to make them quickly. Eventually it will take only a few minutes to brainstorm and map your ideas.

EXERCISE 32a

Make a map of the ideas you want to keep from your brainstorm about a childhood birthday. (You did the brainstorming in Exercise 31a on page 175.)

There are no entries for this exercise in the answer section.

Numbering

Numbering a cluster is another way to organize ideas you have brainstormed. Numbering a cluster saves time when your cluster is already partly organized.

The following steps tell how to number a cluster.

How to Number Brainstorm Notes in a Cluster

STEP 1: Think about all the words in your cluster. Cross out words that you don't need.

STEP 2: Decide which idea should come first, and choose an order for the remaining ideas. Number the ideas in the order you choose.

The cluster on page 175 shows the beginnings of some organization. This is the way it looks with the ideas in it numbered. The ideas that won't be used are crossed out.

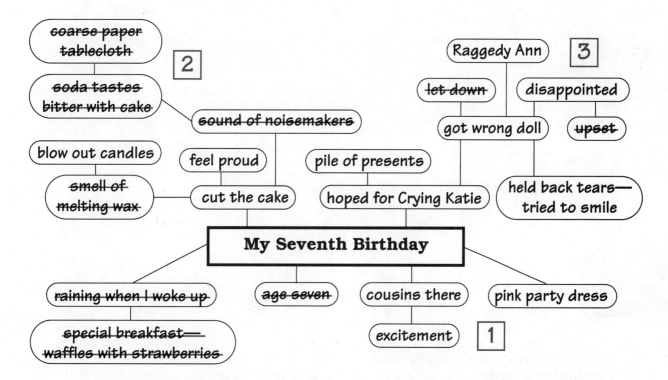

The cluster is numbered in the time order that was already apparent in the original cluster.

If you compare the numbered cluster with the map on page 178, you will see that the ideas in both are grouped the same way. This shows that either method is useful for planning a paragraph.

Number the ideas you want to keep from your cluster about an adult birthday you have had. (You made the cluster in Exercise 31b on page 176.)

There are no entries for this exercise in the answer section.

**Lesson
33**

Writing the Paragraph

After you have organized your ideas for a paragraph by mapping or by numbering a cluster, it is time to write the first draft of the paragraph. This is Step 3 of the writing process.

The draft you write in Step 3 is not the finished paragraph. It is just the first version of the paragraph. You will make changes in it in Steps 4 and 5.

To begin a draft, it is usually a good idea first to write a sentence that might serve as your topic sentence. You might want to write more than one possible topic sentence and then choose the best one. Then, using the organization plan you made in Step 2, write the supporting sentences for the paragraph. Most of your draft will be made of these supporting sentences. Finally, write an ending sentence to tie the paragraph up.

The following steps summarize the procedure for writing a first draft of a paragraph.

How to Write the First Draft of a Paragraph

STEP 1:   Write possible topic sentences for your paragraph and choose the best one to use in your draft.

STEP 2:   Using the map or numbered cluster you made, write the supporting sentences that will make up the bulk of the paragraph.

STEP 3:   Write a final sentence for your paragraph, a sentence that sums up or ends the paragraph.

The following example shows how the woman who planned a paragraph about her seventh birthday wrote her first draft.

STEP 1:   The woman wrote three possible topic sentences for her paragraph and decided that the second one was the best:

(a) ~~Some childhood birthdays is memorable.~~

(b) My seventh birthday was a letdown ll'l never forget.

(c) ~~When people think about there childhood , birthdays stand out most.~~

The woman chose Sentence (b) because it introduced her topic well and would capture a reader's attention. She rejected Sentence (a) because it is rather dull and too general. She was writing about a specific birthday, not memorable birthdays as a whole. She rejected Sentence (c) because it is off the point. She wasn't planning to write a paragraph that would compare birthdays with other childhood memories.

STEP 2:   The woman used the map she'd made to write the supporting sentences that would make up the bulk of her paragraph. The map is reprinted here so that you can see how the woman followed it to write her supporting sentences.

My Seventh Birthday

Before Cake: pink party dress
                 cousins there
                 excitement

During Cake: blow out candles
                 cut the cake
                 feel proud

After Cake: pile of presents
hoped for Crying Katie
got wrong doll
Raggedy Ann
disappointed
held back tears—tried to smile

The organization of the woman's first draft basically follows the organization of her map. All the ideas in the map are included.

My Seventh Birthday

My seventh birthday was a letdown Il'l never forget. My cousins was all at the table, I had on a pink dress. We were all very excited. On my cake I blowed out all the candles. I cut it and gave each of my cousins a piece. I was proud to be the center of attention. I seen a pile of presents. There was lots of presents at Chrismas too. I wanted a Crying Katie doll. She cryes real tears. I came to the last box. Raggedy Ann inside. The wrong doll. I held my tears was in my eyes. You try to smile you know Mom wants me to. Being so disappointed.

STEP 3: The woman wrote a final sentence for her paragraph.

I had never wanted anything as much as the doll I didn't get.

The woman's first draft is not very smooth and has several errors in it. When she wrote the draft, she knew she could improve it and correct its mistakes when she got to Steps 4 and 5 of the writing process.

EXERCISE 33

Follow the directions below to write the first draft of a paragraph about one of your birthdays. Decide whether you want to write about a childhood or an adult birthday. Use the map you made in Exercise 32a (page 178) to write about a childhood birthday. To write about an adult birthday, use the cluster you numbered in Exercise 32b (page 180).

1. Write three possible topic sentences for your paragraph and choose the best one.

   (a) _____

   (b) _____

   (c) _____

2. Using the map or numbered cluster you made, write the supporting sentences that will make up the bulk of the paragraph.

_____

_____

_____

_____

_____

_____

_____

3. Write a final sentence for your paragraph—a sentence that sums up or ends the paragraph.

_____

_____

_____

There is no entry for this exercise in the answer key.

Lesson
34

Revising the Paragraph

First drafts of paragraphs are often choppy and repetitive and use sentence structures that can be improved. First drafts often present the writer's ideas less effectively than they might. You use Step 4 of the writing process to revise the first draft of a paragraph. You make your sentences smoother, your ideas clearer, and the whole paragraph more interesting to read. You bring your paragraph closer to its final form.

When you revise the first draft of a paragraph, you check that each of the three main parts of your paragraph—the topic sentence, the supporting sentences, and the final sentence—are good. (You learned about the parts of a paragraph in Lesson 30.) To improve the structure and clarity of the sentences in your paragraph, you use the skills you practiced in Lessons 18–23.

Note: Correcting mistakes in usage or mechanics is not part of Step 4 of the writing process. You correct such errors when you edit your paragraph in Step 5.

The following guidelines tell you what you should do in Step 4.

Guidelines for Revising a Paragraph

- Make sure that your topic sentence effectively states the topic of your paragraph.
- Check that you have good supporting sentences that support the topic sentence.
- See that the final sentence in the paragraph sums up or ends the paragraph well.
- Add, remove, change, or rearrange words and sentences to make your writing clearer or more vivid.
- Use connecting words to combine short sentences into compound or complex sentences so that the relationships between your ideas are as clear as possible.
- Correct any run-on sentences and sentence fragments.
- Make sure that adjective phrases and sentence parts that function as adjectives are placed correctly in sentences.

As a result of revising, your ideas will be presented more clearly, your sentences will be smoother, and your paragraph will be more interesting.

The following example shows how the woman who drafted the paragraph about her seventh birthday revised her paragraph. The sentences from the original paragraph are numbered to make the discussion about the revision easier to follow.

My Seventh Birthday

began wonderfully but ended as
(1) My seventh birthday ~~was~~ a letdown I'l'l never forget. (2) My cousins was all at the table, ~~I had on a pink dress.~~ *and we* (3) ~~We~~ were all very excited. (4) *After* ~~On my cake,~~ I blowed out all the candles. (5) I cut it and gave each of my cousins a piece. (6) I was proud to be the center of attention. (7) I seen a pile of presents. (8) ~~There was lots of presents at Chrismas too.~~ (9) I wanted a Crying Katie doll. *, which* (10) ~~She~~ cryes real tears. (11) *When* I came to the last box. (12) *I found* Raggedy Ann *instead of Crying Katie* inside. (13) ~~The wrong doll.~~ (14) I held my tears ~~was in my eyes.~~ *and* (15) ~~You~~ try to smile *because* you know Mom wants me to. (16) ~~Being so~~ *I was very* disappointed. (17) *because* I had never wanted anything as much as the doll I didn't get.

184   UNIT 2: Writing

The following notes explain the revisions the woman made.

SENTENCE (1): The woman realized that her topic sentence didn't mention the pleasant parts of her seventh birthday, even though some of the supporting sentences do. She added some words to her topic sentence so that it introduced the *whole* paragraph.

SENTENCE (2): She realized that this was a run-on sentence. She decided to leave out the words *I had on a pink dress* because they weren't too important. Then she used the connecting word *and* to combine Sentences (2) and (3) into a compound sentence.

SENTENCE (4): The woman realized that the adjective phrase *on my cake* was in the wrong place. It made it sound as though *she* were on the cake. She moved the phrase to follow *candles*. She then used the connecting word *After* and a comma after *candles* to combine Sentences (4) and (5) into a complex sentence.

SENTENCE (8): The woman realized that this was not a good supporting sentence for her paragraph because it was about Christmas. She crossed it out.

SENTENCES (9) AND (10): Because Sentences (6), (7), (9), and (10) were all short, the woman decided to combine the last two of them into a complex sentence by using a comma and the connecting word *which.* This gave her sentences variety in length. The complex sentence also read more smoothly than the separate sentences had.

SENTENCES (11) AND (12): Because Sentence (12) was a sentence fragment, the woman added some words to it and connected it to Sentence (11) in a complex sentence by using *When.*

SENTENCE (13): Because this was a sentence fragment and contained information that was not really necessary, the woman crossed it out.

SENTENCES (14) AND (15): To make the relationship between the ideas in these sentences clear, the woman combined them by using a compound predicate: *held my tears* and *try to smile.* She deleted the words *was in my eyes* from the former Sentence (14). She added the word *because* to the former Sentence (15) so that it was no longer a run-on sentence.

SENTENCES (16) AND (17): Because Sentence (16) was a sentence fragment, the woman added some words to it. She used the connecting word *because* to combine it with Sentence (17) in a complex sentence. She felt that this longer sentence ended her paragraph well.

All the changes the woman made in her paragraph made it easier for a reader to see how its ideas related to each other. The paragraph reads very smoothly because it no longer has only short sentences. All in all, the revision made great improvement to the paragraph.

Use the Guidelines for Revising a Paragraph on page 184 to revise the paragraph you wrote in Exercise 33 on page 183. If you need to make only a few changes, you can make them, as the woman did, by crossing out and inserting words and sentences on your original draft. If you need to make many changes, you can write your revised paragraph on the lines that follow.

_____

_____

_____

_____

_____

_____

_____

_____

_____

_____

_____

_____

_____

_____

_____

_____

_____

_____

_____

_____

_____

_____

There is no answer key entry for this exercise.

Editing the Paragraph

Revised paragraphs often contain usage and mechanical errors. You use Step 5 of the writing process to correct them and put your paragraph in its final form. When you edit the revised paragraph, you use the skills you practiced in Lessons 1–17.

Sometimes it is hard to see mistakes in your own writing, especially after you have worked with it for some time. When you edit, it is a good idea to read your paragraph over more than once, checking it carefully each time you read it.

The following guidelines tell you what you should check in Step 5.

Guidelines for Editing a Paragraph

Make sure that
- subjects and verbs agree.
- verbs are in the correct tense and form.
- pronouns are appropriate.
- there are no pronoun shifts and unclear references.
- spelling is correct.
- punctuation is correct.

The following example shows how the woman who revised the paragraph about her seventh birthday edited her paragraph. The sentences from the revised paragraph are numbered to make the discussion about the editing easier to follow.

My Seventh Birthday

(1) My seventh birthday began wonderfully but ended as a letdown I'll never forget. (2) My cousins ~~was~~ *were* all at the table, and we were all very excited. (3) After I ~~blowed~~ *blew* out all the candles on my cake, I cut it and gave each of my cousins a piece. (4) I was proud to be the center of attention. (5) I ~~seen~~ *saw* a pile of presents. (6) I wanted a Crying Katie doll, which ~~cryes~~ *cries* real tears. (7) When I came to the last box, I found Raggedy Ann instead of Crying Katie inside. (8) I held my tears and ~~try to~~ *tried* smile because ~~you know~~ *I knew* Mom ~~wants~~ *wanted* me to. (9) ~~Being so~~ *I was very* disappointed because I had never wanted anything as much as the doll I didn't get.

The following notes explain the corrections the woman made.

SENTENCE (1): The woman corrected the spelling of the contraction *I'll*.

SENTENCE (2): She realized that the subject of this sentence, *cousins*, was plural, so she changed *was* to *were* to make it agree.

SENTENCE (3): She remembered that *blow* is an irregular verb. Since the verb in this sentence needs to be in the simple past tense, she changed *blowed* to *blew*.

SENTENCE (5): In this sentence, she realized that she had used the past participle of the verb rather than the simple past tense, so she changed *seen* to *saw*.

SENTENCE (6): She remembered the rule about *s* endings after the letter *y*: When a letter other than a vowel comes before *y*, change the *y* to *i* and add *es*. She changed the spelling of *cryes* to *cries*.

SENTENCE (7): She realized that she needed a comma after the dependent part of this sentence, so she inserted it.

SENTENCE (8): She discovered that she had written most of this sentence in the wrong tense. Because the whole paragraph is in the simple past tense, she changed the last three verbs in this sentence to the simple past tense. She also noticed that she had shifted from the pronoun *I*, which begins the sentence, to *you*. She corrected that mistake.

After her editing, the woman's final paragraph looked like this:

My Seventh Birthday

My seventh birthday began wonderfully but ended as a letdown I'll never forget. My cousins were all at the table, and we were all very excited. After I blew out all the candles on my cake, I cut it and gave each of my cousins a piece. I was proud to be the center of attention. I saw a pile of presents. I wanted a Crying Katie doll, which cries real tears. When I came to the last box, I found Raggedy Ann instead of Crying Katie inside. I held my tears and tried to smile because I knew Mom wanted me to. I was very disappointed because I had never wanted anything as much as the doll I didn't get.

The paragraph has no usage, sentence-structure, or mechanical errors. It should communicate the woman's ideas to her readers easily because they won't be distracted by mistakes.

Use the Guidelines for Editing a Paragraph on page 187 to edit the paragraph you wrote in Exercise 34 on page 186. If you need to make only a few changes, you can make them, as the woman did, on your revised draft. If you need to make many changes, you can write your edited paragraph on the lines that follow.

_____

_____

_____

_____

_____

_____

_____

_____

_____

_____

_____

_____

_____

_____

_____

_____

_____

_____

_____

There are no entries for this lesson in the answer key.

Chapter

3 WRITING PARAGRAPHS

The pattern of organization a writer chooses for a paragraph depends on the purpose of the paragraph. The signal words a writer uses in a paragraph help the reader see how one idea leads to the next. In the following lessons you will learn about five different patterns for paragraph organization and the signal words appropriate for each. You will practice writing paragraphs using the various organization patterns.

Lesson
36

Writing a Paragraph Organized by Time

In Chapter 2 you used the five steps of the writing process to develop a paragraph about a memorable birthday. Like the woman who wrote about her seventh birthday, you probably organized your paragraph in time order, the order in which things happened. Time order is one of five common ways paragraphs are organized.

Writers often use time order when their purpose is to tell a story, to describe a series of events, or to explain how to do something. Usually the earliest event to happen comes at the beginning of the paragraph. Sometimes, however, events are described in reverse-time order with the last event described first. The signal words a writer uses are clues to the order used in the paragraph.

Read the following example of a paragraph organized by time order. Notice the signal words in dark print.

> Four steps you can take when handling chicken reduce the chances of food poisoning. **First**, if you freeze a raw chicken, wrap it tightly and put it in a freezer no warmer than 32°F. **Second**, defrost the chicken only in a microwave oven or in a refrigerator no warmer than 40°F—not on a counter top. **Then**, when you prepare the chicken to cook it, wash it thoroughly, inside and out, and thoroughly wash everything that touches the raw meat. **Finally**, cook the chicken until no part of it is pink, not even the meat near the bone. If you take these precautions, the chance of food poisoning is almost nil.

The paragraph gives steps for avoiding food poisoning from chicken. The first sentence is the topic sentence. Four details that support the topic sentence follow. The first step, freezing the chicken, is described first; the last step, cooking the chicken, is described last. Notice how the signal words *First, Second, Then,* and *Finally* make the order of the steps clear. The last sentence sums up the paragraph.

The following chart lists signal words commonly used when a paragraph is organized by time order.

```
┌──────────────────────────────────────────────────────────────┐
│  Signal Words Used in Paragraphs Organized by Time             │
│                                                                │
│  after              as soon as              before             │
│  during             earlier                 finally            │
│  first (second, third, etc.)  last week (month, year)  later   │
│  meanwhile          next                    now                │
│  then               today                   tomorrow           │
│  when               while                   yesterday          │
└──────────────────────────────────────────────────────────────┘
```

The following exercise will give you practice arranging ideas in both time order and reverse-time order.

EXERCISE 36

Part A. Following are two sets of sentences for paragraphs that have not been organized. Each includes a topic sentence and four supporting sentences. Number the supporting sentences in each set as indicated.

1. Number the four supporting sentences in time order. (The first detail has been numbered for you.)

Topic Sentence:

> I feel that my schooling and work history qualify me for the job you advertised.

Supporting Sentences:

_____ Right after my father died, I worked as a plumber for five years on my own.

_____ After graduation, I worked for my father, putting the plumbing in the houses he built.

_____ Until last month I was a pipe fitter at the Groton Boatyard.

___1___ I graduated from Horwich Technical School in 1968.

2. Number the four supporting sentences in reverse-time order. (One detail has been numbered for you.)

Topic Sentence:

I feel that my work history and schooling qualify me for the job you advertised.

Supporting Sentences:

_____ I had learned plumbing by working with my father on the houses he built.

_____ Before that I worked for five years on my own as a plumber.

_____ Until last month I was a pipe fitter at the Groton Boatyard.

___4___ That was just after I graduated from Horwich Technical School in 1968.

Part B. Insert signal words in the following paragraph to make clear its organization by time. (One signal word has been inserted for you.)

The IRS has a huge computer system containing information in its data base about each taxpayer—information from past returns, banks, employers, and the DMV. To process tax returns, the IRS follows a careful procedure that involves using its computer system. First, the ~~The~~ IRS receives a taxpayer's return. A worker enters the return's information into the computer. The computer searches its data base and compares the information there to that from the taxpayer's return. If the taxpayer's figures agree with those in the data base, the IRS either credits the taxpayer's account or sends out a check.

Part C. Use the writing process to develop a paragraph on one of the following topics. Organize your paragraph by time order. You may find the list of signal words in the chart on page 191 helpful as you revise your paragraph.

Topic 1: Tell what steps you followed to enter the adult education program you are in.

Topic 2: Suggest steps to prepare for the Writing Skills Test of the GED.

Topic 3: Describe parting from someone you will probably never see again.

Check your answers to Parts A and B of this exercise on page 255.

Writing a Paragraph Organized by Space

Have you ever tried describing your surroundings over the phone? If so, you may have helped the listener "see" what you were describing by arranging the details in space order, by indicating the locations of things in reference to each other. Like time order, space order is one of five common ways paragraphs are organized.

Space order is often used to describe the appearance or location of a place or thing. When you use space order, you need to decide where to start and in which direction to go in your description. You might move from the top to the bottom of an object you are describing or from the bottom to the top. You might move from the front to the back or from the back to the front. You might go from left to right or from right to left. The important thing is to be consistent. Don't change directions in the middle of a paragraph. Describing how something looks is like drawing a picture with words. The more orderly the description is, the clearer the reader's mental picture becomes.

Whatever direction you choose for organizing a space-ordered paragraph, you can help the reader "see" what you are describing by using signal words.

Can you "see" the bookcase described in the following paragraph? There are many signal words in the paragraph (those in dark print) to make the positions of the objects mentioned clear.

The bookcase in my living room is five feet tall. **On top** of it there are two sculptures **on either side** of a large piece of quartz. **The top two shelves** hold compact disks. **On the two shelves below** the disks are small hardbound books. **The bottom shelf** has records **on the left** and tall books **on the right**. The bookcase looks well balanced because the lighter objects are near the top and the heavy objects are near the bottom.

The purpose of the paragraph is to describe the contents of a bookcase. The first sentence is the topic sentence. The description moves from the top of the bookcase to its bottom shelf in four supporting sentences. The last sentence sums up the description.

The following chart lists signal words commonly used when a paragraph is organized by space order.

Signal Words Used in Paragraphs Organized by Space

above	among	around	below
beneath	beside	between	east
front	in back of	in the center of	near
next to	north	on the left side	on the right side
on top of	opposite	over	rear
south	under	upon	west

The following exercise will give you practice arranging ideas by space order.

Part A. Following are two sets of sentences for paragraphs that have not been organized. Each includes a topic sentence and four supporting sentences. Number the supporting sentences in each set as indicated.

1. Number the four supporting sentences in space order from top to bottom. (The first detail has been numbered for you.)

   Topic Sentence:

   　　　The computer keys are arranged in rows.

   Supporting Sentences:

   _____ The three central rows contain the letter keys.

   _____ The numbers are arranged across the second row from the top.

   _____ The space bar and cursor keys lie in the bottom row.

   ___1___ In the top row are the function keys.

2. Number the four supporting sentences in space order from bottom to top. (The first detail has been numbered for you.)

   Topic Sentence:

   　　　The computer keys are arranged in rows.

   Supporting Sentences:

   _____ The three central rows contain the letter keys.

   _____ The numbers are arranged across the second row from the top.

   _____ In the top row are the function keys.

   ___1___ The space bar and cursor keys lie in the bottom row.

Part B. Insert signal words in the following paragraph to make clear its organization by space. (One signal word has been inserted for you.)

　　　The employment pages are located in the classified section of a newspaper. ___At the top___ of the first employment page is the heading, *Employment*. _____ this heading job openings are usually listed alphabetically. _____ side of the page, the first column might begin with a listing for automotive technicians. At the top of the column _____ side of the page, there might be several listings for babysitters. _____ the first page there may be several other pages of job listings. _____ of the last column of the last employment page, there might be a listing for a zoo worker.

Part C. Use the writing process to develop a paragraph on one of the following topics. Organize your paragraph by space order. You may find the list of signal words in the chart on page 193 helpful as you revise your paragraph.

Topic 1: Describe a house in which a party has just ended.

Topic 2: Describe yourself for a stranger who is meeting you at an airport.

Topic 3: Describe an object you own.

Check your answers to Parts A and B of this exercise on page 255.

Writing a Paragraph Organized by Cause and Effect

In Lessons 36 and 37 you learned about paragraphs organized by time and paragraphs organized by space. In this lesson you will look at a third way to organize paragraphs—by cause and effect.

Between any two events there may or may not be a cause-effect relationship. For example, you may send your children off to school and then sit down to have a cup of coffee. There is no cause-effect relationship between these two events: sending children to school does not cause you to have coffee. If you drink too much coffee, you may experience indigestion. There is a cause-effect relationship here. The first event, drinking too much coffee, is the cause; the second event, experiencing indigestion, is the effect.

Cause-effect paragraph organization is used to describe events that make other events occur. The following sentences describe events that are have cause-effect relationships. Notice the signal words in dark print.

This part of the sentence tells the cause.	→ One afternoon my son Vaughn was bored,
This part of the sentence tells the effects.	→ **so** he pinched the baby and pulled the cat's tail.
This part of the sentence tells the effect.	→ Vaughn was sent to the time-out chair
This part of the sentence tells the causes.	→ **because** he had pinched the baby and pulled the cat's tail.
This part of the sentence tells the cause.	→ Because he had misbehaved,
This part of the sentence tells the effect.	→ Vaughn was sent to the time-out chair.
This part of the sentence tells the cause.	→ **Since** he was in the time-out chair,
This part of the sentence tells an effect that is also the cause of this effect.	→ he missed out on a snack → and **thus** spent the afternoon hungry.

In the first and third sentences above the cause appears first and is followed by the effect(s). In the second sentence the effect comes first. The first sentence mentions more than one effect; the second sentence, more than one cause. The fourth sentence describes a chain of events in which a cause produces an effect that becomes the cause of another effect.

When you are writing about causes and effects, you can use one of two basic organizations in your paragraph.

- You can organize the paragraph so that it moves from cause to effect, as the following paragraph does.

> Baseball **causes** arm injuries for millions of youngsters. The twists pitchers' arms make when they throw curve balls **cause** the most arm injuries. These twists can **cause** unusual strain on parts of the arm. The strain can **result in** torn muscles. During healing, torn muscle tissue is often replaced by stiff scar tissue, which **causes** pain and loss of strength.

- You can organize the paragraph so that it moves from effect to cause, as the following paragraph does.

> Millions of youngsters experience pain and loss of strength **as a result of** baseball injuries. The pain and weakness are often **caused by** the stiff scar tissue that replaces torn muscle tissue during healing. Muscles tear when they are subjected to unusual strain. Such strain can be the **result of** the twisting a pitcher's arm muscles undergo when throwing curve balls.

Either method of organization can be effective as long as it is consistent throughout the paragraph.

It is important to use signal words when you describe a cause-effect relationship. They often provide the only clue about which are the causes and which the effects described in a sentence or a paragraph. The following chart lists signal words commonly used when a paragraph is organized by cause-effect.

Signal Words Used in Paragraphs Organized by Cause-Effect

Words That Introduce Causes	Words That Introduce Effects
as a result of	cause(s)
because	consequently
because of	result(s) in
caused by	so
since	therefore
the cause	the effect/result
	thus

The following exercise will give you practice writing about events that have cause-effect relationships.

Part A. For each of the following topic sentences, which state effects, write two supporting sentences that state causes.

Example: Effect: I deserve a raise.

    Cause: ___I have been with the company for twenty-five years.___

    Cause: ___Several of my ideas have earned money for the company.___

1. Effect: The workers decided to go on strike for two main reasons.

    Cause: _____

    Cause: _____

2. Effect: The child is having trouble at school because of family problems.

    Cause: _____

    Cause: _____

3. Effect: Karen decided to learn to use a computer.

    Cause: _____

    Cause: _____

4. Effect: We decided on two tickets to the Bahamas for Jay's retirement present.

    Cause: _____

    Cause: _____

Part B. For each of the following topic sentences, which state causes, write two supporting sentences that state effects.

Example: Cause: The voters decided to cut the budget.

    Effect: ___Therefore, the town will not be getting a new fire truck.___

    Effect: ___We will not be able to buy lights for the track.___

1. Cause: The smoke detector's batteries were dead.

    Effect: _____

    Effect: _____

2. Cause: Fred left the groceries in the car overnight.

    Effect: _____

Effect: _____

3. Cause: Wanda never eats vegetables.

Effect: _____

Effect: _____

4. Cause: We recycle as much of our waste materials as we can.

Effect: _____

Effect: _____

Part C. Insert signal words in the following paragraph to make its organization by cause-effect clear. Make any changes in wording, capitalization, and punctuation that are necessary as a result of the additions. (One signal word has been inserted for you.)

                                                Because

    I am asking for a raise for several reasons. I have turned down several offers to work elsewhere. I have proven my loyalty to the company. The company has saved money. It has adopted several of my suggestions for running itself more efficiently. I am responsible for supervising two other employees. To do that, I put in more time than I used to. I feel I deserve more pay.

Part D. Use the writing process to develop a paragraph beginning with one of the following topic sentences. Organize your paragraph by cause-effect order. You may find the list of signal words in the chart on page 196 helpful as you revise your paragraph.

    Topic Sentence 1: Learning to use a computer has increased my career options.
    Topic Sentence 2: Susan's fear of heights causes several effects in her life.
    Topic Sentence 3: Connie's life changed after her divorce.

Check your answers to Parts A, B, and C of this exercise on pages 255 and 256.

Writing a Paragraph Organized by Comparing and Contrasting Ideas

Suppose you see a movie and then read the book. You might point out to a friend how the movie and the book are alike and how they are different. When you tell how two things are alike, you are comparing them. When you tell how two things are different, you are contrasting them. One of the five common ways paragraphs are organized is by making comparisons and/or contrasts.

When a writer's purpose is to describe two people, places, or things—or to persuade a reader that one is preferable to the other—comparison/contrast organization is often used. Usually the similarities between two things are grouped together in one part of a paragraph and the differences in another.

Read the following example of a paragraph that makes a comparison. Notice the signal words in dark print.

> The human brain and a computer have many similarities. **Like** the brain, a computer has a memory. The brain and a computer can **both** make calculations. Messages are sent from one part of the brain to another. **Likewise**, messages travel from one part of a computer to another. There are other similarities too numerous to mention here.

The paragraph tells how the human brain is similar to a computer. The first sentence is the topic sentence, followed by three examples that support the topic sentence. The signal words *Like*, *both*, and *Likewise* make it clear that ideas are being compared. The last sentence closes the paragraph.

The following paragraph points out contrasts. Again, notice the signal words in dark print.

> There are several differences between the human brain and a computer. The brain is capable of creative thought, **but** computers seem not to be truly creative. **On the other hand**, a computer can solve a complicated math problem in a few seconds, **but** the same problem could take the brain years to solve. Further, most human brains are about the size of two fists, **whereas** most computers are much larger. Other differences are numerous.

The paragraph tells how the human brain is different from a computer. The first sentence is the topic sentence. It is followed by three examples that support the topic sentence. Notice how the signal words *but*, *On the other hand*, and *whereas* make it clear that ideas are being contrasted. The last sentence closes the paragraph.

The following chart lists signal words commonly used when a paragraph compares or contrasts two things.

Signal Words Used in Paragraphs Organized by Comparison/Contrast

Words Used When Comparing		Words Used When Contrasting	
alike	just as	although	in contrast
also	likewise	but	on the other hand
both	same	differ	unlike
common	similar	different	whereas
equally	too	however	
in the same way			

The following exercise will give you practice writing comparisons and contrasts.

Part A. Complete each idea below by making a comparison.

1. Both my mother and my father _____

2. Men and women are equally _____

3. Ben and Michelle _____ in similar ways.

4. Like eating with chopsticks, using a fork _____

5. A camera is like an eye in that _____

Part B. Complete each idea below by making a contrast.

1. A dime used to buy an ice cream cone, but _____

2. Unlike speaking, writing _____

3. Although some people enjoy horror movies, _____

4. While life in the city _____,

   life in the country _____

5. Donna seems to find writing difficult, but Hettie, on the other hand,

   _____

Part C. Insert signal words in the following paragraph to make its organization by comparison clear. Make any changes in wording, capitalization, and punctuation that are necessary as a result of the additions. (One signal word has been inserted for you.)

      Lynne reminds me of my cat. Their eyes have *the same* a slanted shape and

green color. Lynne and my cat are quiet and graceful. They even have

eating habits. Lynne and Shmo drink a cup of milk for breakfast and

eat fish for dinner. Whenever she can, Lynne curls up on the couch for

a nap. Shmo takes every opportunity to doze on the sofa.

Part D. Insert signal words in the following paragraph to make its organization by contrast clear. Make any changes in wording, capitalization, and punctuation that are necessary as a result of the additions. (One signal word has been inserted for you.)

Pedestrians and drivers follow different rules. Walkers often cross at lights when they are red. , but a A driver must stop for a red light. A driver should always stay on the right side of the road. A pedestrian should walk on the left side if there is no sidewalk. A driver who comes upon a pedestrian in a crosswalk must stop. A pedestrian who has stepped into a crosswalk should not have to stop for a car.

Part E. Use the writing process to develop a paragraph on one of the following topics. Organize your paragraph by comparison or contrast. You may find the list of signal words in the chart on page 199 helpful as you revise your paragraph.

Topic 1: Tell how two different people you know are alike or different.
Topic 2: Tell how you are different from the person you were ten years ago.
Topic 3: Explain how two restaurants you've eaten in are alike or different.

Check your answers to Parts A, B, C, and D of this exercise on page 256.

Lesson
40

Writing a Paragraph Organized by the Order of Importance of Ideas

The last of the five common ways paragraphs are organized is by the order of importance of ideas. In such paragraphs ideas are arranged from most important to least important or vice versa. When a writer wants to persuade a reader about something, he or she might organize the ideas in a paragraph by the order of their importance.

Suppose you are writing an ad for a local bulletin board about a car you want to sell. You will probably list the car's strongest features at the beginning of your ad to make a good first impression on potential buyers. If a possible buyer is impressed by the first details, he or she will probably read all the ad.

Read the following example of a paragraph whose ideas are organized by their order of importance. The most important ideas come first. Notice the signal words in dark print.

Adults should not hit children. **The most important reason** is that children can be physically injured by such treatment. **A second reason** is that children learn by adults' examples. They may learn that it is all right to hit other people. **Third**, hitting children usually does nothing to correct their behavior because they often continue to do the very thing they were punished for. **Finally**, adults usually do not feel good about themselves when they hit children. They need to find ways to correct children's behavior without resorting to corporal punishment.

The paragraph tries to convince readers that adults should not hit children. The first sentence is the topic sentence. It is followed by four reasons that support it. The most important reason comes right after the topic sentence. The second reason is somewhat less important than the first, and so on. Notice how the signal words *The most important, A second reason, Third,* and *Finally* make the rank of each idea's importance clear. The last sentence draws a conclusion based on the content of the paragraph.

Sometimes it is useful to organize a paragraph so that it builds from the less important ideas to the more important ideas. Such organization creates suspense that keeps the reader reading. The following example is a paragraph whose ideas are organized from the least to the most important. Again, notice the signal words in dark print.

Smoking on school grounds should be banned at all times. **For one thing**, smokers often litter school grounds with cigarette butts and empty packages. **In addition**, children may not respect teachers who smoke but try to teach them about good health habits. **Even more important** is the health risk caused by inhaling others' smoke. **Also**, when young nonsmokers see older students or teachers smoking, they may decide to try it themselves. **The main reason** smoking should be banned, of course, is that it is hazardous to the health of smokers and the people around them.

The paragraph tries to convince readers that smoking should be banned on school grounds. The first sentence is the topic sentence. It is followed by five reasons that support it. The least important reason comes right after the topic sentence. The other reasons are organized so that the paragraph builds to the most important reason. Notice how the signal words *For one thing, In addition, Even more important, Also,* and *The main reason* make the rank of each idea's importance clear.

Either way you order the ideas in a paragraph organized by their importance, the most important ones will make more of an impression than if they were in the middle of the paragraph. Readers tend to pay more attention to the beginnings and endings of paragraphs than to the parts in the middle.

The chart on page 203 lists signal words commonly used when a paragraph's ideas are organized by the order of their importance.

**Signal Words Used in Paragraphs Organized
by the Order of Importance of Ideas**

above all	also
another reason	chiefly
equally important/significant	even more important/significant
finally	first (second, third, etc.)
for one thing	in addition
less important/significant	the least important/significant
the main reason	the most important/significant

The following exercise will give you practice arranging ideas by the order of their importance.

EXERCISE 40

Part A. Following are two sets of sentences for paragraphs that have not been organized. Each includes a topic sentence and four supporting sentences. Number the supporting sentences in each set as indicated.

1. Number the four supporting sentences by the order of their importance with the most important first. (One detail has been numbered for you.)

   Topic Sentence:

   > Our community needs an area reserved for skateboarders.

   Supporting Sentences:

   _____ Some of the cars in the lot have been scratched and dented during skateboarding maneuvers.

   _____ A second reason is that some skateboarders ride down the sidewalks on Main Street, which makes the walkway hazardous to pedestrians.

   _1_____ Above all, many young skateboarders now risk their lives in traffic for lack of a special skateboarding area.

   _____ Another reason is that when skateboarders use the town parking lot, some customers who might otherwise park there refuse to.

2. Number the four supporting sentences by the order of their importance with the least important first. (One detail has been numbered for you.)

Topic Sentence:

        I think daylight savings time should be kept in effect all year.

Supporting Sentences:

_____ A third reason is that most adults don't like leaving work in the dark in the winter.

_____ Also, many workers are late and many appointments are missed whenever we change to daylight savings time in the spring.

_____ The annoyance of having to change every clock and watch in the house twice a year is one small reason.

_4_____ Most important, every year more and more children walking home from their school-bus stops are hit by cars in dark winter months.

Part B. Insert signal words in the following paragraph to make its organization by order of importance clear. Make any changes in wording, capitalization, and punctuation that are necessary as a result of the additions. (One signal word has been inserted for you.)

        Wearing a motorcycle helmet is important for many reasons. Helmets prevent fatal head injuries when riders are thrown from their bikes.

In addition, helmets

~~Helmets~~ protect wearers from injury when rocks are thrown into the air by

other vehicles. Helmet visors reduce the damaging force of wind on the

wearers' eyes. Helmets keep riders' heads dry during trips through storms.

Part C. Use the writing process to develop a paragraph on one of the following topics. Organize your paragraph by order of importance of ideas. You may find the list of signal words in the chart on page 203 helpful as you revise your paragraph.

Topic 1: Explain why women should or should not be involved in combat.

Topic 2: Tell why cross-country truck drivers should or should not be allowed to drive eighty hours a week.

Topic 3: Explain why companies should or should not require drug testing for applicants and/or employees.

Check your answers to Parts A and B of this exercise on page 257.

Choosing a Way to Organize a Paragraph

In Lessons 36–40 you studied five ways to organize paragraphs. As soon as you know the topic of a paragraph, you may have a good idea which of the five organization patterns you'll use when you write the paragraph. More often it is easier to see how to organize a paragraph during Step 2 of the writing process when you organize your notes. In either case, you need to choose an organization pattern that serves your purpose in writing the paragraph.

Organizing a paragraph is like organizing a filing system for your bills. The way you arrange your bills depends on your purpose in arranging them. Suppose you think that your bills are getting higher every month. You would probably arrange your bills by months to find out. If you want to compare your grocery bills to your bills for rent, you would put all bills of each type together. You put the bills in the order that makes them most useful to your purpose.

When you organize and write a paragraph, you arrange the ideas and sentences in the way that makes them clearest to your reader. Decisions about what to put first, in the middle, and last depend on what you are trying to get across.

Read the following two paragraphs. Which is organized better?

Making muffin pizzas is quick and easy. First, split some English muffins and toast them lightly. Second, spoon on a little pizza sauce. Next, top with shredded cheese. Finally, bake for a few minutes until the cheese is melted.

Making muffin pizzas is quick and easy. Once they're put together, you only need to bake them for a few minutes until the cheese is melted. Don't forget to spoon a little pizza sauce on the English muffins. The muffins should be toasted. Split them ahead of time and add some shredded cheese.

The first paragraph is better organized than the second because the steps for making muffin pizzas are presented in order—time order. The paragraph uses signal words that make its organization clear. It accomplishes the writer's purpose—to tell how to make a muffin pizza.

The second paragraph contains pretty much the same information as the first. Because the steps are mixed up and there are no signal words, the directions for making muffin pizzas are confusing.

Here is a plan you can use to select an order for your ideas in a paragraph.

How to Choose a Pattern of Paragraph Organization

STEP 1: Examine your topic.

STEP 2: Decide on your purpose.

STEP 3: Brainstorm with that purpose in mind.

STEP 4: Study your brainstormed ideas.

To understand your purpose, you need to think carefully about your topic. The following table makes some suggestions about how to do that.

How to Determine Your Purpose in Writing a Paragraph

Ask yourself the following questions:	If "yes," use this organization:
Am I telling a story or explaining the steps in a process?	Time
Am I describing how a person, place, or thing looks?	Space
Am I explaining why or how something happens?	Cause and effect
Am I describing the similarities or differences between two things?	Comparing and contrasting ideas
Am I trying to persuade my readers to accept my opinion?	Order of importance of ideas

---

Two writers were given the following topic:

Explain why you have gone back to school for your GED diploma.

The first writer examined the topic and decided that he would describe the chain of events that led him to return to school. With this purpose in mind, he brainstormed this list:

Why I Want a GED

dropped out when 16	family needed me on the farm
farming has changed	you need more math
you need computer knowledge	I need business courses
I need a GED for community college	I want a degree

A look at his notes told the writer that most of the events he listed caused other events on his list. For instance, he dropped out of high school because his family needed his help on the farm. Changes in modern farming methods caused him to need courses in math, computers, and business. To take those courses he needs a GED. The writer decided that the cause-effect pattern of organization would be best for organizing his ideas into a paragraph.

The second writer decided that she wanted to list the several different reasons she had for returning to school. With this purpose in mind, she brainstormed this list:

Why I Want a GED

can't get a raise	can't get a new job
can't help kids with homework	don't want kids to do like me
don't like being a dropout	want to know I can go to community college

While examining her notes, the woman noticed that in general they followed an order of importance. The first two ideas she put down were about stumbling blocks to her career. The second two ideas had to do with her children; the last two, with her self-image. Based on the notes she brainstormed, the woman decided to organize her paragraph according to the order of importance of her ideas.

In the two examples above the same topic led two different people to two different patterns for organizing their paragraphs.

Sometimes the way a topic is stated suggests an organization pattern for a paragraph. Consider this topic: Explain what causes hiccups. The word *causes* indicates that a cause-effect organization may be the logical one to use to develop a paragraph on the topic.

Now consider this topic: Tell what would happen if there were no laws. The topic doesn't actually contain the word *cause* or *effect*, but it suggests cause-effect organization. It requires you to think about possible results (the effect) of getting rid of laws (the cause).

The following chart may help you choose a pattern of organization for paragraphs you write.

Five Patterns for Paragraph Organization

Organization Pattern	Characteristics	Common Uses	Sample Topics
Time	Organizes the description of events by the order in which they happened (or in the reverse order).	To tell a story. To describe a series of events. To explain a procedure.	How to use a microwave oven. How to get unemployment benefits.
Space	Organizes the description of the appearance of something from top to bottom (or vice versa) or from left to right (or vice versa).	To tell how something looks. To describe the layout of a place. To explain where something is located.	The view from my bedroom window. The arrangement of the articles in my medicine cabinet.
Cause and Effect	Organizes the description of linked events to show how one leads to another or was caused by another.	To explain why an event or a series of events occurred. To tell about the result of or reason for an event or series of events.	How being over-weight contributes to poor health. The beneficial effects of fasting.
Comparing and Contrasting Ideas	Organizes the description of two things so that their differences or similarities are empha-sized.	To describe one thing by reference to another. To argue that one thing is better (or worse) than another.	How marriage today is different from marriage in my grandparents' generation. How life is like a football game.
Order of Importance of Ideas	Organizes the ideas in a paragraph from most to least important (or vice versa).	To give reasons for holding a certain opinion. To persuade a reader to accept your opinion.	Why people should or should not be forced to retire at age 65. The benefits of a single life.

The exercise below will give you practice recognizing and choosing organizational patterns.

Part A. Read the following paragraphs. List at least three of the signal words used in each paragraph and tell the pattern of organization the paragraph uses.

1.   You remind me of your mother. Both of you are tall. Like her, you have brown eyes. She is quiet; you are similarly reserved. Whenever she gets angry, she leaves the room. Likewise, you tend to walk off when you are mad. On the other hand, you like to read but she doesn't. Unlike you, she is athletic. In contrast with the way you drive, she is a careful driver. You are hot-tempered, but she is more of a slow burner.

     (a) Three signal words: _____

     (b) Pattern of organization: _____

2.   I like my neighborhood. On both sides of my house are brownstones. On the right I have three elderly sisters as neighbors. On the left are two young families. Across the street is a grocery store. Only a block away is a movie theater.

     (a) Three signal words: _____

     (b) Pattern of organization: _____

3.   The sky darkened suddenly. Then pounding rain began. Right after that lightning started to flash and thunder to crash. Immediately the couple changed their minds. At first they had planned to drive to the lake for a picnic. Once the storm started, they pulled off the road.

     (a) Three signal words: _____

     (b) Pattern of organization: _____

4.   Several things about my boss annoy me. For example, a little thing that bothers me is that she asks me to bring her coffee every morning. She also sends me out to buy her lunch. Worse yet, she sometimes sends me to the cleaners with a load of her dirty clothes. Furthermore, she acts as though I were a criminal when I come in five minutes late. Besides that, she complains whenever I call in sick. Worst of all, she refuses to give me a raise.

     (a) Three signal words: _____

     (b) Pattern of organization: _____

5.   One person's bad mood can affect a whole group. Last week our teacher walked into class with a frown on his face and called roll as if he wanted to bite off our heads. Consequently, we were all tense. Because our teacher seemed angry with us, we all started feeling angry with him. The reason we usually enjoy his class so much is that our teacher is ordinarily upbeat. As a result, when he is down, we all feel down.

(a) Three signal words: _____

(b) Pattern of organization: _____

Part B. The following five paragraph topics are presented with a set of brainstorm notes for each. Based on the topic and the notes, tell what the writer's purpose seems to be. Then tell the pattern of organization you think would be best for each set of ideas.

1. Topic: Describe a photograph that shows you as you really are.
    Brainstorm Notes:

    taken in my backyard   grass around me uncut
    house paint peeling   railroad cap on my head
    squinting in the sun   smile on my face
    sweaty tee-shirt   model train under my hand

(a) Writer's purpose: _____

(b) Best pattern of organization: _____

2. Topic: Explain how asthma and hay fever are similar yet different.
    Brainstorm Notes:

    both affect breathing   uncomfortable medicines
    allergy   asthma—wheezing
    hard to breathe out   coughing
    relax   hay fever—sneezing
    watery eyes   get away from plants

(a) Writer's purpose: _____

(b) Best pattern of organization: _____

3. Topic: Tell how you get ready for job interviews.
    Brainstorm Notes:

    write down questions   press clothes
    arrange transportation   set alarm
    go to bed early   get up early
    good breakfast   collect paper and pen
    leave home in plenty of time

(a) Writer's purpose: _____

(b) Best pattern of organization: _____

4. <u>Topic</u>: Explain how cars contribute to acid rain.

Brainstorm Notes:

cars give off gases   gases pollute air
bad air gets full of water   water droplets condense around particles
polluted rain falls   harms forests, lakes, coast

(a) Writer's purpose: _____

(b) Best pattern of organization: _____

5. <u>Topic</u>: Argue for or against allowing gambling in your town.

Brainstorm Notes:

no more small-town feeling   too much traffic
need bigger sewage system   big brassy casino buildings
might attract criminals   might attract mobsters looking for jobs
might attract pickpockets   encourages bad habits
gamblers who can't stop   kids want to win money instead of earn it

(a) Writer's purpose: _____

(b) Best pattern of organization: _____

Check your answers on page 257.

Lesson 42

Practicing Paragraph Writing

Whenever you learn a new skill, it is important to practice that skill over and over. The exercise at the end of this lesson offers a number of topics you can write about to practice the skill of paragraph writing. Because of your study in this unit, you should have the skills you need to be able to write a good paragraph. You know what to do at each step in the writing process:

STEP 1: You brainstorm for ideas by

     having in mind your purpose for writing a paragraph
     using discovery questions for help in coming up with ideas
     making observations to help you write vivid descriptions
     jotting notes or clustering your ideas.

STEP 2: You organize your brainstormed ideas by

     crossing out brainstormed ideas you decide not to use
     choosing an organization pattern for presenting your ideas
     deciding on the order in which to present your ideas within the organization pattern you choose.

mapping the jotted notes or numbering the clustered notes you brainstormed.

STEP 3: You write your paragraph by

drafting a few possible topic sentences for your paragraph and choosing one to use

drafting the supporting sentences for your paragraph based on your mapped or clustered notes

drafting the final sentence for your paragraph.

STEP 4: You revise your paragraph by

checking that your topic sentence is effective, that your supporting sentences all support the topic sentence, and that your final sentence sums up the paragraph well

adding, removing, changing, or rearranging words—especially signal and connecting words—and sentences to make your writing clear and vivid

correcting run-on sentences, sentence fragments, and misplaced adjective phrases and sentence parts.

STEP 5: You edit your paragraph by

correcting all errors in spelling, grammar, and punctuation—especially mistakes in subject-verb agreement, in your choice of verb tenses, and in your choice of pronouns.

Now it's time to take up your pen or sit at your computer keyboard and practice putting it all together.

EXERCISE 42

Over the next several weeks, write paragraphs of about 50 words on any of the following topics, on other topics assigned to you, or on topics you think of yourself.

1. Tell about the best (or worst) day you had this week.

2. Explain how you make your favorite snack.

3. Describe your favorite pair of shoes.

4. Describe the parts of a check (or money order).

5. Explain how the heat affects you.

6. Explain why you are voting for a particular candidate.

7. Describe how colds and flu are alike (or different).

8. Describe how dogs and cats are alike (or different).

9. Argue for (or against) joining a union.

10. Argue for (or against) lie-detector tests.

11. Tell what to do when a family member with a drug or alcohol problem won't seek help.

12. Tell how to prepare for a test.

13. Tell how to deal with spouse abuse or child abuse.

14. Tell how you relax when you're stressed out.

15. Describe your bedroom closet.

16. Describe a friend of yours.

17. Describe a snowstorm.

18. Describe something you bought but shouldn't have.

19. Explain why people drop out of high school.

20. Explain why it is important to have a high school diploma.

21. Explain why exercise makes you feel better (or worse).

22. Explain what happens when you lose your temper.

23. Explain why people get the Monday-morning (or after-vacation) blues.

24. Explain how a household appliance works.

25. Explain how you were named.

26. Tell about the most useful information you have learned from TV.

27. Tell what the differences (or similarities) are between a lie and a fib.

28. Tell what the differences (or similarities) are between a divorce and a death.

29. Tell what the differences (or similarities) are between two super heroes.

30. Tell what the differences (or similarities) are between two bosses you've had.

31. Tell what the differences (or similarities) are between yourself and your parent.

32. Tell how you waste money or use money wisely.

33. Argue that all high school graduates in this country should (or should not) have to pass the same test.

34. Tell what you like (or dislike) about TV programming.

35. Tell why you're for (or against) adoption by single parents.

36. Tell why you're for (or against) banning smoking in public places.

37. Give the reasons you are for (or against) a position taken by the president recently.

38. Explain why you like (or don't like) computers.

39. Explain why you like (or don't like) your job.

40. Tell what items you cut out of your budget when you need to save money.

41. Explain why you are (or are not) going to make an effort to vote in the next presidential election.

42. Explain why drivers should be exempted from high car insurance payments if they haven't had any accidents.

43. Argue for (or against) the worth of your hometown.

44. Argue for (or against) staying single.

45. Give reasons for learning to speak Russian, Japanese, Arabic, or some other language not your own.

46. Explain what you like or don't like about daylight savings time.

47. Tell how to get by in a drinking crowd without drinking.

48. Argue for the one TV program you would watch if you had to choose only one.

49. Tell why you would or would not sell an organ such as a kidney or liver from a deceased relative's body in order to save another person's life.

50. Explain why there are outbreaks of large-scale violence in the United States.

51. Tell where you would rather go in your spare time—to a shopping mall, to a museum, to a movie, or to some other place. Explain why.

52. Tell what should be done to stop the spread of AIDS.

53. Explain what to do about the problem of people who drink and drive.

54. Explain why you favor (or don't favor) a federal law prohibiting the hire of permanent replacements for striking workers.

55. Tell why you think the United States should (or should not) remove pennies from circulation.

56. Tell why you think it would (or would not) be a good idea for students to attend school year-round rather than for only nine months of each year.

57. Tell why you think executions should (or should not) be shown on television.

58. Explain whether or not you would consider suicide if you were ill with a terminal disease.

59. Tell whether or not you think it is right for a woman to act as a surrogate mother by bearing a child for another couple.

60. If your employer needed to cut expenses to stay in business, tell whether you think he or she should cut everyone's pay by 10 percent or lay off a tenth of the work force.

There are no entries for this exercise in the answer section.

Posttest

The following Posttest is similar to the Writing Skills Test of the GED. Taking it will help you find out what lessons in this book you should review.

Part 1 of the Posttest consists of 31 multiple-choice items based on paragraphs with numbered sentences. Most of the sentences contain errors or need improvement. After reading each set of paragraphs, answer the multiple-choice items that follow. Some items refer to sentences that are correct as written, but most refer to sentences that need to be corrected or made clearer.

Part 2 of the Posttest asks you to write a short paragraph on an assigned topic.

Work through the Posttest at a pace that is comfortable for you. When you have finished, check your answers. After that, refer to the chart on page 222. It shows which lessons in this book contain instruction and practice related to each of the items in the Posttest.

WRITING SKILLS POSTTEST

Part 1

<u>Directions</u>: Choose the <u>one best answer</u> to each item.

<u>Items 1 through 10</u> refer to the following paragraphs.

(1) What are the population of the United States now? (2) Every ten years the U.S. Bureau of the Census tries to answer this question. (3) Counting every man woman and child in the United States is a huge undertaking. (4) For each census researchers now use computers to tally and analyze the raw data. (5) The raw data are gathered both by mail and by canvassers. (6) When clerks did the tallying and analysis by hand. (7) Then it took several years. (8) With today's computers those tasks took approximately one year. (9) Census results are important because they affect many big decisions. (10) Politics, as well as business, are influenced by census results. (11) For example, the amount of federal dollars a state receives often depends on their population. (12) The birth rate is falling a crib manufacturer will probably cut back on production.

1. Sentence 1: **What <u>are</u> the population of the United States now?**

   Which of the following is the best way to write the underlined portion of this sentence? If you think the original is the best way, choose option (1).

   (1) are
   (2) is
   (3) was
   (4) were
   (5) will be

2. Sentence 2: **Every ten years the U.S. Bureau of the Census tries to answer this question.**

   What correction should be made to this sentence?

   (1) change the spelling of <u>tries</u> to <u>trys</u>
   (2) change <u>tries</u> to <u>try</u>
   (3) change <u>tries</u> to <u>tried</u>
   (4) change <u>tries</u> to <u>trying</u>
   (5) no correction is necessary

3. Sentence 3: **Counting every <u>man woman and child</u> in the United States is a huge undertaking.**

   Which of the following is the best way to write the underlined portion of this sentence? If you think the original is the best way, choose option (1).

   (1) man woman and child
   (2) man woman and child,
   (3) man, woman and child
   (4) man, woman, and child,
   (5) man, woman, and child

4. Sentences 4 and 5: **For each census researchers now use computers to tally and analyze the raw data. The raw data are gathered both by mail and by canvassers.**

   The most effective combination of sentences 4 and 5 would include which of the following groups of words?

   (1) data that are
   (2) data both by mail
   (3) data and to gather
   (4) data since they are
   (5) data being that they are

5. Sentences 6 and 7: **When clerks did the tallying and analysis by <u>hand. Then it</u> took several years.**

   Which of the following is the best way to write the underlined portion of these sentences? If you think the original is the best way, choose option (1).

   (1) hand. Then it
   (2) hand it
   (3) hand, it
   (4) hand, then it
   (5) hand, so it

6. Sentence 8: **With today's computers those tasks <u>took</u> approximately one year.**

   Which of the following is the best way to write the underlined portion of this sentence? If you think the original is the best way, choose option (1).

   (1) took
   (2) taken
   (3) take
   (4) takes
   (5) will take

7. Sentence 9: **Census results are <u>important because they</u> affect many big decisions.**

   Which of the following is the best way to write the underlined portion of this sentence? If you think the original is the best way, choose option (1).

   (1) important because they
   (2) important, because they
   (3) important. They
   (4) important even though they
   (5) important unless they

8. Sentence 10: **<u>Politics, as well as business, are</u> influenced by census results.**

   Which of the following is the best way to write the underlined portion of this sentence? If you think the original is the best way, choose option (1).

   (1) Politics, as well as business, are
   (2) Politics, as well as business, is
   (3) Politics as well as business are
   (4) Politics as well as business is
   (5) Politics and business is

9. Sentence 11: **For example, the amount of federal dollars a state receives often depends on their population.**

   What correction should be made to this sentence?

   (1) change <u>receives</u> to <u>receive</u>
   (2) change <u>depends</u> to <u>depend</u>
   (3) change <u>their</u> to <u>they're</u>
   (4) change <u>their</u> to <u>its</u>
   (5) no correction is necessary

10. Sentence 12: **<u>The birth rate is falling a crib</u> manufacturer will probably cut back on production.**

    Which of the following is the best way to write the underlined portion of this sentence? If you think the original is the best way, choose option (1).

    (1) The birth rate is falling a crib
    (2) The birth rate is falling. A crib
    (3) The birth rate is falling, and a crib
    (4) The birth rate is falling if a crib
    (5) If the birth rate is falling, a crib

Items 11 through 21 refer to the following paragraphs.

(1) Theft from and of cars drive the cost of everyone's car insurance premiums up. (2) Because insurance companies must pay to replace stolen articles and cars, they must be increased. (3) You can take steps that will reduce theft. (4) You can take steps that will keep car insurance costs down. (5) Everyone should always park his or her car in a well lighted area at night.

(6) Whenever you left your car, close the windows and lock the doors. (7) If you install a car security system, it will pay for itself in no time. (8) Packages may tempt thieves in plain view, so you should put them in the trunk when you leave your car. (9) Your tape deck or radio are safest hidden in or removed from your car. (10) Don't store important papers in your cars pockets or glove compartment.

(11) These guidelines have protected my friends and I from thieves many times in the past. (12) Because we use the guidelines, we have probably helped a little to keep insurance premiums from rising.

11. Sentence 1: **Theft from and of cars drive the cost of everyone's car insurance premiums up.**

What correction should be made to this sentence?

(1) insert a comma between of and cars
(2) change cars to car's
(3) change cars to cars'
(4) change drive to drives
(5) change everyone's to everyones'

12. Sentence 2: **Because insurance companies must pay to replace stolen articles and cars, they must be increased.**

Which of the following is the best way to write the underlined portion of this sentence? If you think the original is the best way, choose option (1).

(1) they
(2) it
(3) insurance companies
(4) stolen articles and cars
(5) everyone's premiums

13. Sentences 3 and 4: **You can take steps that will reduce theft. You can take steps that will keep car insurance costs down.**

The most effective combination of sentences 3 and 4 would include which of the following groups of words?

(1) and keep
(2) but keep
(3) unless you keep
(4) if you keep
(5) which you keep

14. Sentence 5: **Everyone should always park his or her car in a well lighted area at night.**

Which of the following is the best way to write the underlined portion of this sentence? If you think the original is the best way, choose option (1).

(1) Everyone should always park his or her car
(2) Everyone should always park their car
(3) Everyone should always park their cars
(4) You should always park your car
(5) Drivers should always park their cars

15. Sentence 6: **Whenever you left your car, close the windows and lock the doors.**

What correction should be made to this sentence?

(1) replace <u>Whenever</u> with <u>After</u>
(2) change <u>left</u> to <u>leave</u>
(3) remove the comma after <u>car</u>
(4) insert a comma after <u>windows</u>
(5) no correction is necessary

16. Sentence 7: **If you install a car security system, it will pay for itself in no time.**

What correction should be made to this sentence?

(1) change <u>install</u> to <u>installed</u>
(2) remove the comma after <u>system</u>
(3) replace <u>it</u> with <u>you</u>
(4) replace <u>itself</u> with <u>themselves</u>
(5) no correction is necessary

17. Sentence 8: <u>**Packages may tempt thieves in plain view, so**</u> **you should put them in the trunk when you leave your car.**

Which of the following is the best way to write the underlined portion of this sentence? If you think the original is the best way, choose option (1).

(1) Packages may tempt thieves in plain view, so
(2) Packages may tempt thieves in plain view so
(3) Packages may tempt thieves in plain view unless
(4) Packages in plain view may tempt thieves, so
(5) Packages tempts thieves in plain view, so

18. Sentence 9: **Your tape deck or radio are safest hidden in or removed from your car.**

What correction should be made to this sentence?

(1) replace <u>Your</u> with <u>Anyone's</u>
(2) insert a comma after <u>radio</u>
(3) change <u>are</u> to <u>is</u>
(4) insert a comma after <u>in</u>
(5) no correction is necessary

19. Sentence 10: **Don't store important papers in your cars pockets or glove compartment.**

What correction should be made to this sentence?

(1) change the spelling of <u>Don't</u> to <u>Do'nt</u>
(2) change <u>cars</u> to <u>car's</u>
(3) change <u>cars</u> to <u>car</u>
(4) change <u>pockets</u> to <u>pockets'</u>
(5) insert a comma after <u>pockets</u>

20. Sentence 11: **These guidelines have protected my friends and I from thieves many times in the past.**

What correction should be made to this sentence?

(1) change <u>have</u> to <u>has</u>
(2) change <u>have protected</u> to <u>protect</u>
(3) change <u>I</u> to <u>me</u>
(4) change <u>I</u> to <u>myself</u>
(5) no correction is necessary

21. Sentence 12: **Because we use the <u>guidelines, we probably help</u> a little to keep insurance premiums from rising.**

Which of the following is the best way to write the underlined portion of this sentence? If you think the original is the best way, choose option (1).

(1) guidelines, we probably help
(2) guidelines we probably help
(3) guidelines, we had probably helped
(4) guidelines, we were probably helping
(5) guidelines, we probably helped

Items 22 through 31 refer to the following paragraphs.

(1) The ability to speak before groups often affects a person's success in their careers. (2) Because speaking ability aren't inborn, effective public speaking requires practice. (3) Anyone who have learned to speak in public can tell you that.

(4) You should always rehearse before you give a speech. (5) When you practice, give your speech to a mirror, deliver it to a friend or use a tape recorder. (6) If you practice on a friend, ask for criticism and suggestions.

(7) Just before you gave a speech, sing or talk to warm up your voice. (8) While you spoke, breathe with a regular rhythm. (9) Regular breathing is keeping your voice strong and your nerves calm. (10) When you are speaking, half of the battle is keeping calm.

(11) Learning to speak well in public takes time and practice. (12) The effort often pays for itself in career success.

22. **Sentence 1: The ability to speak before groups often affects a person's success in their careers.**

Which of the following is the best way to write the underlined portion of this sentence? If you think the original is the best way, choose option (1).

(1) affects a person's success in their careers
(2) affect a person's success in their careers
(3) affects a persons success in their careers
(4) affects a person's success in your career
(5) affects a person's success in his or her career

23. **Sentence 2: Because speaking ability aren't inborn, effective public speaking requires practice.**

What correction should be made to this sentence?

(1) change the spelling of aren't to are'nt
(2) change aren't to isn't
(3) remove the comma after inborn
(4) change requires to require
(5) no correction is necessary

24. **Sentence 3: Anyone who have learned to speak in public can tell you that.**

Which of the following is the best way to write the underlined portion of this sentence? If you think the original is the best way, choose option (1).

(1) Anyone who have learned
(2) Any one who have learn
(3) Anyone, who have learned
(4) Anyone who has learned
(5) Anyone who has learn

25. **Sentence 5: When you practice, give your speech to a mirror, deliver it to a friend or use a tape recorder.**

Which of the following is the best way to write the underlined portion of this sentence? If you think the original is the best way, choose option (1).

(1) friend or use a tape recorder
(2) friend, or use a tape recorder
(3) friend, or speak it into a tape recorder
(4) friend or a tape recorder
(5) friend, but use a tape recorder

26. **Sentence 6: If you practice on a friend, ask for criticism and suggestions.**

What correction should be made to this sentence?

(1) change practice to practices
(2) change practice to practiced
(3) remove the comma after friend
(4) insert a comma after criticism
(5) no correction is necessary

27. **Sentence 7: Just before you <u>gave a speech, sing or talk</u> to warm up your voice.**

Which of the following is the best way to write the underlined portion of this sentence? If you think the original is the best way, choose option (1).

(1) gave a speech, sing or talk
(2) gave a speech sing or talk
(3) gave a speech, sang, or talked,
(4) give a speech, sing or talk
(5) give a speech, sing, or talk,

28. **Sentence 8: While you spoke, breathe with a regular rhythm.**

What correction should be made to this sentence?

(1) replace <u>While</u> with <u>Even though</u>
(2) change <u>spoke</u> to <u>are speaking</u>
(3) change <u>spoke</u> to <u>have spoken</u>
(4) delete the comma after <u>spoke</u>
(5) no correction is necessary

29. **Sentence 9: Regular breathing <u>is keeping your voice strong and</u> your nerves calm.**

Which of the following is the best way to write the underlined portion of this sentence? If you think the original is the best way, choose option (1).

(1) is keeping your voice strong and
(2) is keeping your voice strong, and
(3) keeps your voice strong and
(4) keep your voice strong and
(5) kept your voice strong and

30. **Sentence 10: When you are speaking, half of the battle is keeping calm.**

What correction should be made to this sentence?

(1) change <u>are speaking</u> to <u>spoke</u>
(2) remove the comma after <u>speaking</u>
(3) change <u>is</u> to <u>are</u>
(4) change <u>is</u> to <u>was</u>
(5) no correction is necessary

31. **Sentences 11 and 12: Learning to speak well in public takes time and <u>practice. The</u> effort often pays for itself in career success.**

Which of the following is the best way to write the underlined portion of this sentence? If you think the original is the best way, choose option (1).

(1) practice. The
(2) practice, and the
(3) practice, but the
(4) practice, or the
(5) practice, so the

Part 2

<u>Directions</u>: This part of the Writing Skills Posttest is intended to see how well you write. You are asked to write a short paragraph on an assigned topic. To develop your paragraph you should take the following steps:

1. Read the topic carefully.

2. Use scratch paper to make notes about what you want to include in your paragraph.

3. Before you write your paragraph, decide how you will organize it.

4. Write your paragraph on a piece of lined paper.

5. Make changes in your paragraph that will improve it, including corrections in sentence structure, spelling, punctuation, capitalization, and usage.

TOPIC

Some situations require quick thinking. Write a paragraph of about 50 words that tells about a time you had to make a quick decision. Describe what the problem was and what you did.

Check your answer on page 257.

POSTTEST SKILLS CHART

To review the writing skills covered by the items in Part 1 of the Posttest, refer to the following lessons in this book. The answers and explanations beginning on page 257 tell which part of each lesson pertains to each item.

The skills covered by Part 2 of the Posttest are covered in Unit 2 of this book.

Chapter 1	Subject-Verb Agreement	Item Number
Lesson 1	The Two Parts of Action Sentences	All items related to Chapter 1
Lesson 2	Finding Verbs and Subjects in Action Sentences	All items related to Chapter 1
Lesson 3	Subject-Verb Agreement in Action Sentences	26
Lesson 4	Subject-Verb Agreement in Describing Sentences	23
Lesson 5	Subject-Verb Agreement with Special Subjects	24
Lesson 6	Subject-Verb Agreement with Compound Subjects	18

Answers and Explanations

In this section are the answers for the items in this book's Pretest, Exercises, GED Practices, and Posttest. For Pretest, GED Practice, and Posttest items, there are both explanations and references to the lesson or lessons that contain instruction most directly related to each item.

PRETEST (PAGE 1)

Part 1

1. **(3)** *Myself*, which is a "-self" pronoun, cannot be used in a compound subject. Instead, the subject pronoun *I* is needed. (Lesson 14: "Mistake 4," pg. 91)

2. **(4)** The subject in Sentence 2 is a compound subject. The pronouns in both parts of the subject must be subject pronouns. (Lesson 13: "Pronouns in Compound Subjects and Objects," pg. 88)

3. **(4)** The subject and verb of the first sentence part in this sentence must both be singular because *Anybody* is singular. Therefore, the verb must be *knows*. (Lesson 5: "Subjects That End in *-body*, *-one*, and *-thing*," pg. 28)

4. **(4)** In sentences and sentence parts that begin with *there*, the subject follows the verb. The subject of the second sentence part in Sentence 4 is *causes*. Because this subject is plural, its verb must also be plural. Therefore, the contraction *There's*, which means "There is," must be replaced by the words *There are* so that the verb is in the plural form. (Lesson 7: "Sentences That Begin with *There* or *Here*," pg. 34)

5. **(4)** The parts of a compound subject must have parallel structures. In this sentence, *Heart disease*, *lung disease*, and *gall-bladder disease* are parallel. Because these first three parts of the subject contain no *ing* words, the last part of the subject cannot

have one either. Therefore, the word *experiencing* has to be removed. (Lesson 18: "Using Parallel Structures in Compounds," pg. 114)

6. **(3)** The phrase *as well as anxiety* begins with words that replace *and*. There are commas before and after the phrase. It is not a part of the subject of the sentence. The subject is *Depression*. It is singular and agrees with the singular verb *keeps*. (Lesson 8: "Phrases with Words That Replace *and*," pg. 42)

7. **(5)** The parts of the compound subject, *medicines* and *drugs*, are connected by *and*. Therefore, the subject agrees with the plural verb *contribute*. (Lesson 6: "Compound Subjects with *and*," pg. 31)

8. **(4)** The parts of the compound subject, *wife* and *I*, are connected with *Neither . . . nor*. The verb *have* agrees with *I*, the closer part of the subject once its parts are in the proper order with *I* last. (Lesson 6: "Compound Subjects with *Either . . . or* and *Neither . . . nor*," pg. 32)

9. **(1)** In this reverse-order statement the singular subject *wife* agrees with the singular verb *does*. (Lesson 7: "Reverse-Order Statements," pg. 37)

10. **(2)** *Club* is singular because it names a group. Since it is the subject of the sentence (*of dieters* is an interrupting phrase), it agrees with the singular verb *helps*. (Lesson 5: "Subjects That Name Groups or Amounts," pg. 29)

11. **(2)** The present continuous tense, *I'm* (*I am*) *watching*, is used here because it tells about ongoing regular action that is interrupted by regular action that is not ongoing, *I don't* (*do not*) *eat*. (Lesson 11: "The Present Continuous Tense," pg. 65)

12. **(1)** *Electronics* is singular and agrees with *has*. (Lesson 5: "Singular Subjects That End with S," pg. 26)

13. **(4)** The singular verb *uses* agrees with its singular subject, *company*. *Customers* is not the subject; it is an object in the dependent part of the sentence. (Lesson 3: "Basic Rules for Subject-Verb Agreement," pg. 17)

14. **(5)** The pronoun *them* could refer to either *customers* or *computers* in Sentence 2. (Because it is plural, it could not refer to the singular noun *company*.) The correction uses *the computers* instead of *them* to make the meaning of Sentence 3 clear. Because *computers* is plural, it agrees with the verb *have*. (Lesson 17: "Avoiding Unclear References," pg. 102)

15. **(1)** The reverse order of the subject and verb in this question does not change how they agree. The subject *you* agrees with *Have*. (Lesson 7: "Questions," pg. 35)

16. **(1)** To agree with the pronoun *you* in Sentence 4, the first pronoun in Sentence 5 cannot shift to *anyone*. It must be *you*. (Lesson 17: "Avoiding Pronoun Shifts Within Paragraphs," pg. 100)

17. **(2)** The verbs in Sentence 5 are in the simple present tense because the sentence is about things that occur regularly. Sentence 6 continues telling about regularly occurring events, so its verb must also be in the simple present tense. Because the subject, *voice*, is singular, the correct form of the verb is *comes*. (Lesson 12: "Clues to Tense in a Paragraph," pg. 73)

18. **(4)** The pronoun in the second part of this compound sentence refers to two nouns in the first part of the sentence, *words* and *numbers*. Therefore, it must be the plural pronoun *they*, which agrees with the verb form *were*. (Lesson 16: "Pronoun Agreement with Nouns," pg. 95)

19. **(2)** The most effective combination of Sentences 8 and 9 is a complex sentence: *The computer, which controls calls made from pay phones, senses each number dialed.* Commas and the connecting word *which* are used because the sentence part it begins contains additional, not essential, information. (Lesson 20: "Using *That* and *Which*," pg. 125)

20. **(3)** Sentence 10 is a describing sentence because its verb is a form of *be*. Since it states a fact, its verb, which must be singular to agree with *the computer*, needs to be in the simple present tense. (Lesson 4: tables "Verbs Common in Describing Sentences," pg. 23, and "Patterns for Subject-Verb Agreement with *Be*," pg. 24)

21. **(2)** The words *from the computer's "voice"* form an interrupting phrase between a subject and its verb in this sentence. The plural subject *sounds* agrees with the plural verb *tell*. (Lesson 8: "Identifying Interrupting Phrases," pg. 40)

22. **(1)** The connecting word that makes the relationship between the two parts of this complex sentence clear is *After*, not *Until*. (Lesson 21: table "Connecting Words Used in Some Complex Sentences," pg. 129)

23. **(4)** The word *once* in the dependent part of this sentence indicates that its verb describes something that happened in the past. The simple past form of the irregular verb *do* is *did*. (Lesson 10: table "Some Irregular-Verb Patterns," pg. 62)

24. **(4)** An adjective phrase too far away from the noun it describes can confuse the reader. In the correction, the adjective phrase *from Martin Peterson* appears directly after *letter*, the word it describes. (Lesson 23: "Adjective Phrases," pg. 142)

25. **(3)** Sentence 2 is a run-on sentence. The best way to correct it is to split it into two separate and complete sentences. Each ends with a period. (Lesson 22: "Correcting Run-On Sentences," pg. 133)

26. **(5)** The letter in this sentence "owns" its author, so it is possessive. Since *letter* is singular, its possessive form is correct in the original sentence. (Lesson 15: table "Forming Possessive Nouns," pg. 93)

27. **(5)** Both parts of this compound sentence state facts, so both verbs must be in the simple present tense. The simple present tense of *I'm* (the contraction of *I am*) serves as a further clue to the correct tense for the verb in the second part of the sentence. (Lesson 9: "The Simple Present Tense," pg. 58; Lesson 12: "Clues to Tense in a Paragraph," pg. 73)

28. **(4)** The words *welfare lines* and *food stamps* are the two parts—connected by *and*—of the compound object of the preposition *of.* Commas are used between the parts of a compound object only when there are three or more. (Lesson 18: Spotlight on Punctuation, pg. 111)

29. **(3)** The pronouns *who, whom,* and *whose* are used to refer to one or more people. *That* and *which* should not be used to refer to people. In Sentence 6 *who* is used because it is a subject pronoun—the subject of the dependent part of the sentence. (Lesson 20: "The Uses of *That, Which, Who, Whom,* and *Whose,*" pg. 123)

30. **(2)** Sentence 7 is a run-on sentence. The best way to correct it is to rewrite it as a complex sentence using the connecting word *because,* which shows a cause-effect relationship between the two parts of the sentence. (Lesson 22: "Choosing Between a Compound and a Complex Sentence," pg. 138)

31. **(4)** The most effective combination of Sentences 8 and 9 is a compound sentence with a connecting word that shows the cause-effect relationship between their ideas. The connecting word *so* shows that the idea in Sentence 9 is an effect of the information in Sentence 8. (Lesson 19: table "Connecting Words Used in Compound Sentences," pg. 118)

32. **(3)** Sentence 10 is a sentence fragment. The best way to correct it is to combine it (as a dependent sentence part) with Sentence 11 in a complex sentence. Because the dependent part comes at the beginning of the complex sentence, it must be followed by a comma. (Lesson 22: "Correcting Sentence Fragments," pg. 135; Lesson 21: the bullet about commas in complex sentences, pg. 129)

Part 2

Following are two sample paragraphs—with comments about each—on the topic of the Pretest paragraph. The sentences in the paragraphs are numbered to make the discussion about them easier to follow. Although your paragraph will be different from either of these, you may be able to make a judgment about its strong and weak points by reference to the comments below.

(1) I am against the idea of community service for teens caught drinking. (2) Education or rehab pro-grams would be better. (3) Young people need to learn what alcohol does to your sistem. (4) They need to know what the law will *do* to them if they are caught drinking. (5) Not all kids who are arrested have a drinking problem. (6) A lot of kids who are alcoholics slip through the cracks on community service.

Comment:

This paragraph would be stronger if it had more, better-supporting sentences and clearer organization.

Sentence 1, the topic sentence, states the writer's opinion clearly. However, only Sentence 6 provides any support for the topic sentence. Sentences 2–4 state opinions about the need for education about alcohol. They are not about the topic of the paragraph—the appropriateness of community service as a penalty for underage drinking. Sentence 5 is off the topic, altogether: the paragraph is about underage drinkers, not arrested teens.

Overall the paragraph is not well organized; its ideas aren't presented in a logical order. There are no signal words to help the reader see how ideas relate to each other. There are mechanical errors in the paragraph that further weaken its effect.

(1) I do not feel that the courts should assign underage drinkers community service because the punishment doesn't fit the crime. (2) First, cleaning up parks or putting library books on shelves has nothing to do with alcohol. (3) Second, community service will not inform teen drinkers about the legal consequences of underage drinking. (4) Third, it will not teach them what alcohol does to their bodies and minds. (5) Most important, it will not force them to think about the danger they pose to themselves and others, especially if they get behind the wheel. (6) Underage drinkers should have to attend classes on alcohol.

This paragraph states a position clearly in Sentence 1, the topic sentence, and defends it well in Sentences 2–5, the supporting sentences. Sentence 6 ties up the paragraph neatly with the conclusion that underage drinkers should have to attend classes on alcohol.

Overall, the paragraph is well organized; its ideas are presented in a logical order. There are signal words to help the reader see how ideas, which are organized by order of their importance, relate to each other. There are only a few minor mechanical errors in the paragraph, which do not seriously weaken its effect.

UNIT 1: USAGE, SENTENCE STRUCTURE, AND MECHANICS

EXERCISE 1 (PAGE 13)

Part A

1. Calculators | multiply numbers quickly.
2. Liquids | evaporate fast here.
3. Solid stone walls | last for years.
4. Tourists | travel for fun.
5. Gas stoves | work for a long time.
6. Some subway trains | stop here.
7. My metal files | hold important papers.
8. Reporters | gather the news.
9. I | toss all night sometimes.
10. Some people | suffer terrible pain.

Part B

Sample answers follow. Be sure that you capitalized the first word in each of your sentences and that you ended your sentences with periods.

1. **Car horns honk a lot.**
2. **Express buses stop at that corner.**
3. **Large cargo planes roar overhead.**
4. **Loud police sirens wail all night long.**
5. **Some noisy delivery vans drop morning newspapers there.**

EXERCISE 2a (PAGE 15)

1. Monkeys **play**.
2. Some dolphins **perform**.
3. Whales **talk** to each other.
4. Some parrots **live** in cages.
5. Most apes **learn** quickly.
6. Hippopotamuses **stay** under water a lot.
7. Bats **hunt** at night.
8. Some bees **make** honey.
9. These ants **build** underground nests.
10. Many dogs **howl** like wolves.

EXERCISE 2b (PAGE 16)

Part A

1. **Monkeys play**.
2. Some **dolphins perform**.

3. **Whales** **talk** to each other.
4. Some **parrots** **live** in cages.
5. Most **apes** **learn** quickly.
6. **Hippopotamuses** **stay** under water a lot.
7. **Bats** **hunt** at night.
8. Some **bees** **make** honey.
9. These **ants** **build** underground nests.
10. Many **dogs** **howl** like wolves.

Part B

Sample answers follow. Be sure that you capitalized the first word in each of your sentences and that you ended your sentences with periods.

1. **Baseball** **fans** **cheer** loudly at games.
2. **Catchers** **stay** behind home plate.
3. **League** **teams** **play** against each other.
4. **Professional baseball** **players** **make** a lot of money.
5. **Some** **batters** **hit** home runs frequently.

EXERCISE 3a (PAGE 19)

1. **plural** (*They* can replace *Tourists*.)
2. **singular** (*He/She* can replace *This tourist*.)
3. **plural** (*They* can replace *These tourists*.)
4. **plural** (*They* can replace *Most tourists*.)
5. **plural** (*They* can replace *Many people*.)
6. **singular** (*It* can replace *The underground train*.)
7. **plural** (*They* can replace *Bells*.)
8. **plural** (*They* can replace *Many animals*.)
9. **plural** (*They* can replace *Most reptiles*.)
10. **singular** (*It* can replace *The zoo*.)

EXERCISE 3b (PAGE 20)

1. A bailiff **acts** as an usher in a courtroom.
2. Guards **bring** the defendant in and out.
3. One lawyer **pleads** for the defendant.
4. **No correction is necessary.**
5. **No correction is necessary.**
6. **No correction is necessary.**
7. Jurors **listen** to the case.
8. **No correction is necessary.**
9. A stenographer **writes** down the whole conversation.
10. **No correction is necessary.**

EXERCISE 3c (PAGE 21)

Part A

1. I **hate** my job now.
2. **No correction is necessary**.
3. Some workers **bark** back at him.
4. **No correction is necessary**.
5. **No correction is necessary**.
6. **No correction is necessary**.
7. Other bosses **behave** better.
8. Your boss **treats** people right.
9. She **mixes** with the workers easily.
10. **No correction is necessary**.

Part B

Sample answers follow. The verbs in your sentences should follow the patterns described in parentheses.

1. I **go to work** every day. (verb with **no** ending)
2. You **talk too much** every day. (verb with **no** ending)
3. The guards **change posts** every day. (verb with **no** ending)
4. My doctor **draws blood** every day. (verb with **s** ending)
5. Her daughter **cooks her food** every day. (verb with **s** ending)
6. We **relax here after work** every day. (verb with **no** ending)
7. It **rains** every day. (verb with **s** ending)
8. My friend **talks to me** every day. (verb with **s** ending)
9. Her co-workers **give her a hard time** every day. (verb with **no** ending)
10. Their friends **call them** every day. (verb with **no** ending)

EXERCISE 4a (PAGE 24)

1. One **dream is** a repeating dream.
2. **I seem** anxious at the beginning.
3. **My wife** looks upset.
4. **We feel** frightened by something.
5. The **air becomes** hot and steamy.
6. **It smells** awful.
7. Loud **noises grow** unbearable.

8. **Objects appear** evil.
9. My **heart sounds** like a bass drum.
10. **I am** suddenly awake with a scream.

EXERCISE 4b (PAGE 25)

Part A

1. I **feel** comfortable there.
2. The older people **seem** unchanged.
3. **No correction is necessary**.
4. Our wooden house **appears** a little worn.
5. **No correction is necessary**.
6. The air **smells** sweet with pine in those mountains.
7. **No correction is necessary**.
8. Spring water **tastes** silver there.
9. I **am** at home in the mountains.
10. It **stays** the same there through all my changing.

Part B

Sample answers follow. The verbs in your sentences should be the same as the verbs in the samples.

1. We **are** dissatisfied.
2. My youngest child **becomes** tired easily.
3. The union president **feels** angry.
4. You **look** terrific.
5. The mayor **is** a sound leader.
6. She **seems** happy.
7. This kitchen **smells** dirty.
8. I **am** a student.
9. The guitar **sounds** romantic.
10. The meals here **taste** good.

EXERCISE 5a (PAGE 27)

1. Some exercises **have** benefits for the heart.
2. Aerobics **is** a popular type of such exercise.
3. **No correction is necessary**.
4. Mumps **causes** swelling in glands near the ears.
5. Politics **makes** strange bedfellows.
6. Some games **have** a lot of rules.
7. **No correction is necessary**.
8. **No correction is necessary**.

9. Gymnastics **is** my favorite sport.

10. Mathematics **has** many uses in my job.

EXERCISE 5b (PAGE 28)

1. Tweezers **remove** splinters easily most of the time.

2. His trousers **clash** with his shirt.

3. **No correction is necessary**.

4. Your pants **have** a hole in the seat.

5. The scissors **are** part of my pocket knife.

6. **No correction is necessary**.

7. These jeans **are** too tight for you.

8. **No correction is necessary**.

9. Those sunglasses **block** out too much light.

10. Some shorts **are** just plain too short.

EXERCISE 5c (PAGE 29)

1. **No correction is necessary**.

2. Everything **costs** something.

3. Someone **has** an income in every household.

4. **No correction is necessary**.

5. Everybody **benefits** from taxes.

EXERCISE 5d (PAGE 30)

Part A

1. **No correction is necessary**.

2. Three years **is** a long time to wait.

3. The audience **seems** angry at the comedian.

4. The committee **watches** its spending closely.

5. A hundred dollars **is** not enough for rent.

6. **No correction is necessary**.

7. My class **has** an excellent teacher.

8. Two tablespoons **is** a lot of hot sauce.

9. **No correction is necessary**.

10. Twenty-six miles **is** the length of the marathon.

Part B

Sample answers follow. The verbs in your sentences should be the same as the verbs in the samples.

1. Molasses **looks** like thick motor oil.

2. Your shorts **have** a hole in them.

3. Five hundred dollars **pays** my rent.

4. The rock group **plays** every night.

5. No one **is** at home.

6. These swimming trunks **cost** quite a lot of money.

7. One hundred yards **is** the length of a football field.

8. My class **likes** coffee breaks.

9. Chest colds **last** a week.

10. My scissors **work** well enough.

EXERCISE 6a (PAGE 31)

1. The main library **runs** a literacy program.

2. **No correction is necessary**.

3. Julio, Katie, and Ron **help** them with reading and math.

4. Clarence **needs** a lot of help right now.

5. He and a co-worker **are** in line for the same promotion.

6. People **take** written tests for promotions at their company.

7. Clarence **has** difficulty with reading.

8. Mathematics **is** also not easy for him.

9. **No correction is necessary**.

10. Clarence **needs** high test scores.

EXERCISE 6b (PAGE 32)

Part A

1. **No correction is necessary**.

2. Either Julio or Ron **helps** Lonny with math on Tuesday evenings.

3. Lonny **helps** his wife with the same math at home later in the week.

4. Either Lonny or Latisha **helps** their children with their homework.

5. Their son and daughters **respect** their parents for that.

6. Lonny and Latisha **show** interest in their children that way.

7. **No correction is necessary**.

8. Neither their son nor their daughters **have** much trouble with schoolwork.

9. **No correction is necessary**.

10. Neither Lonny nor Latisha **is** comfortable with that.

Part B

1. **Julio and Ron tutor people at the library.**

2. **Either my son or I drive Julio to the library.**

3. **Clarence, Lonny, and Latisha benefit from their help.**

4. **Either Julio or Ron helps Lonny with math each night.**

5. **Neither reading nor mathematics is easy for Clarence.**

6. **Lonny and Latisha are better at math now.**

7. **Either their son or their daughters need attention tonight.**

8. **Their son and their daughters admire Lonny and Latisha.**

9. **Clarence, Lonny, and Latisha have new skills.**

10. **Neither Julio nor Ron takes the credit.**

EXERCISE 7a (PAGE 35)

1. There **are** several interesting new models.

2. There **are** some new features.

3. Here **is** my favorite design.

4. **No correction is necessary**.

5. There **are** the old floor models.

6. Here **is** the sale price for the floor models.

7. Here **comes** a hopeful couple.

8. There **is** their old wreck.

9. **No correction is necessary**.

10. There **goes** one old floor model.

EXERCISE 7b (PAGE 36)

1. What **goes** with corned beef?

2. **No correction is necessary**.

3. Where **are** your tools?

4. Why **are** the pliers broken?

5. How **are** Junior and his sister?

6. **No correction is necessary**.

7. Who **repairs** computers?

8. **No correction is necessary**.

9. **Is** everyone at the office?

10. What **are** your new hours?

EXERCISE 7c (PAGE 37)

Part A

1. Over there **are** more trees.

2. **No correction is necessary**.

3. On the top shelf **are** the cereals.

4. Below them **is** the sugar.

5. **No correction is necessary**.

6. In December **come** the shortest days.

7. In June **are** the longest days.

8. **No correction is necessary**.

9. Under the car seat **are** the ice scrapers.

10. **No correction is necessary**.

Part B

Sample answers follow. The subjects in your sentences should be like those described in parentheses.

1. There are **no right answers**. (**plural** subject)

2. Here comes **my eldest son**. (**singular** subject)

3. When are **church services**? (**plural** subject)

4. How is **your father**? (**singular** subject)

5. Where are **my slippers**? (**plural** subject)

Part C

Sample answers follow. The verbs in your sentences should be the same as the verbs in the samples.

1. In the closet **are** my shirts, pants, and sweaters.

2. Who **takes** care of him?

3. How **are** John and Sylvia?

4. During the morning rush hour **is** the heaviest traffic.

5. Under the bed **is** the most dust.

EXERCISE 8a (PAGE 40)

1. The short man near the windows **carries** a lot of money around.

2. **No correction is necessary**.

3. Several stories around town **cast** suspicion on them.

4. One tale about some bad debts **curls** my hair.

5. The debtors in the story **use** wheel chairs now.

6. Anyone with any brains **stays** away from Shorty.

7. **No correction is necessary**.

8. Everybody within miles **respects** him.

9. People without power **are** his clients.

10. Anyone with problems **gets** Poppy's ear.

EXERCISE 8b (PAGE 41)

1. Two pans of sliced turkey **are** in the oven.

2. Those pots of water **have** salt in them.

3. **No correction is necessary**.

4. A bowl of carrots **adds** more color.

5. A large pot of greens **is** a must.

6. Two pounds of cranberries **makes** enough sauce.

7. **No correction is necessary**.

8. A mound of potatoes **satisfies** him.

9. That batch of cookies **looks** fattening.

10. The loaves of bread **are** still warm.

EXERCISE 8c (PAGE 43)

1. A job, as well as a career, **appeals** to me now.

2. **No correction is necessary**.

3. My hopes, together with my fears, **make** me nervous.

4. My children, together with my husband, **encourage** my hopes.

5. Jobs and careers **are** the focus of this fair.

6. A hospital, together with the junior college, **sponsors** an interesting program.

7. A paid job, along with free classes, **is** available at the hospital.

8. **No correction is necessary**.

9. Neither long hours nor hard work **scares** me.

10. The application and a pen **are** in front of me.

EXERCISE 8d (PAGE 45)

Part A

1. All of the tenants **know** about the situation.

2. Part of our current problem **comes** from a lack of tenant unity.

3. All of the tenants **have** strong opinions.

4. Most of the people **favor** some kind of action.

5. **No correction is necessary**.

6. None of our plans **are** foolproof.

7. Some of the older tenants **are** afraid.

8. All of those tenants **need** courage.

9. Most of the solution **rests** in their hands.

10. Most of my patience **is** gone.

Part B

Sample answers follow. The verbs in your sentences should be the same as the verbs in the samples.

1. The man on crutches **walks** slowly.

2. Those cartons of milk **are** sour.

3. The salary, along with the benefits, **suits** me fine.

4. All of the strikers **need** money.

5. Some of those movies **have** too much violence.

Part C

Sample answers follow. The verbs in your sentences should be the same as the verbs in the samples.

1. A child with problems **goes** to school here.

2. Some bags of groceries **weigh** too much for me.

3. The boss over that department **supports** our petition.

4. Some of the others **are** against it.

5. Most of us **make** up our own minds.

Part D

Sample answers follow. The verbs in your sentences should be the same as the verbs in the samples.

1. This child, along with my children, **goes** to that high school.

2. Those bags, in addition to his books, **weigh** him down.

3. The boss, together with the others, **works** late every day.

4. My sister, as well as her family, **is** here for a visit.

5. Her friend, as well as my sister, **seems** tired.

Part 1

1. **(2)** Neither *There* nor *concerns* is the subject of the sentence; *list* is. *List* is singular and agrees with the singular verb *is*. (Lesson 7: "Sentences That Begin with *There* or *Here*," pg. 34; Lesson 8: "Identifying Interrupting Phrases," pg. 40)

2. **(4)** In this reverse-order statement the plural subject *concerns* agrees with the plural verb *are*. (Lesson 7: "Reverse-Order Statements," pg. 37)

3. **(5)** The subject *public* is singular because it names a group. It agrees with the singular verb *demands*. (Lesson 5: "Subjects That Name Groups or Amounts," pg. 29)

4. **(2)** The subject in the question is *What*; it agrees with the singular verb *makes*. (Lesson 7: the last paragraph under "Questions," pg. 36)

5. **(1)** In this question, the singular subject *seal* comes after the verb. It agrees with the singular verb *Is*. (Lesson 7: "Questions," pg. 35)

6. **(2)** The parts of the compound subject, *wrappings* and *seal*, are connected with *Either . . . or*. The singular verb *provides* agrees with *seal*, the closer part of the subject. (Lesson 6: "Compound Subjects with *Either . . . or* and *Neither . . . nor*," pg. 32)

7. **(3)** When a sentence tells something, it ends with a period. (Lesson 1: Spotlight on Capitalization and Punctuation, pg. 13)

8. **(3)** The parts of the compound subject, *food* and *items*, are connected by *and*. The subject agrees with the plural verb *come*. (Lesson 6: "Compound Subjects with *and*," pg. 31)

9. **(4)** When a sentence asks something, it ends with a question mark. (Lesson 7: Spotlight on Capitalization and Punctuation, pg. 37)

10. **(3)** *On each shelf* is an interrupting phrase between the plural subject *labels* and the plural verb *have*. (Lesson 8: "Finding Subjects Separated from Verbs," pg. 39; "Identifying Interrupting Phrases," pg. 40)

11. **(2)** *There* is not the subject of the sentence; *labels* is. *Labels* is plural and agrees with the plural verb *are*. (Lesson 7: "Sentences That Begin with *There* or *Here*," pg. 34)

12. **(3)** *Of rice* is an interrupting phrase between the plural subject *boxes* and the plural verb *cost*. (Lesson 8: "Finding Subjects Separated from Verbs," pg. 39; "Identifying Interrupting Phrases," pg. 40)

13. **(1)** The phrase *along with most other foods* begins with words that replace *and*. There are commas before and after the phrase. The subject of the sentence is *rice*. It is singular and agrees with the singular verb *costs*. (Lesson 8: "Phrases with Words That Replace *and*," pg. 42; Spotlight on Punctuation, pg. 43)

14. **(1)** In this sentence, the subject *Some* is plural because it refers to *prices*, which is plural. *Some* agrees with the plural verb *are*. (Lesson 8: "Words That Can Be Singular or Plural as Subjects," pg. 44)

15. **(2)** Even though it has a plural meaning, *Everyone* is singular and agrees with the singular verb *has*. (Lesson 5: "Subjects That End in *-body*, *-one*, and *-thing*," pg. 28)

16. **(1)** *Two hours* is singular because it names an amount. It agrees with the singular verb *is*. (Lesson 5: "Subjects That Name Groups or Amounts," pg. 29)

17. **(3)** When three or more parts of a subject are connected by *and*, commas go between the parts. The last comma goes before the *and*. (Lesson 6: Spotlight on Capitalization, Punctuation, and Style, pg. 32)

18. **(3)** *Electronics* is singular and agrees with the singular verb *is*. (Lesson 5: "Singular Subjects That End with *S*," pg. 26)

19. **(3)** When a word ends with *ch*, add an *e* before an *s* ending. (Lesson 3: Spotlight on Spelling, pg. 21)

20. **(4)** When three or more parts of a subject are connected by *and*, commas go between the parts. The last comma goes before the *and*. When *I* is part of a list of people in a sentence, it usually comes last. (Lesson 6: Spotlight on Capitalization, Punctuation, and Style, pg. 32)

Part 2

Paragraph 1 (3 errors)

Dogs guard property well. They barks⁽²¹⁾ warn-

ings. My collie watch⁽²²⁾es my house. ⁽²³⁾She barks at

strangers.

Comment:

21. *They* is plural and agrees with a verb with
no *s* ending. (Lesson 3: "Basic Rules for
Subject-Verb Agreement," pg. 17)

22. *Collie* is singular and agrees with a verb with
an *s* ending. Because *watch* ends with *ch*,
add an *e* before the *s* ending. (Lesson 3:
"Basic Rules for Subject-Verb Agreement,"
pg. 17; "Test to Decide If a Subject Is
Singular or Plural," pg. 18; Spotlight on
Spelling, pg. 21)

23. The first word in a sentence is capitalized.
(Lesson 1: Spotlight on Capitalization and
Punctuation, pg. 13)

Paragraph 2 (3 errors)

Natural events causes⁽²⁴⁾ homelessness some-

times. Erupting volcanoes destroy whole towns.

E⁽²⁵⁾earthquakes wreck houses and large apartment

buildings. People is⁽²⁶⁾are homeless because of wind,

rain, and fire.

Comment:

24. *Events* is plural and agrees with a verb with
no *s* ending. (Lesson 3: "Basic Rules for Subject-Verb Agreement," pg. 17; "Test to Decide
If a Subject Is Singular or Plural," pg. 18)

25. The first word in a sentence is capitalized.
(Lesson 1: Spotlight on Capitalization and
Punctuation, pg. 13)

26. *People* is plural and agrees with *are*. (Lesson
4: "Editing for Subject-Verb Agreement in
Describing Sentences," pg. 24)

Paragraph 3 (6 errors)

The problem of poverty worry⁽²⁷⁾ies many people in

this city. It is easy to see here. A lot of people

begs⁽²⁸⁾ on our streets. Some of them looks⁽²⁹⁾ simply

poor. There is⁽³⁰⁾are others with mental illnesses.

Either drugs or alcohol control⁽³¹⁾s the lives of many

others. Is a solution possible in our society⁽³²⁾?

Comment:

27. *Of poverty* is an interrupting phrase between
the singular subject *problem* and the singular verb *worries*. To add an *s* ending when a
letter other than a vowel comes before the *y*
at the end of the word, change the *y* to *i* and
add *es*. (Lesson 8: "Finding Subjects
Separated from Verbs," pg. 39; "Identifying
Interrupting Phrases," pg. 40; Spotlight on
Spelling, pg. 40)

28. In this sentence the subject *lot* is plural
because it refers to *people*, which is plural.
Lot agrees with the plural verb *beg*. (Lesson
8: "Words That Can Be Singular or Plural as
Subjects," pg. 44)

29. In this sentence the subject *Some* is plural
because it refers to *them*, which is plural.
Some agrees with the plural verb *look*.
(Lesson 8: "Words That Can Be Singular or
Plural as Subjects," pg. 44)

30. *There* is not the subject of the sentence; *others* is. *Others* is plural and agrees with the
plural verb *are*. (Lesson 7: "Sentences That
Begin with *There* or *Here*," pg. 34)

31. The parts of the compound subject, *drugs*
and *alcohol*, are connected with *Either . . . or*.
The singular verb *controls* agrees with *alco-
hol*, the closer part of the subject. (Lesson 6:
"Compound Subjects with *Either . . . or* and
Neither . . . nor," pg. 32)

32. When a sentence asks something, it ends
with a question mark. (Lesson 7: Spotlight
on Capitalization and Punctuation, pg. 37)

Paragraph 4 (6 errors)

I look(33)s a lot better now. Aerobics keep(34)s me

slim. My group exercises a half hour every day.

Thirty minutes (35)is are a good workout. We wear(36)s

sweat pants. The sweat pants (37)are is loose for easy

movement. Everybody (38)has have a lot of fun in our

group.

Comment:

33. Even though *I* is singular, it agrees with *look*, a verb with no *s* ending. (Lesson 3: "Agreement with *I* and *You*," pg. 20)

34. *Aerobics* is singular and agrees with the singular verb *keeps*. (Lesson 5: "Singular Subjects That End with S," pg. 26)

35. *Thirty minutes* is singular because it names an amount. It agrees with the singular verb *is*. (Lesson 5: "Subjects That Name Groups or Amounts," pg. 29)

36. *We* is plural and agrees with the plural verb *wear*. (Lesson 3: "Basic Rules for Subject-Verb Agreement," pg. 17; "Agreement with *I* and *You*," pg. 20)

37. *Pants* is a plural subject that names one thing. It agrees with the plural verb *are*. (Lesson 5: "Plural Subjects That Name One Thing," pg. 27)

38. Even though it has a plural meaning, *Everybody* is singular and agrees with the singular verb *has*. (Lesson 5: "Subjects That End in *-body*, *-one*, and *-thing*," pg. 28)

Paragraph 5 (7 errors)

Nobody grow(39)s as fast as my teenage son. He

stretch(40)es an inch taller every two months. His

clothes and food cost(41)s a fortune. Either a bigger

shirt or longer pants cost(42)s me $20 or more every

month. My food bill is higher by $10 a week

now. Sixty dollars eat(43)s quite a hole in my month-

ly income(44). My money stretch(45)es less than my son.

Comment:

39. *Nobody* is singular and agrees with the singular verb *grows*. (Lesson 5: "Subjects That End in *-body*, *-one*, and *-thing*," pg. 28)

40. When a word ends with *ch*, add an *e* before an *s* ending. (Lesson 3: Spotlight on Spelling, pg. 21)

41. The parts of the compound subject, *clothes* and *food*, are connected by *and*. The subject agrees with the plural verb *cost*. (Lesson 6: "Compound Subjects with *and*," pg. 31)

42. The parts of the compound subject, *shirt* and *pants*, are connected with *Either . . . or*. The plural verb *cost* agrees with *pants*, the closer part of the subject. (Lesson 6: "Compound Subjects with *Either . . . or* and *Neither . . . nor*," pg. 32)

43. *Sixty dollars* is singular because it names an amount. It agrees with the singular verb *eats*. (Lesson 5: "Subjects That Name Groups or Amounts," pg. 29)

44. When a sentence tells something, it ends with a period. (Lesson 1: Spotlight on Capitalization and Punctuation, pg. 13)

45. *Money* is singular and agrees with a verb with an *s* ending. Because *stretch* ends with *ch*, add an *e* before the *s* ending. (Lesson 3: "Basic Rules for Subject-Verb Agreement," pg. 17; "A Test to Decide If a Subject Is Singular or Plural," pg. 18; Spotlight on Spelling, pg. 21)

Paragraph 6 (10 errors)

(46)T This city (47)is are more dangerous now than before.

The television news report(48)s violence all the time.

In the newspaper (49)are is more crime stories. There (50)are is

murders every day. What cause(51)s all this crime(52)? Is

there an answer? You and I live(53)s in fear. Nobody

enjoy(54)s that. We need a solution(55).

Comment:

46. The first word in a sentence is capitalized. (Lesson 1: Spotlight on Capitalization and Punctuation, pg. 13)

47. *City* is singular and agrees with *is*. (Lesson 4: "Editing for Subject-Verb Agreement in Describing Sentences," pg. 24)

48. *News* is singular and agrees with the singular verb *reports*. (Lesson 5: "Singular Subjects That End with *S*," pg. 26)

49. In this reverse-order statement, the plural subject *stories* agrees with the plural verb *are*. (Lesson 7: "Reverse-Order Statements," pg. 37)

50. *There* is not the subject of the sentence; *murders* is. *Murders* is plural and agrees with the plural verb *are*. (Lesson 7: "Sentences That Begin with *There* or *Here*," pg. 34)

51. The subject in the question is *What*; it agrees with the singular verb *causes*. (Lesson 7: the last paragraph under "Questions," pg 36)

52. When a sentence asks something, it ends with a question mark. (Lesson 7: Spotlight on Capitalization and Punctuation, pg. 37)

53. The parts of the compound subject, *You* and *I*, are connected by *and*. The subject agrees with the plural verb *live*. (Lesson 6: "Compound Subjects with *and*," pg. 31)

54. *Nobody* is singular and agrees with the singular verb *enjoys*. (Lesson 5: "Subjects That End in *-body*, *-one*, and *-thing*," pg. 28)

55. When a sentence tells something, it ends with a period. (Lesson 1: Spotlight on Capitalization and Punctuation, pg. 13)

EXERCISE 9a (PAGE 57)

1. He <u>requests</u> an extension every year. **Present**

2. His brother Fred <u>is</u> just the opposite. **Present**

3. He <u>sets</u> aside nine hours in early February. **Present**

4. He <u>sorts</u> his canceled checks. **Present**

5. He <u>gets</u> special tax forms from the library. **Present**

6. Then he <u>calls</u> a toll-free number for tax advice. **Present**

7. Last winter Fred <u>mailed</u> his taxes on February 12. **Past**

8. His refund <u>arrived</u> on March 7. **Past**

9. He <u>will begin</u> even earlier next year. **Future**

10. Next year Vaughn <u>will give</u> Fred's method a try. **Future**

EXERCISE 9b (PAGE 59)

Part A

1. These phony schools <u>offer</u> worthless degrees. **Present: d**

2. My friend Wesley <u>passed</u> the GED Tests last year. **Past: b**

3. Soon afterward he <u>learned</u> about a certain college from a well-known magazine. **Past: b**

4. The magazine <u>printed</u> an advertisement for the school every week. **Past: c**

5. It <u>painted</u> a glowing picture of the school. **Past: a**

6. Unfortunately Wesley <u>swallowed</u> the bait. **Past: b**

7. He <u>wasted</u> a lot of time and money on worthless courses. **Past: b**

8. He <u>will</u> never <u>make</u> the same mistake again. **Future: i**

9. Now he <u>examines</u> advertisements and catalogs very carefully. **Present: f**

10. He <u>applies</u> only to schools with accreditation. **Present: f**

11. He <u>knows</u> the ropes now. **Present: e**

12. This afternoon he <u>will write</u> to the American Council on Accreditation about the Hayes School. **Future: h**

Part B

1. **referred**
2. **stressed**
3. **works**
4. **prevents**
5. **provide**
6. **receive**
7. **experience**
8. **uses**
9. **will fill**
10. **will take**

Part C

Sample answers follow. (Your sentences do not have to tell a story the way the sample sentences do.) In Sentences 1, 4, 9, and 10 your verbs should be in the same tense as those in the samples. In the other sentences, you may have correctly used tenses different from those in the samples.

1. Before choosing a clinic now, I always **ask about the doctors there**.
2. My family **needs a doctor with sound knowledge about diabetes**.
3. We **want good care**.
4. My last doctor always **seemed in a rush**.
5. The waits in her office **wearied me**.
6. She **preferred payment right away**.
7. Our medical costs **exceeded our ability to pay**.
8. I **resented the doctor's impatience, the waiting, and the bills**.
9. A year ago I **looked for a different clinic**.
10. In the future, I **will avoid clinics like that**.

EXERCISE 10 (PAGE 63)

Part A

1. **took**
2. **put**
3. **had**
4. **fed**
5. **stood**
6. **got**
7. **bought**
8. **brought**
9. **lost**
10. **went**

Part B

1. He **did** it for himself and his family.
2. **No correction is necessary**.
3. He even **brought** his review books with him on concert tours.
4. Last week he **sang** a song about it.
5. **No correction is necessary**.
6. The diploma **gave** him more self-respect.
7. He **began** every concert with that song.
8. I **saw** his show on my birthday.
9. My friend and I **went** together.
10. She **bought** the tickets as a surprise.

Part C

Sample answers follow. The verbs in your sentences should be the same as the verbs in the samples.

1. I **drank too much last year**.
2. You **wrote notes to yourself last year**.
3. We **heard raccoons in the trash last year**.
4. They **blew the whistle on us last year**.
5. You **knew more about this last year than now**.
6. My father **spoke little last year**.
7. Politicians **spent a lot of money on campaigns last year**.
8. Computers **ran many business operations last year**.
9. A burglar **stole my television last year**.
10. My parents **were here last year**.

EXERCISE 11a (PAGE 67)

Part A

1. **was working**
2. **was talking**
3. **were finding**
4. **was going**
5. **were trying**

Part B

1. **am taking**
2. **is showing**
3. **are learning**
4. **am making**
5. **am planning**

Part C

1. **will be taking**
2. **will be staying**
3. **will be earning**
4. **will be complaining**
5. **will be griping**

EXERCISE 11b (PAGE 70)

Part A

1. **had worked**
2. **had promoted**
3. **had regained**
4. **had become**
5. **had been**

Part B

1. **have taken**
2. **have learned**
3. **have held**
4. **has continued**
5. **have received**

Part C

1. **will have taken**
2. **will have worked**
3. **will have made**
4. **will have complained**
5. **will have gone**

EXERCISE 12 (PAGE 75)

Part A

1. Right now I**'m looking** at this envelope. I frequently **receive** mail like this. A message usually **appears** on the envelope. The messages often **sound** like ones from the government.

2. My writing **is** usually full of spelling mistakes. So, I **bought** a new computer program last week. The program **corrects** spelling mistakes. I**'m loading** the program into my computer right now. In the future my writing **won't have** spelling mistakes.

3. My brother **changes** his mind about his future career frequently. Once he **told** me he would become a chef. For a while he **was talking** about being a stunt man. Then he **decided** acting was for him. Last year he **announced** that he wanted to get his trucking license. Now he**'s talking** about a career with the police department. He**'s filling** out his application right this minute.

4. When Janice went to the consumer discount store last night, it **was holding** its grand opening. She**'d driven** around the parking lot for fifteen minutes before she found a space. Shoppers were swarming into the new store like ants, and satisfied customers **were leaving** with carts piled high. Some store employees were passing out flyers, and others **were giving** balloons to the children. Janice **found** some good bargains inside. She**'ll shop** there often in the future.

Part B

Dear Gabby,

A short time ago ~~I'm~~ **I was** buying groceries. I ~~find~~ **found** an empty wallet under some grapes in the fruit section. I ~~was turning~~ **turned** the wallet in at the checkout counter.

A little later a woman ~~is claiming~~ **claimed** the wallet. The clerk point**ed** me out to her. She marche**d** up to me: "You ~~steal~~ **stole** my twenty-dollar bill! ~~I~~ **I'll** tell the police about this!"

Right now ~~I waited~~ **I'm waiting** for an apology. I ~~will not~~ **won't** return~~ing~~ lost items in the future.

Do you think my decision is right?

Unjustly Accused

GED PRACTICE 2 (page 77)

Part 1

1. **(2)** The time words *last fall* tell you that the action in the sentence happened in the past. The past continuous is used here because the bike ride continued (a) for a while and (b) until the bike flew into the ditch. (Lesson 11: "The Past Continuous Tense," pg. 65; Lesson 12: table "Tenses: Uses and Related Time Words," pg. 71; and Lesson 10: table "Some Irregular-Verb Patterns," on subject agreement with *was* and *were*, pg. 62)

2. **(1)** The action described in Sentence 2 (*looked*) took place while the action in Sentence 1 (*was taking*) continued. The action in Sentence 1 was a past action, so the action in Sentence 2 must also be in a past tense. Only one option (Choice 1) is in a past tense. (Lesson 9: "The Simple Past Tense," pg. 57; Lesson 11: "The Past Continuous Tense," pg. 65; and Lesson 12: "Clues to Tense in a Paragraph," pg. 73)

3. **(1)** The combined sentence has a compound subject. Because Sentences 3 and 4 continue the story that began with Sentences 1 and 2, the verb in the combined sentence must be in a past tense. Since the event described in the combined sentence is a one-time past event, the simple past tense is needed. (Lesson 10: table "Some Irregular-Verb Patterns," pg. 62; Lesson 9: "The Simple Past Tense," pg. 57; and Lesson 12: "Clues to Tense in a Paragraph," pg. 73)

4. **(4)** The context lets you know that Sentence 5 tells about a one-time past event. The verb, which is irregular, must be in the simple past tense. (Lesson 10: table "Some Irregular-Verb Patterns," pg. 62; Lesson 9: "The Simple Past Tense," pg. 57; and Lesson 12: "Clues to Tense in a Paragraph," pg. 73)

5. **(5)** The context lets you know that Sentence 6 tells about a one-time past event. The verb, which is irregular, must be in the simple past tense. (Lesson 10: table "Some Irregular-Verb Patterns," pg. 62; Lesson 9: "The Simple Past Tense," pg. 57; and Lesson 12: "Clues to Tense in a Paragraph," pg. 73)

6. **(2)** The context lets you know that Sentence 8 tells about a fact that was true. The verb, which is irregular, must be in the simple past tense. (Lesson 10: table "Some Irregular-Verb Patterns," pg. 62; Lesson 9: "The Simple Past Tense," pg. 57; and Lesson 12: "Clues to Tense in a Paragraph," pg. 73)

7. **(4)** The context lets you know that Sentence 10 tells about a fact that was (probably) true. The verb must be in the simple past tense. (Lesson 9: "The Simple Past Tense," pg. 57; Lesson 12: "Clues to Tense in a Paragraph," pg. 73)

8. **(1)** The words *each year* and the use of the simple present tense in Sentence 11 let you know that it states a fact. With Sentence 11, the tense in the passage shifts from past to present. Sentence 12 states a fact, so its verb must be in the simple present tense. The subject of Sentence 12 is *Most*. It refers to *deaths*, so the verb must be plural. (Lesson 8: "Words That Can Be Singular or Plural as Subjects," pg. 44; Lesson 9: "The Simple Present Tense," pg. 58; and Lesson 12: table "Tenses: Uses and Related Time Words," pg. 71)

9. **(4)** Sentence 13 states a fact, so its verb must be in the simple present tense. The subject of Sentence 13, *helmets*, is plural, so the verb must be plural. (Lesson 3: "Basic Rules for Subject-Verb Agreement," pg. 17; Lesson 9: "The Simple Present Tense," pg. 58; and Lesson 12: "Clues to Tense in a Paragraph," pg. 73)

10. **(1)** With Sentence 15, the tense in the passage shifts from present to future. The word *someday* is a clue that the simple future tense is needed. (Lesson 9: "The Simple Future Tense," pg. 59; Lesson 12: table "Tenses: Uses and Related Time Words," pg. 71)

Part 2

⑪ L

Leonardo and ⑫ T Tanisha are Melida's children.

has ⑬ t

Since they were born, Melida spends every

Mother's Day with them.

Last Mother's Day the sister and brother

brought ⑭

bring their mother breakfast in bed. On her tray

were ⑮   , ⑯

was scrambled eggs, cereal, fresh fruit and

⑰ was

toast. There were also a vase of ragweed and

⑱ a

dandelions. The children give their mother a

⑲

cake, a bracelet, and a plant. Melida smiled and

⑳ ed

thanks them.

Next Mother's Day Leonardo and Tanisha

will take ㉑

took Melida to a city park for a picnic.

Comment:

11. The first word in a sentence is capitalized. (Lesson 1: Spotlight on Capitalization and Punctuation, pg. 13)

12. A person's name is capitalized. (Lesson 6: Spotlight on Capitalization, Punctuation, and Style, pg. 32)

13. The present perfect tense is used. The words *Since they were born* let you know that the sentence tells about an action that began in the past and continues in the present. (Lesson 11: "The Present Perfect Tense," pg. 68)

14. The words *Last Mother's Day* begin the second paragraph. They let you know that the first sentence in that paragraph has to be in a past tense. Since the sentence tells about a one-time past event, the verb, which is irregular, must be in the simple past tense. (Lesson 10: table "Some Irregular-Verb Patterns," pg. 62; Lesson 9: "The Simple Past Tense," pg. 57; and Lesson 12: "Clues to Tense: Time Words," pg. 71)

15. In this sentence the compound subject—*scrambled eggs*, *cereal*, and *fresh fruit*—follows the verb. Because the subject is plural, the verb must be plural. The context lets you know that the sentence tells about a fact that was true, so the verb, which is irregular, must be in the simple past tense. (Lesson 7: "Reverse-Order Statements," pg. 37; Lesson 10: table "Some Irregular-Verb Patterns," pg. 62; Lesson 9: "The Simple Past Tense," pg. 57; and Lesson 12: "Clues to Tense in a Paragraph," pg. 73)

16. When three or more parts of a subject are connected by *and*, commas go between the parts. The last comma goes before the *and*. (Lesson 6: Spotlight on Capitalization, Punctuation, and Style, pg. 32)

17. In this sentence the subject, *vase*, follows the verb. Because the subject is singular, the verb must be singular. The context lets you know that the sentence tells about a fact that was true, so the verb, which is irregular, must be in the simple past tense. (Lesson 7: "Sentences That Begin with *There* or *Here*," pg. 34; Lesson 10: table "Some Irregular-Verb Patterns," pg. 62; Lesson 9: "The Simple Past Tense," pg. 57; and Lesson 12: "Clues to Tense in a Paragraph," pg. 73)

18. The context lets you know that the sentence tells about a one-time past event. The verb, which is irregular, must be in the simple past tense. (Lesson 10: table "Some Irregular-Verb Patterns," pg. 62; Lesson 9: "The Simple Past Tense," pg. 57; and Lesson 12: "Clues to Tense in a Paragraph," pg. 73)

19. When a sentence tells something, it ends with a period. (Lesson 1: Spotlight on Capitalization and Punctuation, pg. 13)

20. The context lets you know that the sentence tells about a one-time past event. The verb must be in the simple past tense. (Lesson 9: "The Simple Past Tense," pg. 57; Lesson 12: "Clues to Tense in a Paragraph," pg. 73)

21. The words *Next Mother's Day* begin the last sentence in the passage. They let you know

that it has to be in a future tense. Since the sentence tells about an event that will happen, the verb must be in the simple future tense. (Lesson 9: "The Simple Future Tense," pg. 59; Lesson 12: "Clues to Tense: Time Words," pg. 71)

EXERCISE 13a (PAGE 84)

1. **George** dropped out of high school.
2. The young **man** soon realized his mistake.
3. Many **jobs** in law enforcement require a high school diploma.
4. That **door** slammed in his face.
5. The **U.S. Navy** accepted him.
6. **George** took correspondence courses.
7. His **GED** paved the way to college.
8. George's **wife** left high school at 15.
9. **Ellen** returned for her GED ten years later.
10. Her **sister-in-law** convinced her.

EXERCISE 13b (PAGE 85)

1. **They** told Maria about the class.
2. **She** passed the test.
3. **We** got high scores on each of the tests.
4. **They** hope to get associates degrees.
5. **We** want to get jobs in the state capital.

EXERCISE 13c (PAGE 87)

1. **No correction is necessary**.
2. Manuel told **me**.
3. I phoned **him**.
4. **No correction is necessary**.
5. You informed **us**.
6. We told **him**.
7. We avoided **her**.
8. Brian notified **her**.
9. Sylvia advised **them**.
10. Secrets bother **us**.
11. I would recommend this career counselor to **you**.
12. She helped **me**.
13. Without **her** I probably would never have known.
14. She helped all of **us** get back on the right track.

15. She gives good advice, so don't ignore **her**.

1. **No correction is necessary**.
2. The baby is **she**.
3. **No correction is necessary**.
4. It was **she** behind Grandpa.
5. It was **he** taking the pictures.

EXERCISE 13e (PAGE 89)

1. Luanne sometimes helps Jeff and **me** make the baked goods downstairs.
2. You will be working upstairs with **her** and Dick.
3. Sometimes Luanne brings a coffee cake down to Jeff and **me** in the morning.
4. **She** and I will soon be assigned to the front office.
5. Dick and **I** share an office.
6. **No correction is necessary**.
7. There have been clashes between Daphne and **him** about the radio in their office.
8. **No correction is necessary**.
9. The noise is too distracting for **him**.
10. Next Friday night Daphne and **he** are going bowling with Luanne and **me**.

EXERCISE 14 (PAGE 91)

Part A

1. Sitting alone, Arlene is humming a little tune to **herself**.
2. Dan arrived by **himself**.
3. **No correction is necessary**.
4. **No correction is necessary**.
5. My husband and **I** are fidgeting.
6. We are trying to keep our nervousness to **ourselves**.
7. I have to remind **myself** that I survived last week.
8. When I found **myself** up in front of all those people, I nearly fainted.
9. The curtain seems to be opening by **itself**.
10. Those kids should be proud of **themselves**.

Part B

Sample answers follow. The pronouns you used to replace the words in dark type should be the same as the pronouns in the samples.

1. This check is **for him**.
2. **She** is very nosy.
3. She plays checkers with **him**.
4. The other tenants rely on **us**.
5. Tina bought **herself** a watchdog.
6. Some of the best ideas come from Kathy and **him**.
7. Next month **they** are organizing a block party.
8. **We** have volunteered to help.
9. The wall is wet behind **it**.
10. The pigeons make a racket under **them**.

Part C

1. **She'll** need to wear safety glasses.
2. **He'll** buy a power saw.
3. **I'm** going to wear earplugs.
4. **It's** a noisy tool.
5. **You've** plugged in an extension cord.

EXERCISE 15a (PAGE 93)

1. **mouse's**
2. **boys'**
3. **doors'**
4. **window's**
5. **men's**
6. **women's**
7. **rugs'**
8. **chair's**
9. **people's**
10. **tooth's**

EXERCISE 15b (PAGE 95)

1. The rug and **its** owner are over there.
2. **No correction is necessary**.
3. For twenty cents it can be **yours**.
4. **No correction is necessary**.
5. **Its** handle is a bit chipped.
6. **Her** sunglasses were a bargain.
7. **Their** lenses are a little scratched.
8. The sneakers in the box of free items are **mine**.

9. **Their** laces are missing.

10. Where are **our** customers?

11. We received these notices in **our** mail.

12. My sister entered the sweepstakes and now the stereo is **hers**.

13. **No correction is necessary**.

14. **No correction is necessary**.

15. I wish those prizes were mine and not **theirs**.

EXERCISE 16a (PAGE 96)

Part A

1. **his**
2. **his**
3. **its**
4. **their**
5. **their**
6. **she was**
7. **they**
8. **their**
9. **he**
10. **it**

Part B

1. I watch the news, but I find **it** disturbing.

2. The team almost lost **its** chance.

3. He does gymnastics because he enjoys **it**.

4. The audience showed **its** appreciation by clapping.

5. **No correction is necessary**.

6. Her father enjoyed politics, and she enjoys **it** too.

7. Those scissors need **their** blades sharpened.

8. The FBI headquarters closed **its** doors.

9. My family is going to have **its** reunion this summer.

10. Athletics has **its** place in the school day.

EXERCISE 16b (PAGE 99)

Part A

1. Anybody can improve **his or her** diet.

2. Most of these fruits offer vitamins, but **they** can be high in calories.

3. **No correction is necessary**.

4. Some of those canned fruits owe **their** sweetness to added sugar.

5. **No correction is necessary**.

6. Several of these vegetables lose **their** vitamins when peeled.

7. Some of those vegetables contain harmful chemicals in **their** peels.

8. Many like **their** food fried.

9. When most is fried, **it becomes** oily.

10. All of these vegetables keep more of **their** vitamins if cooked quickly in a little water.

Part B

1. **its**
2. **it**
3. **they**
4. **it**
5. **their**
6. **them**
7. **its**
8. **them**
9. **his or her**
10. **they**

EXERCISE 17a (PAGE 100)

1. She also used alcohol because **she** felt less shy after a drink or two.

2. I worried about **her** because I couldn't tell what she would do next.

3. I hoped she'd never mix alcohol with other drugs because **she** could die.

4. Now she wants to stop, but **she is** addicted after years of drinking.

5. Her family wants to help, and **it is** looking for a good treatment center.

EXERCISE 17b (PAGE 101)

1. (a) Someone may be trying to break his or her drug habit. **He or she** can receive one or more kinds of treatment.

   (b) **People** may be trying to break **their** drug **habits**. They can receive one or more kinds of treatment.

2. (a) A person may recognize the problems caused by his or her drug abuse. **He or she** can go to a clinic where doctors can help **him or her** get off drugs.

   (b) **People** may recognize the problems caused by **their** drug abuse. **They** can go to **clinics** where doctors can help **them** get off drugs.

3. (a) Another person may discover that he or she abuses drugs. **He or she** can go to a mental health center where counselors will help **him or her** deal with **his or her** problems.

(b) **People** may discover that **they abuse** drugs. They can go to a mental health center where counselors will help them deal with their problems.

4. (a) A child can develop a drug problem. **He or she** sometimes **lives** in **a** halfway **house** where **he or she gets** treatment.

(b) **Children** can develop drug **problems**. They sometimes live in halfway houses where they get treatment.

5. (a) For someone to get help, he or she must recognize a problem. To get well, **he or she** must want to change.

(b) For **people** to get help, **they** must recognize a problem. To get well, **they** must want to change.

EXERCISE 17c (PAGE 103)

1. When too much hair goes down the drain, **the hair** can cause a problem.

2. If you must wash your hair in the sink, clean **the sink** well afterward.

3. Wipe the hair out of the sink and throw **the hair** away.

4. Hair is clogging our sink, and **we can't** use the sink.

5. Gail's daughter is studying to be a plumber, and she likes **plumbing** very much.

6. Gail told Josephine to go to **Gail's** room.

7. In a shopping bag Josephine found a box; **the box** contained a special powder.

8. When Josephine found the box in the bag, she looked at the bottom of **the box**.

9. The label said to keep the powder out of children's reach, so **the powder** must be strong.

10. She poured the powder down the drain, and thirty minutes later **the drain** started working.

GED PRACTICE 3 (PAGE 104)

Part 1

1. **(2)** The friends belong to Bernard. Since Bernard is one male, the correct possessive pronoun is *his*, not *their*. (Lesson 16: "Pronoun Agreement with Nouns," pg. 95; Lesson 15: table "How Possessive Pronouns Are Formed," pg. 94)

2. **(4)** The sentence begins with the pronoun *They*. The possessive pronoun *their*, not *your*, must be used to avoid a pronoun shift within the sentence. (Lesson 17: "Avoiding Pronoun Shifts Within Sentences," pg. 100)

3. **(5)** The sentence describes a one-time event in the past, so *paid* is correctly in the simple past tense. *Pay* is an irregular verb; its past tense form is spelled correctly in the sentence. (Lesson 10: table "Some Irregular-Verb Patterns," pg. 62)

4. **(3)** The rewritten sentence would say *She gave them vocational interest questionnaires*. The three friends receive the action in that sentence, so the object pronoun *them* is correct. (Lesson 13: "Pronouns as Objects," pg. 86)

5. **(3)** The context tells you that the forms were for the three friends. The forms' questions, therefore, were about Bernard's, Jose's, and Anton's abilities. The plural possessive pronoun that refers to the three friends, *their*, not *your*, must be used to avoid a pronoun shift within the paragraph. (Lesson 17: "Avoiding Pronoun Shifts Within Paragraphs," pg. 100)

6. **(2)** In this sentence the subject, *questions*, follows the verb. Because the subject is plural, the verb must be plural. The context lets you know that the sentence tells about a fact that was true, so the verb, which is irregular, must be in the simple past tense. (Lesson 7: "Sentences That Begin with *There* or *Here*," pg. 34; Lesson 10: table "Some Irregular-Verb Patterns," pg. 62)

7. **(3)** Since the plural possessive pronoun that refers to two people stands alone, it must be *theirs*. (Lesson 15: "Possessive Pronouns," pg. 94)

8. **(3)** Both Sentences 8 and 9 state facts. Sentence 9 must be in the simple present tense just as Sentence 8 is. The correct subject pronoun for Sentence 9 is *He* because it refers to Jose. To agree with the subject, the verb must be *is*—or *isn't* in a contraction with *not*. (Lesson 12: table "Commonly Used Verb Contractions," pg. 74)

9. **(3)** Because the sentence tells about a one-time past event, the verb, which is irregular, must be in the simple past tense. Anton receives the action in the sentence, so the object pronoun *him* is correct. (Lesson 9: "The Simple Past Tense," pg. 57; Lesson 10: table "Some Irregular-Verb Patterns," pg. 62; and Lesson 13: "Pronouns as Objects," pg. 86)

10. **(1)** The sentence describes an action (or the lack of an action) that began in the past and continues in the present, so the verb must be in the present perfect tense. The word *yet* is another clue to the correct tense. Since the subject, *Anton*, is singular, the verb must be *has learned*—or *hasn't learned* in a contraction with *not*. (Lesson 11: "The Present Perfect Tense," pg. 68; Lesson 12: table "Tenses: Uses and Related Time Words," pg. 71)

11. **(5)** The verb in the sentence, *provided*, describes a one-time past event, so it is correctly in the simple past tense. The pronoun that refers to Anton (one male) follows a preposition, so it is correctly the object pronoun *him*. (Lesson 13: "Pronouns as Objects," pg. 86)

12. **(4)** The pronoun after the verb *followed* refers to what was followed, *the directions*. Since *directions* is plural, the plural object pronoun *them* is correct. (Lesson 16: "Pronoun Agreement with Nouns," pg. 95)

13. **(4)** The pronoun that shows possession of *forms* refers to *No one*. Since the possessive pronoun refers to a pronoun that is singular and itself refers only to the three men, it must be *his*. Because *No one* and *his* are singular, *form* must also be singular. (Lesson 16: Spotlight on Agreement with Pronouns That End with *-body* or *-one*, pg. 98)

14. **(4)** *Hisself* is not a word. Since this "-self" pronoun must agree with *Each man* and *his*, the correct form is *himself*. (Lesson 14: "Mistake 1," pg. 90)

15. **(5)** The sentence includes the pronouns *them* and *their*. The possessive pronoun

their, not *our*, must be used to avoid a pronoun shift within the sentence. (Lesson 17: "Avoiding Pronoun Shifts Within Sentences," pg. 100)

Part 2

⑯ *worked*
Michael McVane is working at Finest Boat

⑰,
Company's main plant for over twenty-four

⑱
years. He or she worked at the shipyard as a

pipe fitter and later as a pipe shop superinten-

dent. He died of cancer at age 58 on September

⑲ *the cancer*
23, 1992. Breathing asbestos caused it.

⑳ *me*
This letter is from my children and myself. We

㉑ ㉒ *your*
wants to know why you're company didn't pro-

㉓ *its*
tect it's employees from asbestos. Those in

㉔ ㉕ *themselves It's* ㉖
charge cares only about theirselves. Its a

㉗ *took* ㉘ ㉙ *us*
shame. Yous taken him away from we. Everyone

㉚ *s*
know that you are responsible.

Comment:

16. Because Michael McVane is dead, his employment at the Finest Boat Company was in the past. Therefore the verb in the first sentence must be in the simple past tense, *worked*. (Lesson 9: "The Simple Past Tense," pg. 57)

17. The Finest Boat Company owns the main plant. To show that, the possessive form of the singular noun *Company's* should be used. (Lesson 15: table "Forming Possessive Nouns," pg. 93)

18. One use of the subject pronoun *He or she* is to refer to a person when his or her sex is not known. Here the pronoun that begins this sentence refers to Michael McVane, so *He* should be used. (Lesson 16: Spotlight on Agreement with Pronouns That End with *-body* or *-one*, pg. 98)

19. In this sentence it is not clear what *it* refers to. It could refer to Michael McVane's death or to cancer. For clarity, it is better to use *the cancer*. (Lesson 17: "Avoiding Unclear References," pg. 102)

20. The words that follow *from* in this sentence are a compound object. It is incorrect to use a "-self" pronoun in a compound. In this case, the object pronoun *me* should be used. (Lesson 14: "Mistake 4," pg. 91)

21. The subject of this simple-present-tense sentence, *We*, is plural, so the verb must be plural—*want*. (Lesson 3: "Basic Rules for Subject-Verb Agreement," pg. 17)

22. *You're* means "You are," but this word is meant to show possession. It should be the possessive pronoun *Your*. (Lesson 15: table "How Possessive Pronouns Are Formed," pg. 94)

23. *It's* means "It is," but this word is meant to show possession. It should be the possessive pronoun *Its*. (Lesson 15: table "How Possessive Pronouns Are Formed," pg. 94)

24. The subject of this simple-present-tense sentence, *Those*, is plural. The phrase *in charge* separates it from the verb, which must be plural—*care*. (Lesson 8: "Identifying Interrupting Phrases," pg. 40)

25. *Theirselves* is not a word. Since this "-selves" pronoun must agree with *Those*, the correct form is *themselves*. (Lesson 14: "Mistake 3," pg. 90)

26. The first word in this sentence means *It is*, so it must be spelled with an apostrophe. (Lesson 12: table "Commonly Used Verb Contractions," pg. 74)

27. *Yous* is not a word. The plural form of the subject pronoun is *you*. (Lesson 13: table "Subject and Object Pronouns" and the paragraph below it, pg. 87)

28. This sentence describes a one-time past event, so its irregular verb must be in the simple past tense—*took*. (Lesson 10: table "Some Irregular-Verb Patterns," pg. 62)

29. Any pronoun that follows a preposition must be an object pronoun. In this case *us* is used because it follows *from*. (Lesson 13: "Pronouns as Objects," pg. 86)

30. The subject of this simple-present-tense sentence, *Everyone*, is singular, so the verb must be singular—*knows*. (Lesson 5: "Subjects That End in *-body*, *-one*, and *-thing*," pg. 28)

EXERCISE 18a (PAGE 110)

1. **Many parents and children take part in the program.**

2. **Several mothers and fathers are completing their high school educations.**

3. **Karen and Justina earned their high school degrees after four months.**

4. **All of the parents and children are learning new skills.**

5. **Most of the parents and children get library cards.**

6. **Mason Sr. and Mason Jr. like doing their homework.**

7. **Mason Sr. and Milagros are single parents.**

8. **Mason Sr. and Milagros don't want their children to think it's OK to quit school.**

9. **Mason Sr. and Milagros learn how to help their sons do homework.**

10. **Several libraries and a women's support group are sponsors of the literacy program.**

EXERCISE 18b (PAGE 112)

1. **She bought few steaks and chops.**

2. **I ate a lot of corn, salad, and coleslaw.**

3. **We had some pretzels, chips, and carrot sticks.**

4. **I bought two drinks, a burger, and two hot dogs.**

5. **We visited my mean cousin, my grumpy grandmother, and my spoiled nephew.**

6. **We played a little volleyball, softball, and football.**

7. **The children lost my volleyball, softball, and football.**

8. **My husband had too much sun, soda, and cake.**

9. **We picked some blackberries, raspberries, and blueberries.**

10. **I got a bee sting, a sunburn, and a scratch.**

EXERCISE 18c (PAGE 113)

1. **Suki rides an exercise bike and uses a treadmill.**

2. **Ross quit swimming and started jogging.**

3. **Warm up lightly and stretch slowly before a workout.**

4. **Ronald plays basketball at lunch time and runs after work.**

5. **One day while jogging he became exhausted and felt dizzy.**

6. **His doctor examined him and suggested indoor exercise.**

7. **Yesterday the secretaries left for lunch early and arrived at the rink ten minutes later.**

8. **By skating every lunch hour they burn up calories and save money.**

9. **After dinner Georgina shoots baskets and jumps rope.**

10. **She gets thirsty and stops for a sip of water now and then.**

EXERCISE 18d (PAGE 115)

Part A

1. She felt both disappointed and **relieved** when she didn't get the job as business office clerk.

2. She tells me her hopes, her dreams, and **her fears**.

3. Accepting money, making out receipts, and **helping** people fill out papers are not tasks she wants.

4. She is kind, patient, and **shy**.

5. **The pay**, the duties, and the hours of a medical records clerk are more up her alley.

6. She noticed a job listing, **requested** an application, and completed it.

7. I know that she will like the job and **be** good at it.

8. A medical records clerk must be good at both filing and **typing**.

9. Filing and **typing** don't interest Imogene.

10. She likes to meet people, **to answer** questions, and to help others.

Part B

1. **Ellen, Francine, and Shirley had no money.**

2. **Francine drove to the bank, dropped Shirley off at the door, and parked the car in the lot.**

3. **Shirley pressed, pulled, and twisted the door handle.**

4. **She scratched her head, raised her eyebrows, and looked at her watch calendar.**

5. **The bank closed an hour ago and won't open again until Monday.**

(Notice that the tenses of the verbs in this sentence are different because the actions do not happen at the same time. The first verb is in the simple past tense, and the second is in the simple future tense)

6. **She could call a friend and borrow some money.**

7. **She pulled out her wallet, her change purse, and her checkbook.**

8. **She found her bank card, put it in the slot, typed in her code, and requested some cash.**

9. **The bank's computer received, read, and acted on her message.**

10. **The computer pushed the bills through an opening, returned her card through another opening, and ejected her receipt through a third opening.**

EXERCISE 19 (PAGE 118)

Part A

1. **She will enjoy using the register, but she may not like bagging.**

2. **No correction is necessary.**

3. **She slides the item over a small window, and a laser beam reads the bar code.**

4. **No comma**: Computers can read the name and price of the item.

5. **No comma**: She will not have to deduct coupons or food stamps.

6. **No comma**: Weighing vegetables and approving checks are handled by the computer.

7. **No comma**: She or the customer puts the groceries into bags.

8. **No correction is necessary.**

9. **No comma**: Computers also keep track of popular items and sold-out stock.

10. **No comma**: Computers can tell whether an ad or a special offer raised sales.

Part B

1. Some students explored medical careers, **and** others looked at careers as hair stylists.

2. Dottie found some facts about her career in pamphlets, **and** Raj found information for her in library books.

3. She wrote a list of words that describe her, **and** Raj found words that describe a hair stylist.

4. Dottie examined the want ads, **and** Raj looked for ads in store windows.

5. Dottie looked in the telephone book for the names of hair salons, **and** Raj wrote down their phone numbers for her.

6. She may call a hair salon, **but** Raj thinks she should write a letter.

7. Dottie wants job applications mailed to her, **so** she made up some labels with her name and address on them.

8. Dottie is not a certified beautician, **so** Raj encouraged her to get certification.

9. She filled in applications without making spelling errors, **fo**r employers look at writing skills.

10. Dottie's friend Bonnie is a certified stylist, **so** Bonnie told Dottie about certification requirements.

Part C

Sample answers follow. You may have combined sentences in different ways. You should have used a comma before each of your connecting words.

1. **We will be studying the types of writing people in certain careers do, and some of us will write papers about our findings.**

2. **Shana will write a letter to an editor, and Celestine will write a report to a supervisor.**

3. **Celestine will visit a workplace, so he will find out some things he hadn't known.**

4. **I try to capture the moods of an office, but others notice the decor.**

5. **Writing character sketches of workers was not easy, but it taught them a lot.**

6. **Justin wrote a description of a particular job, and the teacher told him her feelings about his writing.**

7. **Mary prepared an advertisement for a job opening, and Elizabeth listed the job's requirements.**

8. **Conrad didn't like his original application, so Regina helped him make corrections.**

9. **Gloria will prepare a report for your boss, or you may prepare it.**

10. **Felix has never actually worked at a job like this, but he's doing very well.**

EXERCISE 20a (PAGE 122)

1. **That space is for people who are physically disabled.**

2. **A man who is not disabled has a "Disabled Person" sign in his car window.**

3. **I saw him dash into the music store that is across the street.**

4. **A man who isn't disabled doesn't deserve that parking space.**

5. **He probably bought his sign from the woman who sells them from her red van at the weekend flea market.**

6. **I wish someone would put the woman who sells the signs out of business.**

7. **A sign that lets handicapped motorists park in reserved spaces does not rightfully belong to an able-bodied person.**

8. **People who use canes, walkers, or wheelchairs need spaces close to the store.**

9. **The police have computerized information that identifies handicapped drivers.**

10. **The police are able to identify and ticket cars that don't belong in reserved parking spaces.**

EXERCISE 20b (PAGE 124)

1. **that**
2. **who**
3. **that**
4. **who**
5. **that**
6. **who**
7. **who**
8. **that**
9. **that**
10. **that**

EXERCISE 20c (PAGE 125)

1. **Submariners who seem depressed might be interviewed by a computer.**

2. **The computer, which is programmed to ask several questions, might begin by asking how the person feels.**

3. **Many patients find talking to a computer, which doesn't pass judgment, easier than talking to a doctor.**

4. **A question that would usually bother a person is less threatening if it appears on a computer screen.**

5. **Computers, which have modernized methods of suicide prevention, are often better than doctors at predicting suicide attempts.**

EXERCISE 20d (PAGE 126)

Part A

1. who
2. whom
3. whose
4. who
5. whom
6. who's
7. who's
8. whose
9. whose
10. who

Part B

1. **The new town library, which opened last year, cost a lot to build.**

2. **Those sewers that they put in this year were expensive.**

3. **The workers who plow the roads in the middle of the night are paid overtime.**

4. **The three blizzards that we had in February created plenty of overtime work.**

5. **Without the snowplows, people whose houses are in the country would be out of luck.**

6. **Many of those people are the same ones who lost their jobs when the factory closed.**

7. **Many senior citizens who live on limited incomes are going to vote against the budget.**

8. **Some people whose children are grown and gone resent paying for our children's schooling.**

9. **Unfortunately our children, who deserve good schools, cannot vote.**

10. **The newspaper editor who received my letter will publish it (or, my letter).**

EXERCISE 21 (PAGE 130)

Part A

1. It is still interesting to think about other types of jobs **after** you have chosen a career. (**No comma**)

2. Most people try more than one job **before** they settle into a career. (**No comma**)

3. **When** you are learning things about different types of jobs, you also learn things about yourself.

4. **Whenever** my friend finds out something about a job, he tells everyone what he has learned.

5. He visits a lot of job sites **so that** he can talk to people about their work. (No comma)

6. **Because** he wants to find a career, he listens carefully.

7. He doesn't mind **when** people ask him to make an appointment. (**No comma**)

8. **Unless** he has other things to do, he reads about jobs.

9. **If** he does his research carefully, he will probably get all the information he needs.

10. He would probably make a good TV reporter **even though** he isn't sure about that yet. (**No comma**)

Part B
Sample answers. You may have used different connecting words in your sentences and may have combined sentence parts in opposite orders.

1. **Before the budget passes, the town has to vote on it.**

2. **Because the budget would increase taxes, one large group of citizens wants it voted down.**

3. **Another group wants the budget approved although it would result in a higher bill at tax time.**

4. **If taxes are not raised, several teachers will be fired.**

5. **Unless the town collects the money for their salaries, they cannot be kept.**

6. **Whenever cuts are made in the budget, the largest cuts are made in education.**

7. **Wherever I go, I hear people talking about how tight money is.**

8. **Priscilla will vote while Arnie watches the children.**

9. **After she comes home, Arnie will go to the polling place.**

10. **When tomorrow's newspaper hits the stands, I want to see the headline.**

Part C

1. **had examined** or **examined**
2. **showed**
3. **saw**
4. **hoped**
5. **has**
6. **had explained** or **explained**
7. **hurt**
8. **had slammed** or **slammed**
9. **had become**
10. **will receive**

Part D

1. **When doctors and computers work together,** doctors are less likely to forget important details.

2. **Before a patient comes to a doctor's office,** the physician can get his or her records from the computer.

3. The computer holds records in a data base **just as you might keep boxes in a storehouse**.

4. **If Mr. Jones comes in for a yearly checkup,** the doctor can get a computer report of all past physicals.

5. **Even though he may not like to admit it,** Mr. Jones sometimes forgets the names of his medications.

6. **Whenever the doctor needs to know their names,** he can get a report from the computer.

7. Another patient may go to the doctor **because an unusual problem has just come up**.

8. **Once the doctor tells the computer the symptoms,** it can scan thousands of patient records.

9. **Although doctors used to rely mainly on their own experience,** they can now share knowledge with each other by computer.

10. **Before a doctor decides how to treat the symptoms,** he or she can check treatments used by other doctors.

EXERCISE 22a (PAGE 134)

Sample answers follow. You may have corrected the run-on sentences in different ways. You needed to write only one correction for each sentence.

1. METHOD 1: The sidewalks outside the bank are clean. **The** inside of the bank is just as tidy.

   METHOD 3: The sidewalks outside the bank are clean, **and** the inside of the bank is just as tidy.

2. METHOD 1: The heat was smothering on the day of my visit. **The** cool air inside the bank brought me back to life.

   METHOD 3: The heat was smothering on the day of my visit, **but** the cool air inside the bank brought me back to life.

   METHOD 4: **Even though** the heat was smothering on the day of my visit, the cool air inside the bank brought me back to life.

3. METHOD 1: The rug in the bank is burnt orange. **The** curtains are the same shade.

   METHOD 2: The rug **and the curtains** in the bank are burnt orange. (compound subject)

   METHOD 3: The rug in the bank is burnt orange, **and** the curtains are the same shade.

4. METHOD 1: Ten tellers stand behind windows. **Several** other workers sit at desks.

   METHOD 3: Ten tellers stand behind windows, **and** several other workers sit at desks.

5. METHOD 1: Personal bankers help people with new accounts. **They** help with other bank business.

   METHOD 2: Personal bankers help people with new accounts **and with other bank business**. (compound object)

   METHOD 3: Personal bankers help people with new accounts, **and** they help with other bank business.

6. METHOD 1: Only one security guard stands inside the bank lobby. **Another** sits in a control room.

   METHOD 3: Only one security guard stands inside the bank lobby, **but** another sits in a control room.

   METHOD 4: **Although** only one security guard stands inside the bank lobby, another sits in a control room.

7. METHOD 1: Most of the time it is very quiet. **Traffic** noises come in through an open door.

   METHOD 3: Most of the time it is very quiet, **yet** traffic noises come in through an open door.

   METHOD 4: Most of the time it is very quiet **even though** traffic noises come in through an open door.

8. METHOD 1: The vault is in the basement. **People** keep their personal belongings in safe deposit boxes there.

   METHOD 3: The vault is in the basement, **and** people keep their personal belongings in safe deposit boxes there.

   METHOD 4: **Because** the vault is in the basement, people keep their personal belongings in safe deposit boxes there.

9. METHOD 1: Behind two doors is an office with a fireplace. **The** bank's executive officer works there.

   METHOD 3: Behind two doors is an office with a fireplace, **so** (or, **and**) the bank's executive officer works there.

10. METHOD 1: My first job here will be at a teller's window. **I** plan to sit at the desk near the fireplace someday.

    METHOD 3: My first job here will be at a teller's window, **but** I plan to sit at the desk near the fireplace someday.

    METHOD 4: **Although** my first job here will be at a teller's window, I plan to sit at the desk near the fireplace someday.

EXERCISE 22b (PAGE 136)

Sample answers follow. You may have corrected the sentence fragments in different ways. You needed to write only one correction for each sentence.

1. METHOD 2: Pam is a licensed day-care provider **who** takes care of eight children in her home.

   METHOD 3: Pam is a licensed day-care provider. **She** takes care of eight children in her home.

2. METHOD 2: She gives play materials to the children **when** they are with her.

   METHOD 3: She gives play materials to the children. When they are with her, **they enjoy playing**.

3. METHOD 2: I read a newspaper article **that** suggested tips on choosing day care.

   METHOD 3: I read a newspaper article. **It** suggested tips on choosing day care.

4. METHOD 1: Go to a center you can visit any time. **Don't** make an appointment.

   METHOD 2: Go to a center you can visit any time **even if** you don't make an appointment.

   METHOD 3: Go to a center you can visit any time. Even if you don't make an appointment, **you could drop in**.

5. METHOD 2: Many people prefer to hire a child care provider **who** has a license.

   METHOD 3: Many people prefer to hire a child care provider **only if he or she** has a license.

6. METHOD 2: I had a goal, **which was to find** a safe place for my children.

   METHOD 3: I had a goal. **I wanted to find a** safe place for my children.

7. METHOD 2: The state checks on the safety of homes **that** provide care for children.

   METHOD 3: The state checks on the safety of homes **if they** provide care for children.

8. METHOD 2: There are a couple of things I don't want to see **when** I visit a day-care center.

   METHOD 3: There are a couple of things I don't want to see. When I visit a day-care center, **I don't want to see child abuse**.

9. METHOD 3: There should be good discipline, **but there should be** no spanking.

10. METHOD 3: Pam serves the children healthy snacks **that include** cheese, apples, carrots, and crackers.

EXERCISE 22c (PAGE 138)

Sample answers follow. You may have used different connecting words in your corrections.

1. Last week he repaired our door, **but** I fixed the broken window.

2. He works as a handyman in an apartment complex, **but** he is not satisfied with his job.

3. He would rather run his own business **even though** he needs to learn how.

4. **Even though** his friends encouraged him to stay in school, he dropped out.

5. Now he wants to improve his writing skills, **so** he has come back.

6. **No correction is necessary.**

7. **If** a customer requests a written estimate, Eric may have some trouble.

8. Last week he agreed to paint a customer's house, **but** he is unsure about how to write a contract.

9. He will work on his own, **or** he will work with a partner.

10. **Although** he would love to start his own business now, it will have to wait until he finishes his schooling.

EXERCISE 22d (PAGE 139)

Part A

Sample answers follow. You may have rewritten sentences differently to make the relationships between their ideas clearer.

1. **When** she returned from Hawaii, she found her door open.

2. The police **who came to her apartment** gave her ideas for making her apartment more secure.

3. She could replace her flimsy window locks **since** the burglars easily broke one of Karen's.

4. She could make her apartment look lived in **if** she used a timer on her lights.

5. **Whenever** she leaves, she could turn on a radio.

6. A neighbor could pick up her mail **because** an overflowing mailbox is an invitation to a burglar.

Part B

1. **Since his baby had a high fever, Richard rushed him to the hospital.**

2. **Since the doctor needed to make a blood test, he drew blood from the boy's arm.**

3. **It was rushed to the laboratory in order that it could be tested immediately.**

4. **When the blood arrived, the lab worker analyzed it by computer.**

5. **No correction is necessary.**

6. **Unless the doctor gave the boy a shot, he would become sicker.**

EXERCISE 22e (PAGE 140)

1. The police car's siren didn't work well. **The** driver had asked for a new siren.

2. They sped up. **They** were traveling way over the speed limit.

3. **No correction is necessary.**

4. The computer did its job. **The** other car was going 80 miles per hour.

5. **No correction is necessary.**

EXERCISE 23a (PAGE 142)

1. Have you tried **bran** cereal in yogurt?

2. The melons feel **soft**.

3. Someone brought **blueberry** muffins.

4. The muffins were **tasty**.

5. Herman likes **pork** sausages.

6. The sausages taste **spicy**.

7. Lulu put **purple** flowers on the table.

8. The lilacs smell **sweet**.

9. Grandma, **happy** as ever, played with her grandchildren.

10. The **noisy** family began to eat.

EXERCISE 23b (PAGE 143)

Part A

1. She just sits and rocks in the chair **next to the window**.

2. The girl is using a computer **with a recorded voice** to teach her new words.

3. The child sat at the computer and pushed a key **on the keyboard**.

4. A picture **of a dog** appeared on the screen.

5. The girl heard a voice **on the recording** say "dog."

Part B

Sample answers follow.

1. I don't like to eat fish **with bones**.

2. My wife enjoys fish **on Fridays**.

3. The customer **by the counter** seems to be buying ingredients for stew.

4. He has just bought a pound **of beef**.

5. He is pointing at the sign **with the price**.

Part C

1. **Running to his phone,** Charles dialed 911.

2. **Speaking too quickly,** he reported a fire.

3. **No correction is necessary**.

4. **Turning on the message repeater,** the operator listened to a recording of Charles's message.

5. **No correction is necessary**.

6. **Pushing a button next to his terminal,** the operator called for the Fire Department.

7. **Speeding to the scene,** the firefighters put on their siren.

8. **Arriving within minutes,** they quickly put out the fire.

9. **Having forgotten a lighted candle,** the neighbor had fallen asleep on her couch.

10. **No correction is necessary**.

Part D

Sample answers follow. You may have correctly positioned phrases at other points in some sentences.

1. **Memorizing the feel of the raised dots,** she learned to read with her fingertips.

2. **Waiting for her Braille books to arrive in the mail,** she sometimes grew impatient.

3. The Braille books **lining her room** taught her a lot, but she wanted to read other books.

4. **Itching to read her friends' comics,** Sadie told her parents how she felt.

5. **Hearing about the Optaconer,** her father decided to look into it.

6. A small computerized tool **containing a tiny TV camera** is moved across a line of print.

7. **Changing the computer pictures into vibrations,** the device allows the holder to read print.

8. **Opening a gift beside her bed,** Sadie found an Optacon inside.

9. **Holding the device in one hand and feeling the pattern with the other,** she showed her folks how it worked.

10. **Hugging her parents,** she told them how happy they had made her.

EXERCISE 23c (PAGE 146)

1. **No correction is necessary**.

2. He really needs to heed the tips **that are on the last page** about safety in garages.

3. Uncle Bert always smokes the special pipe **that he received for his birthday** in the garage.

4. Garages, **which often contain gasoline,** are not good places for lighting up cigarettes, cigars, or pipes.

5. During cookouts, Uncle Bert often leaves the grill **that he has just lit** to chat with friends.

6. A fire **that is unattended** is a bad idea.

7. Uncle Bert's habit **that bothers me even more** is putting the barbecue near the lawn mower.

8. **No correction is necessary**.

9. The garden tools **that are usually lying all over his yard** should be put in the shed and garage.

10. The clippers **that have those sharp blades** belong on a wall hook.

GED PRACTICE 4 (page 148)

Part 1

1. **(3)** In this sentence the subject, *ways*, follows the verb. Because the subject is plural, the verb must be plural. The words *Until recently* let you know that the sentence tells about an action that began in the past and continues in the present, so the verb, which is irregular, must be in the present perfect tense. (Lesson 7: "Sentences That Begin with *There* or *Here*," pg. 34; Lesson 5: Spotlight on Special Agreement Patterns, pg. 26)

2. **(5)** The parts of a compound predicate must have parallel structures. In this sentence, *mail a letter* and *send a telegram* are parallel. To be parallel with those two parts of the predicate, the last part of the predicate must be made up of a present-tense verb and an object: *make a telephone call.* (Lesson 18: "Using Parallel Structures in Compounds," pg. 114)

3. **(3)** When the dependent part of a complex sentence comes at the beginning of the sen-

tence, it is followed by a comma. In this sentence the connecting word introduces the dependent part of the sentence. (Lesson 21: table "Connecting Words Used in Some Complex Sentences" and the paragraphs above it, pg. 129)

4. **(3)** The most effective combination of Sentences 4 and 5 is a complex sentence: *The paper that bears the message is called a hard copy.* (Lesson 20: "Complex Sentences with *That, Which, Who, Whom,* and *Whose*," pg. 121, and "The Uses of *That, Which, Who, Whom,* and *Whose*," pg. 123)

5. **(1)** In a compound sentence the connecting word should make the relationship between the two parts of the sentence clear. This sentence describes a contrast, so the connecting word *but* is appropriate for the sentence. Because this is a compound sentence, a comma separates the two parts of the sentence from each other. (Lesson 22: "Choosing the Right Connector," pg. 137; Lesson 19: the second paragraph on pg. 116)

6. **(2)** Because this is a compound sentence, a comma separates the two parts of the sentence from each other. The comma goes before the connecting word *but.* (Lesson 19: the second paragraph on pg. 116)

7. **(4)** This run-on sentence can best be corrected by splitting it into two separate sentences. (Lesson 22: "Correcting Run-On Sentences," pg. 113)

8. **(2)** This sentence contains a compound predicate with two parts. No comma is needed between the parts of a compound unless there are at least three parts. (Lesson 18: Spotlight on Punctuation, pg. 111, and "Compound Predicates," pg. 113)

9. **(4)** The tense of *sends,* the first verb in this complex sentence, is simple present. Because the whole sentence states a fact, the tense of the second verb in the sentence must also be simple present. The verb must be singular because *device,* the subject, is singular. (Lesson 12: "Clues to Tense in a Paragraph," pg. 73)

10. **(3)** Sentence 11 is a sentence fragment. The best way to correct it is to make a complex sentence by joining it to Sentence 12. Sentence 11 becomes the dependent sentence part in the complex sentence. Since it comes first in the sentence, it must be followed by a comma. (Lesson 22: "Correcting Sentence Fragments," pg. 135; Lesson 21: table "Connecting Words Used in Some

Complex Sentences" and the paragraphs above it, pg. 129)

11. **(3)** In Sentence 13 the pronoun *them* could refer to either of two nouns in the same sentence: *signals* or *telephone lines.* By changing *them* to a noun, the meaning of the sentence becomes clear. (Lesson 17: "Avoiding Unclear References," pg. 102)

12. **(4)** Sentence parts that function as adjectives should be placed right after the noun they describe. In this sentence, the sentence part *that tell the user how to work the machines* describes the computers, not the fax machines themselves. In order to have that sentence part follow the word it describes, the other sentence part has to be rewritten. (Lesson 23: "Sentence Parts That Function as Adjectives," pg. 146)

Part 2

Stress may be the key element in half of all illnesses. Studies suggest(s) that your stress level affects your nervous system, heart function, and hormone levels. Researchers believe that stress may affect your recovery from an illness.

A group of adult students recently ~~meets~~ met at a stress clinic. They shared ideas about how to handle stress. When the pressure gets too great, ~~so~~ Thelma likes to go somewhere private and yell or cry. Louise likes to close her eyes and imagine ~~yourself~~ herself in a pleasant setting. If a situation upsets Arnold, he often talks it out with a sympathetic friend. He sometimes writes his complaint that he ~~does'nt~~ doesn't send in a letter.

Comment:

13. *Studies* is plural, so the verb in the sentence must be plural—*suggest.* (Lesson 3: "Basic Rules for Subject-Verb Agreement," pg. 17)

14. When three or more parts of an object are connected by *and*, commas go between the parts. The last comma goes before the *and.* (Lesson 18: Spotlight on Punctuation, pg. 111)

15. The general context of this sentence lets you know that it tells about a one-time event in the past. The word *recently* is a further clue. Therefore, the verb must be *met.* (Lesson 9: "The Simple Past Tense," pg. 57; Lesson 12: "Clues to Tense: Time Words," pg. 71)

16. The first "sentence" in the second paragraph is a run-on sentence. The best way to correct it is to split it into two separate sentences. (Lesson 22: "Correcting Run-On Sentences," pg. 133)

17. This sentence has two connecting words, *When* and *so.* The word *When* makes the relationship between the two parts of the sentence clear. Therefore, the word *so* should be deleted. A comma is necessary after the word *great* because the first part of the changed sentence is a dependent sentence part. (Lesson 22: "Choosing the Right Connector," pg. 137; Lesson 21: table "Connecting Words Used in Some Complex Sentences" and the paragraphs above it, pg. 129)

18. This sentence contains a compound predicate with two parts. No comma is needed between the parts of a compound unless there are at least three parts. (Lesson 18: Spotlight on Punctuation, pg. 111, and "Compound Predicates," pg. 113)

19. The "-self," pronoun in this sentences refers to *Louise* and must agree with it. (Lesson 14: table "The '-self/-selves' Pronouns," pg. 90)

20. The subject of the first sentence part in this sentence, *Situation,* is singular, so the verb in the sentence must be singular—*upsets.* (Lesson 3: "Basic Rules for Subject-Verb Agreement," pg. 17)

21. A comma is necessary after the word *Arnold* because the first part of the sentence is a dependent sentence part. (Lesson 21: table "Connecting Words Used in Some Complex Sentences" and the paragraphs above it, pg. 129)

22. The tense of *upsets,* the first verb in this complex sentence, is simple present.

Because the whole sentence tells about something that happens regularly, the tense of the second verb in the sentence must also be simple present. (Lesson 12: "Clues to Tense in a Paragraph," pg. 73)

23. The last "sentence" in the second paragraph is a run-on sentence. The best way to correct it is to split it into two separate sentences. (Lesson 22: "Correcting Run-On Sentences," pg. 133)

24. Sentence parts that function as adjectives should be placed right after the noun they describe. In this sentence the sentence part *that he doesn't send* describes the letter, not the complaint. To have that sentence part follow the word it describes, the words *in a letter* should be moved to follow the word *complaint.* (Lesson 23: "Sentence Parts That Function as Adjectives," pg. 146)

25. The contraction in this sentence should be spelled *doesn't.* (Lesson 12: table "Commonly Used Verb Contractions," pg. 74)

UNIT 2: WRITING

EXERCISE 28 (PAGE 163)

Part B

1. **hearing**
2. **smell**
3. **touch**
4. **taste**
5. **sight**

EXERCISE 30a (PAGE 171)

1. a. The topic of the paragraph is **James Whitmore's career at the container factory**.

   b. The topic sentence is the first sentence in the paragraph: **During his 29 years at the Mosther container factory, James Whitmore worked in almost every phase of the operation**.

2. a. The topic of the paragraph is **difficulties faced by job applicants without high school diplomas**.

   b. The topic sentence is the first sentence in the paragraph: **The lack of a diploma can prevent a capable worker from finding a job**.

3. a. The topic of the paragraph is **hot, crowded graduation ceremony**.

b. The topic sentence is the last sentence in the paragraph: **The room was hotter and more crowded than the graduates' families and friends had expected**.

EXERCISE 30b (PAGE 172)

Part A

1. **(b)** The "supporting sentences" in Paragraph (a) do not give examples of practical jokes played on the paragraph's writer. The supporting sentences in Paragraph (b) do.

2. **(a)** The "supporting sentences" in Paragraph (b) do not give examples of tasks handled by computers in post offices. The supporting sentences in Paragraph (a) do.

3. **(a)** The "supporting sentences" in Paragraph (b) do not explain why the paragraph's writer has decided to disable his or her car alarm. The supporting sentences in Paragraph (a) do.

Part B

1. Sentences **(2)** and **(4)** support the topic sentence. Sentence (3) doesn't offer proof that the writer's little girl is lying about her homework. Sentence **(5)** is not about the writer's little girl.

2. Sentences **(4)** and **(5)** support the topic sentence. Neither Sentence (2) nor Sentence (3) offers evidence that pipe fitting is a good career.

3. Sentences **(2)** and **(3)** support the topic sentence. Sentences (4) and (5) are about things you should do *during* a test, not *in preparation for* a test.

4. Sentences **(4)** and **(5)** support the topic sentence. Sentence (2) doesn't offer support for the writer's desire that public smoking be banned. Sentence (3) is not about public smoking.

EXERCISE 36 (PAGE 191)

Part A

1. You should have numbered the supporting sentences in this order: **3**, **2**, **4**, 1.

2. You should have numbered the supporting sentences in this order: **3**, **2**, **1**, 4.

Part B

Suggested answer:

The IRS has a huge computer system containing information in its data base about each taxpayer—information from past returns, banks, employers, and the DMV. To process tax returns, the IRS follows a careful procedure that involves using its computer system. ~~The~~ First, the IRS receives a taxpayer's return. ~~A~~ Then, a worker enters the return's information into the computer. ~~The~~ After that, the computer searches its data base and compares the information to that from the taxpayer's return. ~~If~~ Finally, if the taxpayer's figures agree with those in the data base, the IRS either credits the taxpayer's account or sends out a check.

EXERCISE 37 (PAGE 194)

Part A

1. You should have numbered the supporting sentences in this order: **3**, **2**, **4**, 1.

2. You should have numbered the supporting sentences in this order: **2**, **3**, **4**, 1.

Part B

Suggested answer:

The employment pages are located in the classified section of a newspaper. <u>At the top</u> of the first employment page is the heading *Employment*. <u>**Below**</u> this heading job openings are usually listed alphabetically. <u>**On the left**</u> side of the page, the first column might begin with a listing for automotive technicians. At the top of the column <u>**on the right**</u> side of the page, there might be several listings for baby-sitters. <u>**After**</u> the first page there may be several other pages of job listings. <u>**At the bottom**</u> of the last column of the last employment page, there might be a listing for a zoo worker.

EXERCISE 38 (PAGE 197)

Part A

Sample answers:

1. **They felt they deserved a pay raise.**
   They wanted a better health plan.

2. **His parents are getting a divorce.**
   His grandmother has been quite ill.

3. **Her company has computerized its billing system.**
   She wants to have as many skills as possible when she applies for another job.

4. **We knew he had never been to the Bahamas.**
   We are able to get a good discount on the tickets.

Part B

Sample answers:

1. **No alarm went off when the fire started.**
   The apartment was heavily damaged by fire.

2. **The frozen foods thawed.**
   The milk turned sour.

3. **Wanda has a vitamin deficiency.**
   Wanda has dull, brittle hair.

4. **We don't throw our old newspapers in the trash.**
   Fewer trees need to be cut down.

Part C

Suggested answer:

I am asking for a raise for several reasons. ~~I~~ *Because* have turned down several offers to work elsewhere,' I have proven my loyalty to the company. The company has saved money.~~It~~ *because it* has adopted several of my suggestions for running itself more efficiently. *Since* I am responsible for supervising two other employees. ~~To do that~~, I put in more time than I used to. *Therefore* I feel I deserve more pay.

EXERCISE 39 (PAGE 200)

Part A

Sample answers:

1. **work in a department store.**

2. **intelligent.**
3. **spend their free time**
4. **becomes natural with practice.**
5. **both view a scene and make a record of it.**

Part B

Sample answers:

1. **now it buys only a mint.**
2. **allows you the time to edit your ideas before you share them with your audience.**
3. **others don't like to be frightened.**
4. **is often quick-paced; is more relaxed.**
5. **writing is easy and enjoyable.**

Part C

Suggested answer:

Lynne reminds me of my cat. Their eyes have *the same* ~~a~~ slanted shape and green color. *Both* Lynne and my cat are quiet and graceful. They even have *similar* eating habits. *They both* ~~Lynne and Shmo~~ drink a cup of milk for breakfast and eat fish for dinner. Whenever she can, Lynne curls up on the couch for a nap. *Likewise,* Shmo takes every opportunity to doze on the sofa.

Part D

Suggested answer:

Pedestrians and drivers follow different rules. Walkers often cross at lights when they are red. *, but a* ~~A~~ driver must stop for a red light. *Although a* ~~A~~ driver should always stay on the right side of the road. *, a* ~~A~~ pedestrian should walk on the left side if there is no sidewalk. A driver who comes upon a pedestrian in a crosswalk must stop. *However, a* ~~A~~ pedestrian who has stepped into a crosswalk should not have to stop for a car.

Part A

1. You should have numbered the supporting sentences in this order: **4**, **2**, 1, **3**.

2. You should have numbered the supporting sentences in this order: **3**, **2**, **1**, 4.

Part B

Suggested answer:

Wearing a motorcycle helmet is important for
many reasons. ~~Helmets~~ prevent fatal head
Above all, helmets

injuries when riders are thrown from their
bikes. ~~Helmets~~ protect wearers from injury
In addition, helmets

when rocks are thrown into the air by other
vehicles. A helmet's visor reduces the damaging
A third reason is that a

force of wind on the wearer's eyes. ~~Helmets~~ keep
Finally, helmets

riders' heads dry during trips through storms.

EXERCISE 41 (PAGE 208)

Part A

1. (a) You should have written three of the following signal words contained in the paragraph: **Both**, **Like**, **similarly**, **Likewise**, **On the other hand**, **Unlike**, **In contrast**, **but**.

   (b) The pattern of organization the paragraph uses is **Comparing and Contrasting Ideas**.

2. (a) You should have written three of the following signal words contained in the paragraph: **On both sides**, **On the right**, **On the left**, **Across**, **away**.

   (b) The pattern of organization the paragraph uses is **Space**.

3. (a) You should have written three of the following signal words contained in the paragraph: **Then**, **Right after that**, **Immediately**, **At first**, **Once**.

   (b) The pattern of organization the paragraph uses is **Time**.

4. (a) You should have written three of the following signal words contained in the paragraph: **For example**, **also**, **Worse yet**, **Furthermore**, **Besides that**, **Worst of all**.

   (b) The pattern of organization the paragraph uses is **Order of Importance of Ideas**.

5. (a) You should have written three of the following signal words contained in the paragraph: **Consequently**, **Because**, **The reason**, **As a result**.

   (b) The pattern of organization the paragraph uses is **Cause and Effect**.

Part B

1. (a) The writer's purpose is **to describe the contents of a photo**.

   (b) The best pattern of organization to use would be **Space**.

2. (a) The writer's purpose is **to tell the likenesses and differences between asthma and hay fever**.

   (b) The best pattern of organization to use would be **Comparing and Contrasting Ideas**.

3. (a) The writer's purpose is **to tell the steps in preparing for a job interview**.

   (b) The best pattern of organization to use would be **Time**.

4. (a) The writer's purpose is **to explain how cars cause acid rain**.

   (b) The best pattern of organization to use would be **Cause and Effect**.

5. (a) The writer's purpose is **to explain why gambling should not be allowed in his or her town**.

   (b) The best pattern of organization to use would be **Order of Importance of Ideas**.

POSTTEST (PAGE 215)

Part 1

1. **(2)** The reverse order of the subject and verb in this question does not change how they agree. The subject *population* agrees with *is*. (Lesson 7: "Questions," pg. 35)

2. **(5)** To add an *s* ending when a letter other than a vowel comes before the *y* at the end of a word, change the *y* to *i* and add *es*. (Lesson 8: Spotlight on Spelling, pg. 40)

3. **(5)** This sentence contains a compound object (the object of *Counting*) with three parts. A comma is needed between the parts of a compound when there are three. (Lesson 18: Spotlight on Punctuation, pg. 111)

4. **(1)** The most effective combination of Sentences 4 and 5 is a complex sentence: *For each census researchers now use computers to tally and analyze the raw data that are gathered both by mail and by canvassers.* The connecting word *that* is used because the sentence part it begins contains essential information. (Lesson 20: "Using *That* and *Which*," pg. 125)

5. **(3)** Sentence 6 is a sentence fragment. The best way to correct it is to combine it as a dependent sentence part with Sentence 7 in a complex sentence. Because the dependent part comes at the beginning of the complex sentence, it must be followed by a comma. (Lesson 22: "Correcting Sentence Fragments," pg. 135; Lesson 21: the bullet about commas in complex sentences, pg. 129)

6. **(3)** The word *today's* in Sentence 8, as well as the general context of the sentence, lets you know that it states a fact. Therefore, the verb must be in the simple present tense— *take.* Because the subject, *tasks*, is plural, the verb is also plural. (Lesson 12: table "Tenses: Uses and Related Time Words," pg. 71, and "Clues to Tense in a Paragraph," pg. 73)

7. **(1)** When the dependent part of a complex sentence comes at the end of the sentence, there is no comma between the two parts of the sentence. (Lesson 21: the bullet about commas in complex sentences, pg. 129)

8. **(2)** The phrase *as well as business* begins with words that replace *and*. There are commas before and after the phrase. It is not a part of the subject of the sentence. The subject is *Politics*. It is singular and agrees with the singular verb *is*. (Lesson 8: "Phrases with Words That Replace *and*," pg. 42; Lesson 5: "Singular Subjects That End with S," pg. 26)

9. **(4)** The possessive pronoun in the sentence refers to *state*. Therefore, it must be the singular pronoun *its*. (Lesson 16: "Pronoun Agreement with Nouns," pg. 95; Lesson 15: table "How Possessive Pronouns Are Formed," pg. 94)

10. **(5)** Sentence 12 is a run-on sentence. The best way to correct it is to change it to a complex sentence by using the connecting word *If* and a comma after the dependent part of the sentence. (Lesson 22: "Correcting Run-On Sentences," pg. 133)

11. **(4)** The words *from and of cars* form an interrupting phrase between the subject and the verb in this sentence. The singular subject *Theft* agrees with the singular verb *drives*. (Lesson 8: "Identifying Interrupting Phrases," pg. 40)

12. **(5)** Because the pronoun *they* is plural, it could refer to *cars* or *insurance premiums* in Sentence 1 or to *insurance companies* or *stolen articles* and/or *cars* in Sentence 2. (Because it is plural, it could not refer to the singular noun *Theft* in Sentence 1) The correction uses *everyone's premiums* instead of *they* to make the meaning of Sentence 2 clear. (Lesson 17: "Avoiding Unclear References," pg. 102)

13. **(1)** Sentences 3 and 4 can be combined into one sentence with a compound predicate by using the word *and*: *You can take steps that will reduce theft and keep care insurance costs down.* (Lesson 18: "Compound Predicates," pg. 113)

14. **(4)** To agree with the pronoun *You* in both Sentences 3 and 4, the first pronoun in Sentence 5 cannot shift to *Everyone*. It must be *You*. Therefore, the second pronoun in Sentence 5 must be *your* to agree with the first pronoun in the sentence. (Lesson 17: "Avoiding Pronoun Shifts Within Sentences" and "Avoiding Pronoun Shifts Within Paragraphs," pg. 100)

15. **(2)** The first part of this complex sentence refers to something that occurs regularly, so the verb must be in the simple present tense. To agree with *you*, the subject, it must be *leave*. (Lesson 9: "The Simple Present Tense," pg. 57)

16. **(5)** Since the "-self" pronoun in this sentence must agree with *it*, the correct form is *itself*. (Lesson 14: "Mistake 5," pg. 91)

17. **(4)** An adjective phrase too far away from the noun it describes can confuse the reader. In this case, the reader could assume that the phrase *in plain view* describes *thieves*. In the correction, the phrase appears directly after *Packages*, the word it is meant to describe. (Lesson 23: "Adjective Phrases," pg. 142)

18. **(3)** The parts of the compound subject in this sentence, *tape deck* and *radio*, are connected with *or*. The verb *is* agrees with *radio*, the closer part of the subject. (Lesson 6: "Compound Subjects with *Either . . . or* and *Neither . . . nor*," pg. 32)

19. **(2)** The car in this sentence "owns" the pockets and the glove compartment, so it is possessive. Since *car* is singular, its possessive form is *car's*. (Lesson 15: table "Forming Possessive Nouns," pg. 93)

20. **(3)** The words *my friends and I* form a compound object. The pronoun *I* is not an object pronoun. It must be changed to *me*. (Lesson 13: "Pronouns in Compound Subjects and Objects," pg. 88)

21. **(1)** The tense of *use*, the first verb in this complex sentence, is simple present because it tells about something that happens regularly. Because the second part of sentence states a "fact" that may result from that regular action, the tense of its verb must also be simple present. Because the dependent part comes at the beginning of the complex sentence, it must be followed by a comma. (Lesson 12: "Clues to Tense in a Paragraph," pg. 73; Lesson 21: the bullet about commas in complex sentences, pg. 129)

22. **(5)** The possessive pronoun in Sentence 1 should refer to the singular possessive noun *person's*. Because *person's* can refer to a person of either sex, the reference to it must be the singular pronoun group *his* or *her*. (Lesson 16: "Pronoun Agreement with Nouns," pg. 95, and the second sentence in the Spotlight on Agreement with Pronouns That End with *-body* or *-one*, pg. 98)

23. **(2)** The dependent part of Sentence 2 has a describing verb, a form of *be*. The verb must be singular to agree with *ability*, so it is *isn't* instead of *aren't*. (Lesson 4: table "Verbs Common in Describing Sentences," pg. 23, and table "Patterns for Subject-Verb Agreement with *Be*," pg. 24)

24. **(4)** The verb in the dependent part of Sentence 3 must be singular because its subject, the pronoun *who*, refers to *Anyone*, which is singular. Therefore, the verb must be *has learned*. (Lesson 5: "Subjects That End in *-body, -one,* and *-thing*," pg. 28)

25. **(3)** This sentence begins with a dependent part followed by three independent parts. The independent parts, since by themselves they form a compound sentence, must have parallel structures. The word groups *give your speech to a mirror* and *deliver it to a friend* are parallel: they begin with a verb, contain *your speech* or *it* (referring to *your speech*), and end with a phrase. In the correction, with some rewording, the third part has the same structure: *speak* (verb) *it* (referring to your speech) *into a tape recorder* (phrase). A comma is needed between the last two parts of the compound because the compound has three parts. (Lesson 18: "Using Parallel Structures in Compounds," pg. 114)

26. **(5)** *You* agrees with *practice*, the verb form with no *s* ending, not with *practices*. The verb must be in the simple present tense because it tells about something that occurs (or should occur) regularly. (Lesson 3: "Agreement with *I* and *You*," pg. 20)

27. **(4)** Sentences 4–6 tell about things that occur (or should occur) regularly. Sentence 7 does the same, so its verbs must be in the simple present tense. *Gave*, the simple past tense form of an irregular verb, must be changed to *give*. There is no comma between *sing* and *or talk*. They are the two parts of the compound verb in the independent part of this complex sentence. A comma is needed before the last part in a compound only when there are three or more parts. (Lesson 10: table "Some Irregular-Verb Patterns," pg. 62; Lesson 12: "Clues to Tense in a Paragraph," pg. 73)

28. **(2)** Sentences 4–7 tell about things that occur (or should occur) regularly. Sentence 8 does the same, so its verb must be in a present tense. The present continuous tense of the first verb, *are speaking*, is used here because it describes an ongoing action that should occur regularly. (Lesson 11: "The Present Continuous Tense," pg. 87)

29. **(3)** This sentence states a fact, so its verb must be in the simple present tense. To agree with *breathing*, the singular subject, it must be *keeps*. (Lesson 9: "The Simple Present Tense," pg. 65)

30. **(5)** The subject of the independent part of this sentence, *half*, is singular because it refers to *battle*, which is singular. *Half* agrees with the singular verb *is*. The verb is in the simple present tense because the sentence states a fact. (Lesson 8: "Words That Can Be Singular or Plural as Subjects," pg. 44)

31. **(3)** Sentences 11 and 12 are more effective written as a compound sentence than as two separate sentences because there is a relationship of contrast between their ideas. The contrast is between the hard work learning to speak in public requires and the rewards it brings. To make the relationship between the two parts of the combined sentence clear, the connecting word *but* is appropriate. (Lesson 19: table "Connecting Words Used in Compound Sentences," pg. 118)

Part 2

Following are two sample paragraphs—with comments about each—on the topic of the Posttest paragraph. The sentences in the paragraphs are numbered to make the discussion about them easier to follow. Although your paragraph will be different from either of these, you may be able to make a judgment about its strong and weak points by reference to the comments below.

(1) *Once I noticed the house next door on fire.* (2) *I turned on the hose but the water didnt reach the window.* (3) *Then I remembered a longer piece of house in the backyard.* (4) *I got it and now the hose was long enough.* (5) *Finally the fire trucks come when I am just putting the last of the fire out.* (6) *They took long enough.* (7) *I had called 911 but I didn't know the house number or even the street.* (8) *So I looked for a letter and found one.* (9) *I gave that to the dispatcher and told her the fire was next door.*

Comment:

This paragraph tells about several quick-thinking actions the writer took, but it would be stronger if it were carefully organized in time order. Using the numbers of the sentences in the paragraph, the events could have been organized in this order: 1, 7, 8, 9, 2, 3, 4, 5. Sentence 6 could be deleted because it is a comment that is not directly on the topic.

The paragraph would be clearer with the addition of more details. It isn't clear, for example, why the writer didn't know what street the house next door was on. Did the writer run into the burning house to look for a letter with an address on it? Did the writer give the letter to the dispatcher, or did he or she read the address from the letter over the phone to the dispatcher?

Overall the paragraph is not well organized because events aren't presented in a logical order. The writer uses some signal words to show the reader something about the sequence of events: *Then* (in Sentence 3), *now* (in Sentence 4), and *Finally* (in Sentence 5). More signal words would have been better, especially if events were told in order. Several mechanical errors in the paragraph further weaken its effect.

(1) *Several years ago I was baby-sitting a friend's children when I happened to glance out a window.* (2) *I saw with a shock that a neighbors curtains were in flames.* (3) *First I called 911.* (4) *When the dispatcher asked for the address of the fire, I realized that I had no idea what street I was on.* (5) *Luckily I found an envelope addressed to my friend on the kitchen table and read the address to the dispatcher.* (6) *After hanging up, I raced outside and turned on a hose.* (7) *It was too short, so I ran to the backyard for a longer one.* (8) *Moments later, I was back in the front yard battling the blaze.* (9) *By the time the fire trucks arrived, all that remained of the fire was a blanket of smoke.*

Comment:

This paragraph tells about several quick-thinking actions the writer took. It is carefully organized in time order. The descriptions of events are lively, and the amount of detail makes it clear how and why events occurred.

The writer uses enough signal words to make the sequence of events clear: *Several years ago* and *when* (in Sentence 1), *First* (in Sentence 3), *When* (in Sentence 4), *After hanging up* (in Sentence 6), *Moments later* (in Sentence 8), and *By the time* (in Sentence 9).

There are only a few minor mechanical errors in the paragraph, which do not seriously weaken its effect.